What Others Say...

"Wonderful read. Beautiful and touching writing ... I had a few laughs and shed a few tears along the way...That must have been some class, with all those colorful characters."

Bill Casteel, columnist, The Chattanooga Times, ret.

"One of the finest writers I ever worked beside in a lifetime of journalism."

Tom Wark, former Associate Managing Editor,
The Philadelphia Inquirer

"It is a masterpiece, a tapestry of unguarded reflections of lives that spanned the full range of emotions — love, joy, pathos, despair, fatalism."

Bob Gilbert, freelance columnist, former Associated Press Writer

"Quite a gripping tale. Tis really a good read."

Sam Venable, Columnist, The Knoxville News Sentinel

D1491256

The Last Reunion

The Class of 1952
Comes Home to the Secret City

Jay Searcy

Copyright© 2010 By Jay Searcy

ISBN: 978-0-692-01233-8

For additional copies of this book
please contact Jay Searcy:

Phone: 865-657-9371
Email: jay@jaysearcy.com
Website: jaysearcy.com

Printed by:
Graphix Network
4104 Colben Blvd.
Evans, Georgia 30809
(706) 210-1000

Cover photo by Ed Westcott.

This book is dedicated to my mother, Dovie Ryan Searcy, and my father, H.J. Searcy Jr., who were part of the Oak Ridge miracle, and to my wife, Jackie, who insisted.

Acknowledgments

I have been collecting Oak Ridge stories all my adult life, as if they would die without my rescue. This is a book of rescued stories about and by my schoolmates who returned for a last reunion in their mid-70s with tales from a half-remembered time long ago.

I am grateful to the Oak Ridge High class of 1952 for its cooperation and contributions. I asked for their stories and they poured their hearts out. I am especially grateful to those who told stories that caused them pain, that brought tears – tears in the telling and tears in the writing. You know who you are.

I cannot give enough credit to Stephany Beane, an electric bolt from a younger generation who energized our reunion. She was a volunteer photographer, sound engineer, and video maker and she put together the pages of this book. She was an adviser, editor and critic, and designer of just about everything that required organization. She expected nothing in return; she just likes geezers. She gave the class a website (jaysearcy.com,) and updated it with text, photos and video.

Marty Gick Tidwell, a classmate who was secretary to longtime city recreation director, Carl "Rabbit" Yearwood, a town legend, read every word of the book for errors. All that punctuation you see is hers. Sophie Brody Ravin spent hours editing and advising me on the phone from Chicago.

The cover was designed and engineered by James "Cowboy" Hodges, a classmate who made his living as an illustrator. He also created a class video and gave a copy to everybody who attended the 2010 reunion.

Long time Oak Ridger Fred Strohle, with X-10 public relations, showed me through the Oak Ridge National Laboratory and, at my request, provided an all-time Top Ten list of Oak Ridge personalities, most of whom he knew. Ed Westcott, Oak Ridge's noted photographer, gave us a free slide show of early Oak Ridge at the reunion, presented by his daughter, Emily, and son-in-law Don Hunnicutt, and gave permission to use some of his pictures in this book including the cover photo.

The reunion was a grand success because of classmates who contributed their stories, photographs, skills and money. There was a little fiddling, guitar picking and singing and a peppy trombone quartet. And we had a surprise; a prancing, twirling majorette, Dottie Hawkins, who strutted for us once more at age 75. The reunion cost almost $11,000. More than $5,000 of that was donated by 28 classmates and their spouses. Thank you all.

And finally, thanks to my loving wife, the former Jackie Hildebrand, for being helpful and kind while this project was under way.

–Jay Searcy

Contents

The Last Reunion

Once, more than 60 years ago, we were kids living in a strange new town protected by soldiers and fences and gunboats. We lived in new houses on new streets, attended new schools, shopped in new stores, made new friends and our parents worked new jobs at new plants. There had never been a town quite like it—off the map, censored and ruled by military decree in the heartland of democratic America. It would become the cradle of the Atomic Age, the most significant story of the 20th Century, the secret town that produced the explosive guts for the first uranium bomb. It was Site X, code name for what became known as the Atomic City, Oak Ridge, Tennessee, the administrative headquarters for the Manhattan Project.

An army of men advanced on this beautiful green East Tennessee Valley in 1943 and peeled it down to an ugly red clay encampment, paved it with asphalt and concrete and set down rows of look-alike houses.

Our parents were part of the massive Oak Ridge work force that built the town and operated its plants, sworn to secrecy in a risky experiment that became the best-kept secret in the history of war. Our parents didn't make the atomic bomb and most of them never even saw one. But their handprints are all over it.

They did it so fast—30 months—it was a veritable miracle, a feat so remarkable that top German scientists could hardly believe it happened. It was done quietly at a torrid, round-the-clock pace and with a patriotic fervor that has not since been equaled in America. We, their children, were with them then and we are now the last of the living to witness it. We watched them go to work around the clock—weekdays, weekends, day, night, summer, winter. We heard them come home after midnight, we kept our voices down so they could sleep during the day, we smelled the ether in their hair.

We lived in plywood homes, some of us, showered in community bathhouses, sat on chamber pots when there was no toilet. We walked to school in construction mud, stood in lines for rationed goods. We lived the mystery—felt it, touched it and smelled it—though we didn't know what it was. And, except for a few, neither did our parents. Then, on August 6, 1945, when the Oak Ridge bomb destroyed some 60 percent of Hiroshima, everybody knew—about the town, about its mission, about our parents.

They are resting now, most of our moms and dads, in graves and urns and scattered ash—forgotten mostly except for their families. They gave their labor, they gave their talents, and some of them gave their lives.

Their names are embedded in a memorial brick sidewalk at Jackson Square, once the town's business center, and engraved in a bronze monument in Bissell Park—blue-collar workers and scientists side by side, as it was back when. A peace bell hangs at a distance in the same park, designed by Oak Ridgers and forged in Japan, observing the renewal of friendship with the Japanese. The mellow bell weighs more than 8,000 pounds, almost as heavy as "Little Boy," the Oak Ridge bomb that exploded above Hiroshima. The bell commemorates the dates of Japan's 1941 attack on Pearl Harbor, which started the war, and the United States' atomic bombing of Hiroshima and Nagasaki in 1945, which ended the war.

In the beginning we were from virtually everywhere, from big cities and little towns, from cotton mills and tobacco patches, from laboratories and big industry, from the military and academia, from England, Hungary, Poland, France—and on the run from Hitler's Germany and Mussolini's Italy. We invaded East Tennessee at a rate of about 1,000 a week until we were a city of 75,000, the fifth largest in the state. Hardly anyone knew we were there—wherever "there" was. We went to school there, played in its woods and on its playgrounds. We dated and danced at its youth centers and formed friendships that have lasted more than six decades. We met our husbands and wives there, many of us, and after 60 years it's still home to some. We are what's left of the Oak Ridge High School Class of 1952, and in the summer of 2010 we returned a final time to remember; thinking of life not as it is today, but as it was.

We drove through our old neighborhoods, down familiar streets, places we lived and loved, scenes and faces we had known long ago in childhood. It was therapy for our souls.

There, on Orchard Lane, on that doorstep, I kissed pretty Jackie Hildebrand for the first time. She became my wife, mother of two sons and grandmother of three. I stopped and looked at that porch and I could see us holding hands and it seemed like yesterday.

Once we were carefree teenagers wearing saddle oxfords and penny loafers, listening to Vaughn Monroe and Patti Paige, rooting for Joe DiMaggio and Joe Louis and taping pinup posters of Hedy Lamarr and Betty Grable on our lockers. We were the first graduating class in what was in 1951 a new, $3 million high school—$23 million in 2010 dollars. Today that school is old like us but, unlike us, it recently received a $53 million face-lift and a new life.

There were 243 graduates listed on our printed 1952 commencement program, but three of them were not recognized by any of us and for good reason. None of them, two girls and boy, had ever attended a class at Oak Ridge High. We wouldn't discover who they were until a half-century later when we were tracking down missing classmates for our 50th reunion. They had been students at Scarboro, we discovered, the isolated "Colored" neighborhood of Oak Ridge, the only three seniors in an all-black school that most of us didn't even know existed. Blacks weren't allowed in white schools in 1952 Tennessee, or in any public school in the south. Putting names of the three Scarboro students in our commencement program was, perhaps, the school board's way of recognizing them, since they had no graduation ceremony of their own. All three were dead, we discovered, when we tried to locate them in 2002. Three years after our graduation, in 1955, Oak Ridge would become the first public high school in Tennessee to desegregate.

The Class of '52 was ordinary in most respects. We didn't produce a great statesman, or a rock star or a famous athlete. We had no grand authors or inventors or war heroes. We had an ordinary number of children and grandchildren and divorces. We fought in Korea and then Vietnam, some of us. And we turned out three decorated colonels and a jet fighter pilot and a Navy pilot who flew groceries to Alaska. We had a Navy frogman and some submariners and submarine chasers, a professional baseball player, four Oak Ridge Sports Hall of Famers, a Bronze Star recipient, a noted potter and a playwright, a state senator and a gubernatorial candidate. We had at least four ministers and missionaries and scores of teachers and nurses and church pianists and choir singers and Sunday school teachers and medical doctors. We had a handful of engineers and professors, an architect, an optometrist, a Navy blimp pilot, a fashion model. And as far as we know, nobody went to jail—for long.

We lost classmates to cancer and heart failure and automobile accidents. A bolt of lightning would kill one of our children and a swimming accident would take another. One of our spouses would go down with American Airlines Flight 191 in Chicago in 1979, the deadliest airline accident ever on American soil. One of us was murdered. Two committed suicide.

Some of us lost parents too early because of work they did at the nuclear plants during World War II and the Cold War that followed. We still don't know much about what it was or how it happened. The Department of Labor has paid nearly $6 billion dollars in compensation to nuclear workers whose lives were shortened or whose health was damaged by something they inhaled or touched or worked around—my mother and father were among them.

For our 50th high school reunion eight years ago we accounted for all but seven of the 240 graduates. Seventy-six are dead at this writing and we are losing a classmate every month or two now. Of those remaining, almost 70 plus spouses attended the last reunion in the summer of 2010, our 58th. We had planned to wait until 2012 and celebrate our 60th graduation anniversary, but we were dying or going lame so quickly that we decided to have it earlier. Still, one classmate died the week of the reunion and another died the month after.

We gathered like family, widows and widowers, most of us retired. We schmoozed at the old Wildcat Den on the Turnpike, our after-school and after-ballgame recreation center hangout named for the school mascot. It is now a visitors' center and an Oak Ridge landmark.

At the 50th reunion we weren't just older, as we had been at other reunions, but old. Now, returning for the last reunion, we are 75-to-77 year-old antiques, bent and crooked, many of us, our eyes a little cloudy and enfeebled, our strength and vigor in steep decline. Yet we came together at the reunion as full of youthful spirit as we were six decades ago, no longer concerned about unfulfilled expectations or dreams abandoned. We met when we were nine and 10, most of us, gathering from virtually everywhere—a farm in Georgia, a mountainside in North Carolina, a cotton mill in Alabama, a steel mill town in Pennsylvania.

For this one June weekend in 2010, we tried to be kids again, singing our fight song and our Alma Mater, standing as straight as we could, leaning on our canes and our walkers or on somebody if we had to.

We talked about our younger ways in our younger days, of old boyfriends and girlfriends, of weddings and grandchildren. And then we talked about our pills and our braces and our doctors and our surgeries. And funerals.

We had a dinner show that featured a surprise performance by one of our cutest majorettes. Marching to Glenn Miller's lively rendition of the St. Louis Blues, 75-year-old Dottie Hawkins Shelton high-stepped across the banquet room wearing white boots and a sequined black outfit. She pranced and twirled and strutted confidently, just as she had done so many times in front of the Oak Ridge High marching band 60 years ago. She sashayed off stage to a standing ovation.

We laughed at a silly skit, making fun of our bald men and baldish women and our big bellies and our turkey necks. And we flirted a little. Some widows had their eyes out for widowers and divorcees and at least two couples exchanged phone numbers with promises to call.

Melvin George, the boy we voted Most Likely to Succeed, flew in from Missouri and played piano accompaniment for the show. He was president at two colleges—St. Olaf and Missouri. He was a math whiz and marched in the band at Northwestern and earned a PhD at Princeton.

Richard "Footsie" Reece, our class president, captain of the basketball team and Most Representative Boy, was the evening's principal speaker. He had never been to any of our previous six reunions, but was shamed into attending this one. He went to Duke on a combined basketball and academic scholarship and became Richard Reece, M.D., a prominent pathologist for 30 years in Minnesota before his retirement to Connecticut. Now he writes books and blogs, mostly about the ills of America's healthcare system.

"A pathologist," he explained to the class, "is a doctor who knows everything but it's too late." He said he had made it through life believing in three things: the power of words, the power of a sense of humor and the power of a sense of humus. "Humus, as you know, is another word for dirt. I learned on my farm in Minnesota that he who throws dirt loses ground."

Sophie Brody, our girl voted Most Likely to Succeed, earned a degree in English literature at the University of Rochester and then a Master's degree and turned down a Fulbright scholarship to marry a college professor. She taught school for some 25 years in a career that took her to the prestigious University of Chicago Lab School. She is a widow now and too worn to attend.

One of our brightest, Charles Franz VandenBulck, became a highly successful engineer, as everyone expected, and established his own firm in Savannah, Georgia. We didn't know, and he didn't know until after the war, that his father was the disbursing officer for the Manhattan Engineer District and signed almost $1.6 billion worth of government checks that paid for most of Oak Ridge and other secret Manhattan Project developments. Colonel Charles VandenBulck, one of the few who knew the bomb secret, was awarded the Legion of Merit by the War Department. A 1963 bridge that spans the Clinch River on Highway 95 on the edge of Oak Ridge now bears his name.

Gene Gardner, the state 440-yard dash champion and record-holder (and voted our Best Looking Boy) chose a military career and became an Air Force colonel. He's in the Oak Ridge and University of Tennessee sports halls of fame. We had another colonel, Roy Loudermilk, but he chose not to attend. "It would just be too painful," he said. Roy lost his wife, Joan Upchurch, our beautiful blonde Miss Oak Ridge High, almost 25 years ago.

Billy Kendrick, a bit of a loner in high school, skipped class too often to be a class star, but he would become one soon after graduation. He learned hairdressing at Antoine's in New York to spite his controlling father and became widely popular under his professional name, "Mr. Kristopher," in neighboring Knoxville. His passion was restoring old architectural treasurers in Knoxville and he is revered there. He died in 2009.

Lefty Gene Pharr, a popular four-sport athlete, signed with the Philadelphia Phillies out of high school and Ed "Sonny" Shackelford, our Mr. ORHS, was an Army captain and chaplain. Quiet, smart Joshua "Sonny" Boyd earned five degrees and spent his career teaching in Texas. Lois Haese, our Prettiest Girl, is a widow now and is still pretty as a 70-something great grandmother.

Dave Griffith, our all-America tailback, 100-yard dash champion and Most Athletic Boy, landed a football scholarship at the University of Tennessee and seemed headed for certain stardom. But Dave, a devout Jehovah's Witness, was dismissed by legendary coach Robert Neyland after one season for refusing to salute the American flag or to pledge allegiance to the United States of America. He never quite made it anywhere. Alcoholism wrecked his life.

Tom Hardin, who had the best legs on the basketball team according to the girls, was our All-Around Boy and one of the nicest. He was still recovering from the 2009 loss of his wife Kathleen, who died of cancer. Kay Mason, the class songbird and our All-Around Girl, led us in singing the alma mater and we hardly missed a note.

Sandy-haired Patty Craig, voted our Most Feminine Girl, and our Most Representative Girl, Carolyn Blakely, died far too soon. And so did Mary Sue Reece, Footsie's twin and our Wittiest Girl.

Our Friendliest Boy, Charles "Pedie" Counts, a highly acclaimed potter, was bitten by a mosquito while he was teaching in Nigeria and died of the West Nile virus. His ashes were sent home to Oak Ridge in a whisky decanter according to his prearranged instructions.

Once upon a fleeting time we were a class, dating and dancing and laughing and never once realizing that 58 years would pass so quickly. Now we are old like our parents before us, running out of time—to mend things, to forgive, to be forgiven, to tell our stories. Who were we? Where did we come from? What did we see and hear and whatever happened to us?

Those questions became the theme of the last reunion, the answers taking the form of stories and parodies and collected for this book. They may not be complete or perfectly accurate, but they are what we remember. They are joyful and they are tragic, they are comical and heartbreaking, inspirational and depressing, triumphant and sorrowful. And yes, some of them may seem insignificant and out of place. But not for us. Some of us told stories about ourselves that we never imagined we would tell, or could tell in public. We did it for ourselves, for our parents, for one another. And we did it so that we will live forever in an inch or two of shelf space in the library of our hometown.

Book One
Early Oak Ridge...

Photos by Ed Westcott

War at Home

World War II was really two wars, the one abroad and the one at home. A widely published article that first appeared in an Army ordinance magazine in 1942 warned us. It read, in part:

For the first time in the history of war, battles are as much tussles between competing factories as between contending armies. The production of weapons, more so than the conscription of men, will be the deciding factor in battle.

And so it was. In a 1946 book, <u>While You Were Gone,</u> (Simon and Shuster) the home front was described in detail. By mid-1942 American typewriter factories were making machine guns. Auto plants were making fighter planes and tanks. A mechanical pencil manufacturer turned out bomb parts and precision instruments. A soft drink company loaded shells with explosives. A company that canned citrus fruit made parts for merchant ships.

Virtually every walking American contributed in some way. Japan's sneak attack on Pearl Harbor on Dec. 7, 1941, sobered the pacifists who had openly opposed the war and all but a radical few Americans bonded like a threatened family.

Eighty-five million Americans bought war bonds and stamps to help finance a war that would cost $400 billion. The Boy Scouts collected rubber, scrap metal, books, paper and were responsible for the purchase of $8 billion in war bonds and stamps. Children took their nickels and dimes to school and bought more than $1 billion in bonds and stamps, enough to buy 2,900 planes, 33,000 jeeps, 11,600 amphibious jeeps and 11,690 parachutes. Newspapers, radio and advertising agencies donated nearly $1 billion worth of space and radio time so the government could get messages quickly to the public.

In 1944 alone, 18 million home-grown victory gardens were planted, enough to preserve 3.5 billion quarts of vegetables and feed 40 percent of the U.S. population. America accepted the rationing of goods with good spirit—cigarettes, sugar, meat, shoes, coffee, chocolate, tires and gasoline. Motorists were limited to three gallons of gas a week and the speed limit across the United States was reduced to 35 miles per hour. Pleasure riding was prohibited. Men's pants were tailored without cuffs. The sale of heavy cream was stopped altogether. Cosmetics, hairpins, tinfoil and alcohol disappeared from shelves, along with alarm clocks, cameras and field glasses. One could buy almost nothing that had metal in it—ice tongs, hair curlers, corn poppers, tools, shellfish crackers, beer steins, bird cages or cocktail shakers. There was no plastic then. There was nothing special on store shelves for Christmas, but hardly anyone complained.

American flags hung from porches and gold stars hung in windows, each star representing a son or daughter serving in the military. War songs blared across the country. *"Praise the Lord and Pass the Ammunition"* was a favorite sing-along tune. One of the most talked-about songs, *"In Der Fuehrer's Face,"* was banned from radio by the FCC because its lyrics were considered inappropriate. The song suggested that America should "bra-a-a-a-a-a-ck" in the fuehrer's face, an action verb meaning to break considerable wind.

At least a fourth of the males in Hollywood—actors, writers, directors—joined the military; including Mickey Rooney, Clark Gable, Jimmy Stewart, Henry Fonda, John Huston and Frank Capra. Others like Bob Hope and Joe E. Brown went around the world to entertain troops on what was called the "foxhole circuit."

Baseball put some 4,000 of its players into military uniforms. Joltin' Joe DiMaggio left the New York Yankees and enlisted in the Army as a private. Ted Williams left the Boston Red Sox and became a Marine fighter pilot, and Detroit slugger

Hank Greenberg was commissioned a second lieutenant. Major League baseball continued throughout the war as a morale booster, filling rosters with mostly Class A talent—flat-footed draft rejects, teenagers and old warriors.

World heavyweight champion Joe Louis donated two of his fight purses to the Army and Navy relief funds, then enlisted in the Army and fought exhibition bouts for the troops.

A teenaged farm boy named Audie Murphy, an orphan reared by poor Texas sharecroppers, became a battlefield star and a symbol of American courage. He was wounded three times, rose from private to a battlefield commissioned lieutenant, won the Congressional Medal of Honor and became the most decorated American soldier in the war with 28 medals. He returned home to a movie star career.

Superman, aka Clark Kent, tried to enlist, too, but was rejected as a 4F when his X-ray vision eyes read a test chart in an adjacent room instead of the one he was supposed to read.

While 12 million American men and women were serving in the U.S. military, almost 70 million worked on the home front to supply them. That figure included 3 million children between 12 and 18 who went to work full time. Those kids, plus thousands of under-aged teens who lied about their ages and enlisted in the military, sent U.S high school enrollment to a record low.

Bobby Cox from Chattanooga, Tennessee was 14 on Pearl Harbor day. "I was walking down Market Street," he said, "and a corner newsboy was holding up The Chattanooga Times yelling 'Japanese attack Pearl Harbor! Read all about it!' I'd never heard of Pearl Harbor. I thought it was a woman. Anyhow, I enlisted and a few months later I'm in a fox hole on Guadalcanal."

While young men fought, young women performed jobs traditionally done by them and, daringly, began wearing slacks to work. Some employers asked women to not wear tight sweaters after some men reportedly stopped working to gape.

Millions of citizens stood in line and gave blood for combat troops. More than 5 million pints were donated in 1944 alone. They saved tin cans, empty toothpaste tubes, scrap metal and paper for recycling.

Sears Roebuck and Company loaned the government its gifted executive vice president, Donald M. Nelson, who was immediately put in charge of the War Production Board. Nelson's mobilization of the nation's productive resources turned into the biggest economic undertaking in history. He turned a $90 billion 1940 economy into a nearly $200 billion economy by war's end. In 1943, United States war factory production equaled that of Germany, Japan and Italy combined, and in 1944 it more than doubled the output of the Axis.

And something more was happening in America, something much bigger than guns and planes and ships, something that would change the world forever. Between some sparsely populated mountain ridges in East Tennessee's rural backwoods, in a highly guarded complex first known only by its code name, Site X, a new kind of factory was making the explosive material for a new kind of weapon—atomic bombs. It was done secretly and miraculously by a collection of physicists, chemists and engineers from around the world, with the help of a skill-and-muscle, all-America blue-collar labor force. By the time my parents arrived in 1944 with three children, it was known as Oak Ridge—but not by many.

War Department's 21-Day Notice

November, 11, 1942

Dear _____:

The War Department intends to take possession of your farm, December 1, 1942. It will be necessary for you to move not later than that date. In order to pay you quickly, the money for your property will be placed into the United States court in Knoxville, Tennessee. The court will permit you to withdraw a substantial part of this money without waiting. This may be done without impairing your right to contest the fixed payment on your property by the War Department.

It is expected that your money will be put in court within 10 days, and as soon as you are notified it is suggested you get in touch with the United Sates attorney to find out how much can be withdrawn. Your fullest cooperation will be a material aid to the war effort.

Signed: Fred Morgan, project manager.

He Left the Farm on a Hay Truck

John Rice Irwin was a young boy when his farm family was displaced by government officials in 1942 so that Oak Ridge could be built. He became a teacher in Anderson County, then a principal and, at age 31, the youngest school superintendent in the state. He is the founder of the Museum of Appalachia, an author, historian and entertaining storyteller.

We had about 325 acres roughly from the top of Pine Mountain to a little ridge above where the Garden Apartments are now. It included the whole valley. The land where the hospital is belonged to my father's brother. He had a little farmhouse there and a barn about where the Snow White Drive-In was on the Turnpike. There was only one blacktop road in the county – Highway 61 from Clinton to Oliver Springs, part of which was the Turnpike. There was one lone power line.

My family was displaced twice, first by TVA in the Thirties when they built Norris Dam in Union County, and then for Oak Ridge. To my knowledge, all the people who lived here were general farmers. There were a few farmhouses along what is now the Turnpike after you left Elza Gate, and there was a beer joint called the Full Moon that was the epitome of sin and degradation. When my grandmother used to get angry at me she'd say, "If you don't mend your ways you'll end up at the Full Moon." It was about the worst thing that could happen to anybody. When people passed by there, respectful citizens, they not only wouldn't stop, they wouldn't even look in that direction because they might be accused of patronizing the place. But apparently, in addition to being a beer joint, I'm sure they bootlegged there and sold most of the moonshine people made around here. Some people would go there, get drunk and stay for days.

But on down below that, there was a farm owned by Andy Stooksbury, a cousin of mine. He never had an automobile. He went to the store in his wagon with a team of mules.

All this land around here was pretty scarce because people moved here after being pushed off their land for the dam. So just about all the land that a mule could stand on was cleared, even if it was terribly steep, and they grew corn on it. Most everybody grew corn and had tobacco patches.

On down the road was Nash Copeland's store and just about everybody traded there. His store was about where the shopping mall is and on down the road were two more stores. One was owned by Bill Key and the other was owned by Bill Lockett. So you had Lockett and Key right across the road.

Bill Key was illiterate but a pretty good businessman, and he drove a school bus from the time I can first remember. When I became superintendent of schools many years later, he was still driving a bus and fibbing about his age. I said, "Now Bill, we can't continue to let you drive a school bus," and he said, "Johnny, I'm just 65." He had no record of his birth, but I knew he was at least 75. We finally talked him into quitting. He came back and wanted a job as a janitor down at Norwood, a new building. He said, "Johnny, I need a job. I'm an old man." I said, "How old are you?" and he said, "I'm 78." I said, "Well, that's funny. Last year you were 65 and now you're 78." He laughed.

He was an interesting man. He served on the county court one time but couldn't sign his name. He made an "X" for his signature. He was a pretty sharp old fellow and accumulated a lot of money. He drove a big Cadillac around here before he died.

The first physical work I saw on the Oak Ridge project was at Elza Gate where they built a little spur off that railroad and started moving some equipment in by train. Then all of a sudden you had people surveying pasture land, farm land and before long the place was crawling with these engineers and everybody was talking about it.

One old gentleman that I remember by the name of Charlie Gamble was going around spreading the rumor that these people were working for the government and that the government was trying to move everyone out in order to get the gold and silver that the Indians buried here when they were taken out by Andrew Jackson. He said his father or grandfather had told him and several people that the Indians had buried enough gold and silver here to shoe the people's horses and that someday, if people ever found it, all the people would be rich.

Before long they began building some temporary housing and by that time they were condemning the land and taking it over. They had what they called hot spots, land they needed in a hurry, and there was this family that went to Clinton for something and when they got back they found a notice tacked on their front porch indicating that they had to be out within 14 days and that's what they called the 14-day notices. In some cases it was disastrous for the farmer. Here's a fellow who has two or three barns of hay, corn and wheat and cattle and all the farm machinery and everything, and he had to find a place to move within 14 days.

My family was given more time than that, but not a great deal more. My grandfather was a Methodist minister and he didn't believe in working on Sunday and neither did my father, but they worked on Sundays until we got moved. We had about 1,500 bushels of wheat for example, and several barns full of corn and hay. The hay was put up loose, wasn't bailed, and you can't move loose hay. You take a barn bigger than a house; fill it with loose hay it would take 10 men all summer to move. We had to get bailers to get all this hay out.

My father bought another place up in the Glen Alpine Community, about 20 miles away. We just had one truck and we made a lot of trips hauling stuff—cows and pigs and chickens. We finally got some help, but it wasn't easy. I left home one day on a hay truck and I never saw the farm again. Just like that it was government property and off limits.

There was this one young man named Elisha Miller. They called him Lash. He used to work for us quite a bit. He lived up on the ridge not far from here and he would walk down from the ridge five or six miles and get here about 7 o'clock. Then he'd work 10 or 11 hours, and I mean really work, and then he'd walk back home. He got 75 cents or $1 dollar a day, which is what my dad paid most people then.

Lash was one of the first people to get a job in Oak Ridge when they started hiring labor. He was a typical son of the depression. He was born up in Union County way up in the ridges somewhere, an illegitimate child with no formal education. He had a very tough life.

He got into a fight with a boy one time and cut the boy up and they put him in reform school. He used to sit and talk about the kind of life he had living in that reform school. He still had big welts and scars on his back where they had whipped him because of the least bit of an infraction of the rules. They would tie him up and whip him with a black snake whip and literally whip the clothes off of him. Some of those boys tried to get away, swimming across a river. Not many got away. Some of them drowned. That was before Lash came to work for my father. By then he was about 30 and lived in what used to be a chicken house. He got one of the first jobs in Oak Ridge in 1942 and he was still working there the last I heard, some 30 years later. It was not an easy life around here.

John Rice Irwin

-- From a 1974 interview with Jay Searcy

Weinberg Waited Outside
On the Day of the Atom

So powerful was the new atomic weapon that the United States was trying to make in 1942, so horrible was its destructive capabilities, some of the scientists at the University of Chicago hoped that the attempt to make the first controlled nuclear chain reaction would fail. If their calculations were correct, heat from an atomic explosion would hit 100 million degrees Fahrenheit, 55 million degrees Centigrade at its center, or about three times the estimated heat at the core of the sun.

Fifty carefully chosen people were in the makeshift laboratory on a squash court beneath the football stadium at Stagg Field on December 2, 1942. They were there to take part in the experiment or to witness the historic occasion. They stood around waiting for the rods to be pulled from the pile that would start the first controlled nuclear chain reaction, thus ushering in the Atomic Age. Two young physicists in the group— Alvin Graves of the University of Texas, and Harold Lichtenberger of Milliken College in Illinois—were selected for what was called the "suicide brigade." They were positioned in silence on a high platform overlooking the pile, each holding a bucket of a potent cadmium solution to quince any fire that might start if the cadmium and boron bonds were broken. For two hours they stood, waiting.

Bernard Feld, a physicist who witnessed the test, described the final moment. "When everything was ready, [Enrico] Fermi had the rods withdrawn one by one and he was sitting there looking at the counter. As the counter started to go up and up and all the rods were withdrawn, we could hear the counter rrrrrRRRRR!—and off the scale. After a minute Fermi said, "That's enough. Put the rods back and let's go to lunch."

Alvin Weinberg, then 27, a native of Chicago and a University of Chicago educated physicist, had been working on the experiment, and was disappointed that he was not among the 50 invited inside the lab. He was No. 54 on the priority list, he said, and so he stood outside with others and talked about the potential of atomic energy.

"There was a lot of speculation," he remembered years later after his retirement from a distinguished career in Oak Ridge. "Some thought we would soon be living in constant fear for the rest of time, that any moment a reign of atomic bombs might come down on us from anywhere and that the tension would become unendurable. Others thought that nations with the bomb would be hesitant to use it knowing that retaliation would start a world nuclear war that everyone would lose. Some thought a few trigger-happy men would frantically push the button, reasoning that they were only beating other nations to the punch."

Some said that a nuclear war was sure to happen someday, and that it would set us back 500,000 years, all the way back to the caves.

Concerns grew among the scientists after the first test bomb was detonated in the Trinity experiment in July, 1945. An anti-bomb petition circulated quietly and was presented to President Truman while plans for the first bombing were being finalized. It changed nothing.

After the war, some spoke out.

Said physicist Eugene Wigner: "I signed the petition because I believed at the time that it would be possible to terminate the war without the use of the nuclear weapon."

Said Albert Einstein, whose letter to President Roosevelt got America's nuclear program moving: "Had I known that the Germans would not succeed, I would have done nothing for the bomb."

A German Error Saved Us

Dr. Alvin Weinberg was an Oak Ridge resident from 1945 until his death in 2006. He helped design the X-10 reactor, the pilot plant that produced the world's first plutonium, when he was in his 20s. After World War II he served as director of Oak Ridge National Laboratory's Physics Division and was soon after appointed ORNL research director. In 1955 he succeeded Eugene Wigner as director of ORNL, a position he held until 1972. He was among the first to produce research suggesting that increased atmospheric levels of carbon dioxide from burning fossil fuels was leading to global warming.

I came in by train from Chicago at 6 a.m. and was driven to the city in an Army staff car. My first look at Tennessee was Knoxville. There were pawnshops everywhere. Oak Ridge was just a farmland, bare ground in the valley and trees up above. They took me in a shuttle car to the lab where I would be working. I spent my first night at the Guest House, the only hotel in town. It was November, 1943.

Later on when I was going back and forth from Chicago, I stayed at a D house at 105 West Malta Road. It was a kind of a bachelor's hideaway for scientists and engineers, mostly from Chicago. It was called the Charlie West Mansion. Charlie was a pretty old guy in those days and he took care of the place. Not many knew about that house.

I'm from Chicago. My parents were Russian immigrants and they settled there. My father was a tailor in Russia but he managed a dress factory in Chicago.

I was a graduate student in the physics department of the University of Chicago when I was recruited by the dean. I didn't know what I was recruited for. I was about to go into radar. My special skill was spectra chemical analysis. Only younger people were available then and the single ones were more likely to be sent to Hanford or Oak Ridge. We didn't know exactly what they were doing or how, but we knew they were separating isotopes. I was 28. Everyone in Oak Ridge seemed to be 28.

I expected an Army town, Army buses to take us to work, Army PX, soldiers everywhere. And it was, somewhat. But at the dormitories we were treated like high school boys rather than adults. The dorms were handled like a boys' boarding school. When my mother came down she couldn't even come to my room because she was of the opposite sex. No women allowed in the men's dorms I went to the front desk and said, "But this is my mother!" Sorry no women allowed in the men's dorm.

I don't remember a lot about what Oak Ridge looked like then. We had the mud and whatever else that represents. But the social and intellectual side of it was wonderful. I used to go to sleep early on Saturday night because I was so exhausted. It was a closed city and you had to make your own entertainment, and we didn't lack for it. I happen to play piano so I got involved in musical events, so that worked out fine. It was a big picnic. The money wasn't bad either. When I first joined the project I think I was making about $200 a month [roughly $2,500 in 2010 dollars] and that wasn't bad back then. Housing was cheap and you didn't have to pay for electricity, coal or water. Everything was people oriented. I met my wife, Marge, in Oak Ridge. She had come to Y-12 from Berkeley. Like me, she never went back.

But the big attraction was the work, the intellectual challenge. You have to realize that the idea of a chain reaction was so bizarre it was hard to really realize. Look, we're going to have it. It's going to work. That was about it. You were driven by the knowledge that you were breaking into something. We never worked so hard before or after. Six, seven days a week—10, 12, 14 hours a day, both here and Chicago.

We were not in production at X-10. We were the pilot plant for Hanford. The first gram of plutonium came from X-10. We made about one pound of it by the summer of 1944 and developed a chemical process that was used at Hanford. They were able to make 100 times a day as much as we made.

It was a great challenge for us, but we never felt we couldn't do it. In my lab, the first spectra of two or three new elements were taken because we had finally separated a big enough amount that we could do that work. I look back on it and realize we were the first ones to see this stuff in big amounts. We were youngsters and we just thought we could do anything. I remember one of the leaders sitting on top of a wastebasket talking to the guys in the lab, arguing about the meaning of what we had just done. It was a wonderful intellectual endeavor.

Along with that, an enormous research program was developed here because we had that reactor and since it could not be put on wheels and moved, it remained and we used it for research. That's what kept a lot of the people here. It was an academic community as much as any university would be.

A lot of people were worried early in the war because we were supposedly in a race for the bomb with Germany because the Germans, who discovered fission in 1939, were about two years ahead of everybody at the start of the war. I remember in 1943 [Eugene] Wigner was always worried more than anybody else. He thought the Germans would have the bomb before we did. We had a little meeting in Arthur Compton's office.

Compton was the big boss. Present at the meeting was [Enrico] Fermi. Wigner went up to the blackboard and tried to calculate how long it would take for the Germans to make a bomb, so he said: "Well, it will take them three months to design a reactor. It will take them three months to build a reactor and in a year they could have the bomb." The big mistake Wigner made was that he assumed that everybody on the German project was either a Wigner or a Fermi. They did have some good people, but their best ones were the Jews who left because of Hitler.

We knew for sure the Germans wouldn't have the bomb in late 1944 when the Allies captured the top German nuclear scientists and their records. Since I know German, I was assigned to analyze their technical data, along with Lothar Nordheim, who was a native German. Looking at their papers, it was obvious that the Germans were not committed. We noticed that their line of thinking was quite parallel to our line of thinking, more or less, although they made one crucial error in the chain reaction.

You know how to get a neutron into the nucleus; it splits into two neutrons, comes out and so on. But one of the keys to making a controlled nuclear reaction is that not all of those neutrons come off immediately. One percent of neutrons come with a delay of maybe 20 seconds. That means if you are subcritical by that amount then they won't explode. It just acts naturally. The Germans never understood about delayed neutrons, which means they really hadn't taken things all that seriously. It was a terrible error on the part of the Germans. They also rejected graphite as the moderator. They made an incorrect measurement on the graphite and so they went after heavy water as the moderator, which is easier to do. But if you don't have heavy water in abundance, that in itself is a big job. And they didn't. In the end they had what they called a reactor, but it was not big enough to go critical. That was a sense of relief, because we didn't know for sure until then. It was exciting, knowing what the world didn't know.

Apparently, the Germans didn't think we were close to getting the bomb. As far as I know, no German spies infiltrated the Manhattan Project, although there were some German spies who were caught; so it came as a big surprise to the captured German scientists when they heard about the Hiroshima bomb. Some of them didn't believe it at first.

It was the Russians who were so successful with their spies, namely Klaus Fuchs and Morris Cohen who were the most damaging. They supplied the Soviet Union with top-secret technical documentation from Los Alamos during the war. They were both caught and convicted, and there were others. But there was another one, an American named Ted Hall, who was never arrested. At age 18, Hall was a Harvard graduate and the youngest physicist working on the Manhattan Project. He was in on the design work and he worked both at Oak Ridge and Los Alamos. He was never interrogated by the FBI and never arrested because the U.S. would have had to expose its source for identifying other Russian spies in order to convict him. He spent most of his life in England after the war, and his work with electron microscopes in biological X-ray microanalysis led to broad acclaim.

I knew some of the spies and worked with them, but I was never suspicious. Alan Nunn, who was British, was one. I knew him in Chicago. He visited Oak Ridge at times. He got 10 years. Then there was a fellow named Bruno Pontecorvo, an Italian Jew who was a protégé of Fermi. I knew him in Chicago and Montreal. He got 15 years. But you know, I really didn't think of spies back then. We were so involved, I was never suspicious of anyone. All those spies were arrested after the war during the cold war, and by then it was over.

I never really thought about leaving Oak Ridge after the war. I moved into my F-house on Moylan Lane in 1945 and never left it. It is a good house and I paid only $7,000 for it in the Fifties. Why move?

Alvin Weinberg

1915 - 2006

The General Was a Bully

Although he was never an Oak Ridger, General Leslie Groves, director of the Manhattan Project, spent much of his time in the city, commuting from Washington on a train with a secretary and a briefcase stuffed with paperwork. He slept at the Guest House, at the Elza House and, on occasion some said, in the maternity ward of the Oak Ridge Hospital (with a guard posted at the door).

He made it a point to hide from the public and dashed from place to place in an unmarked staff car driven by Elmer Brummett, whose family had 40 acres of farmland in Lupton Valley before the government took it over. "I lied about my age when I was 16 to get on at the plant," Brummett told friends, "and ended up being Gen. Groves' chauffeur for 65 cents an hour."

Groves was a huge man, almost 300 pounds, and he had a reputation for throwing his weight around. He was considered arrogant when he was at West Point, where he finished fourth in his class, and that reputation expanded when he was a colonel in the Corps of Engineers in charge of building the Pentagon. Said one critic, "He was conceited, impatient, rude, forceful, ruthless, impetuous and an intimidating know-it-all egomaniac." Lt. Col. Kenneth Nichols, in charge of the Oak Ridge operation under Groves, said after the war that Groves was "the biggest sonofabitch I've ever met in my life, but also one of the most capable individuals. He had an ego second to none; he had tireless energy and absolute confidence in his decisions. I hated his guts and so did everybody else, but we had our form of understanding."

President Franklin D. Roosevelt thought his credentials were just right. He promised him a promotion to brigadier general, appointed him director of the Manhattan Project and made it the top priority of the war. Groves would have to handle scores of brilliant scientists, many of whom were equally egotistical and arrogant. Roosevelt needed a bully.

Photo by Ed Westcott

General Leslie Groves

Nobody ever ignored the Fourth Amendment the way Leslie Groves did. He became a czar. He had no rules restricting him, he had a federally backed blank check for spending, and he created what amounted to a secret empire.

He went against his advisors and appointed physicist Robert Oppenheimer to head the Los Alamos bomb design project, then kept him under surveillance for the rest of the war; bugging his apartment and tapping his phone. He had Albert Einstein's Long Island home bugged, his phone tapped and denied him a security clearance because he was German and had expressed some left wing ideas.

Groves was paranoid, some said, with the fear that Germany would develop the atomic bomb ahead of the United States, and he used that fear to drive his scientists and to keep them from leaving the project.

Until the U.S. had positive knowledge, he wrote in his book Now It Can Be Told, he assumed the most competent German scientists and engineers were working on an atom bomb with the full support of their government and with full capacity of German industry at their disposal.

An indication of just how concerned Groves was: Several times in 1943 and 1944 he considered having top German scientists kidnapped and assassinated. In December, 1944, Germany's top physicist, Werner Heisenberg, director of the Kaiser Wilhelm Institute, was scheduled to speak in Switzerland. An unlikely U.S. intelligence agent, former major league baseball catcher Moe Berg, was instructed to attend the lecture with a pistol and a cyanide pill. If Heisenberg indicated that Germany had the bomb, or was on its way to getting one, Berg was instructed to shoot him. Heisenberg made no mention of a German bomb program in his delivery; Berg put his gun away and returned home.

The United States didn't know it, but in June 1942, Adolph Hitler met with Albert Speer, Reich Minister for German armaments, and issued a general decree forbidding any research program that would not yield quick results for the war effort. Heisenberg, who thought it would take 1,000 pounds of enriched uranium to make a bomb (it took about 90), and his top physicists were virtually ignored. They were afraid to ask for the substantial amounts of money and material needed to build the bomb because if they failed, German science would be embarrassed and the temperamental, vengeful Hitler could have them imprisoned.

Groves continued to run roughshod over his empire until the bombing of Hiroshima. He accomplished his goal but he made many enemies along the way, some of them quite power-ful. He never got the accolades expected for what turned out to be a miraculous accomplishment. His enemies reduced his power drastically after the war when the nuclear program was transferred to civilian authority. Groves eventually left the military and became vice president of Sperry Rand Corporation. He died of a heart attack at age 73.

Groves with P.R. Officer George Robinson

Shhhhhh! It's a Secret

One day at the Pentagon a corporal who worked at Oak Ridge demanded to see Gen. Leslie Groves, director of the Manhattan Project. He knew the secret, he said, and wanted to file a complaint about the Oak Ridge operation. Gen Groves invited him into his office and the corporal blurted out: "I have enough scientific background to know that we are attempting to make an atomic bomb."

Groves nodded to an aide, then asked the corporal to sit down. He chatted with him for a half hour, long enough to enable an aide to photocopy all the papers in the corporal's briefcase. The corporal was detained and eventually arrested.

Groves was urged by advisors to transfer the corporal to a combat unit, but he refused for fear that he might talk loosely or be captured. Instead, he was put under house arrest and guarded for the duration of the war.

August 21, 1944, Arthur Hale, radio commentator, broke a story written for him by a conscientious objector who knew a man at Illinois Tech whose roommate worked on the secret project. He thought the broadcast might make Hitler quit the war. A G-2 agent heard it and called Gen. Groves, who ordered that all associated with the program be brought before him. Hale was taken to task, then ordered to return to the air as if nothing had happened.

Sex at Site X

With more than 100,000 mostly 20-to-34-year olds dashing in and out of Oak Ridge 24 hours a day, many of them single and virtually all of them frisky, sex got as much attention as the atomic bomb in the secret years. And like the nuclear plants, sex was an around-the-clock matter and a race against time. They did it here. They did it there. They did it everywhere.

You had to watch where you were stepping as you walked through any wooded area, especially the picnic grounds where there were tables and boardwalks—day or night. They hid behind trees, in bushes and weeds and under bridges. It wasn't just happening in the woods. It was in grave yards, moving vans, tents, hospital beds, sewer pipes, parking lots, truck beds, back seats, crawl spaces, end zones and centerfield, and on tennis courts, hardwood floors, and hoods of cars. I almost stepped on a soldier and his lady one night walking home through the woods from a movie.

There was a wooden bridge over a small creek in the woods behind the Chapel on the Hill where guys and their girls liked to stand and pet. Sometimes in the moonlight, sometimes in daylight. Some of my friends hid under the bridge, from time to time, and peeked up through the cracks and under the skirts of the ladies. Some of them saw their first vagina under that bridge—and a lot of handiwork. "I swear to you," a buddy told me once about his first bridge experience, "it winked at me."

Nobody ever confirmed it, but the rooftop of one of the nuclear buildings at X-10 was rumored to be a favorite spot—behind the air vents. They did it between shifts, on lunch breaks and on overtime, the story goes. Next to the atomic bomb, that roof was the best-kept secret of the war.

It wasn't just dating singles who were looking for privacy. Some married couples had to search for privacy, too, because the housing shortage kept them apart. Married men and women were often assigned to separate men's and women's dorms with no room visitation rights. It wasn't unusual for a married man to be cited by police for hiding his wife in a dormitory room, and a few women got caught hiding their husbands.

At Oak Ridge's population peak in 1945, about 7,000 mostly single women were concentrated in dormitories in the Townsite area alone; many of them just out of high school or college, most of them unmarried and some living away from home for the first time. Oak Ridge men outnumbered women, 20-1, so the dormitories were popular hangouts. Dormitory women were instructed to meet and entertain their male visitors in a first-floor lounge at the main entrance. But there were fire-escape exits at each end of the two-story, barrack-like buildings, and some boyfriends sometimes received more accommodating invitations.

Maids working at the men's dorms had one of the most hazardous jobs of the war. It wasn't unusual for a housekeeper to be propositioned several times on a single shift. Some pushed men away and others were dragged into rooms, kicking and screaming. The police were called in regularly.

Louise Hill, mother of classmate Gene Pharr, was a supervisor at one of the women's dorms. Among her biggest problems were hot plates and men, both forbidden in the women's rooms. The hot plate issue was easy, but the men just wouldn't stay away. They hung around like dogs at a picnic, looking for dates.

"There weren't enough women to go around," said Louise, who was a pretty, young woman herself at the time, "and some of the guys tried to date *me*."

"'I'm married,' I told them, and they just shrugged and said, 'that doesn't matter,' and I said, 'Well, it matters to *me*.'

"One young man in particular kept begging me to go out with him and one evening he was getting kind of fresh and he didn't know that the man sitting behind me was Freeman, my husband. The man just wouldn't stop and finally Freeman had heard enough and got up to say something to him. But you know, that man grabbed Freeman by his tie, pulled him out on the porch and sat on him. I had to call the police to get him off.

"I was getting a look at the real world in that dorm. Some of those girls were stepping out on their husbands, going off to places with them and I just hated to see that. I talked to a girl about that one time. 'What would you tell your husband, what would you tell your children and your mother and dad?' She just shrugged and said, 'I don't care.' "

Concerned town officials attempted to improve behavior and attitudes at the women's dorms by hiring some employees from fashionable women's colleges, such as Bryn Mawr, Radcliff and Smith, as lifestyle consultants. It was a failed mission. They too were propositioned and went home.

The town's first recreation center for high schoolers, the Wildcat Den, was a favorite hangout for young soldiers. Only Oak Ridge High students were allowed inside, but the GIs waited outside and tried to introduce themselves as coeds came and went. The Den was strictly supervised but many parents wouldn't allow their daughters to attend.

G-road was a favorite go-to place for teens. It was a gravel-and-dirt border road off Outer Drive, curling down a steep, thickly wooded ridge to the secluded grounds of Bacon Springs. A shallow cave above the springs on a ridge was a popular spot for bedrolls and sleeping blankets. So was an abandoned barn at the bottom of G-road, where a lot of teenagers got their first serious kiss.

Oak Ridge's 44,000 or so young construction workers attracted a fair number of shift-working prostitutes in the trailer parks. With 5,000 trailers inside the fences, business boomed. Since every adult had to have a job or a working spouse to get housing, many prostitutes took jobs as waitresses and store clerks to attract after–hours business.

Off-duty civilians and soldiers made the cafeterias a hang-out, for dates and for prostitutes. On my family's first night in Oak Ridge in August, 1944, we got off a bus from Knoxville at the Central Cafeteria after dark in front of a standing crowd of mostly men. Some were waiting for buses, others were just looking. The cafeteria was a wooden Army mess hall, one of 11 in town, and together they served more than 26,000 meals a day. Lines were always out the door and onto the grounds. Mom, Dad and we three children were walking toward the cafeteria when some young soldiers walked by and gave my 13-year-old sister the eye. Mother saw it and jerked Mary Glenn's arm as if she were at fault. "Watch where you're going," mother warned, and she looked at my dad as if to say, "What have we gotten into?" Mother, who was in her mid-30s, got looked at, too, though she pretended not to notice.

Venereal disease was rampant; some studies showed the VD rate in wartime Oak Ridge to be 2 ½ times the national average and 25 times higher among Black residents. Illegitimate pregnancies were common. Pregnant women lost their jobs and were sent home.

While the government didn't exactly endorse promiscuity, the sex issue wasn't a high priority on its list of concerns. A report found among the post-war wartime archives explains the government's position. "Women's need for economic security and desires for independence, including a fair amount of social and sexual freedom, overlapped with the government's need for labor and for 'girls' to keep the important male employees happy." All this was expected, at least from the governmental perspective, to be "temporary."

Near the end of the war, marriages and babies kept Oak Ridge ministers and obstetricians busy. Births in the Secret City numbered more than a thousand in 1945, a rate that made Oak Ridge one of the biggest baby towns in American history. But no one knew it. For security reasons, sites of weddings and births were falsely documented in the earliest days. Birth certificates and marriage announcements placed the events in Knoxville and corrections weren't made until after the war. William Pugh, an Army obstetrician, delivered a high percentage of the secret newborns. In a newspaper interview years after the war he estimated that he delivered between 150 and 200 babies in his first six months in Oak Ridge. Statistics kept in a scrapbook by a fellow Army doctor showed that 581 babies were born at the Oak Ridge hospital in the first six months of 1945. The first Oak Ridge baby was born two weeks before the hospital was officially opened in 1943. Pregnant women virtually swarmed the hospital on opening day.

"Black Folks Wasn't Allowed"

We knew virtually nothing about Negroes, as they were properly addressed in early Oak Ridge. There were none in the school system. You almost never saw any in a grocery store or public building unless they were sweeping up, and even that was rare. Some of us graduated high school without ever knowing a Negro.

Not that we didn't want to. There was just nobody to know. Negro children weren't allowed inside the city gates until the end of the war, even if both parents lived and worked there. Negro children couldn't even visit their parents. Children were left back home with grandparents and assorted relatives. Some lived off-site with their working parents who rode buses to work.

Kathleen Stephens, from Auburn, Alabama, now a retired teacher living in Oak Ridge, was among the children left behind. "It was hard being away from Mom and Dad," she said. "We missed them and wanted to be with them. We stayed with our grandparents and we had other cousins who stayed there with us. We grew up really close, like brothers and sisters. Our grandparents were nice, but it isn't like being with your real parents."

To avoid attracting attention to Oak Ridge, the government determined before the Manhattan Project got under way to follow the cultural policies of the state in order to avoid attracting attention. Officially, the statement read: "The responsibility of the Office of the District Engineer and Roane-Anderson Company is not to promote social changes, whether desirable or undesirable, but to see that the community is efficiently run and that everybody has a chance to live decently in it."

But everybody didn't live decently in it.

About 7,000 Negroes, mostly poor and uneducated and mostly from Alabama, Mississippi, Georgia and Tennessee, were recruited for Oak Ridge. Many of them were rounded up by labor bosses and given free transportation to Site X on so-called labor trains, or on buses. Some were hauled in by the truckload like cattle.

"Here's how that worked," said Hal Williams, a 21-year-old Negro from Mississippi in 1943. "My work boss told me to be down at this government building in Memphis at 10 o'clock on Monday morning if I wanted to work. He said it was good money, but he didn't say nothing about where we was going. I lived about 20 miles outside Memphis in Mississippi, so I hitch-hiked to get there. I had to come in the highway where Elvis Pressley's place is now. It wasn't nothing but a cotton field then. There was a bunch of us Black folks waiting at the government building and when they got there they just gave us a ticket and put us on a bus and I still didn't know where we was going 'til they let us off in Kingston. There wasn't no Oak Ridge."

Williams had a third-grade education. He could read and write, add and subtract, and little more. "If a Black kid learned to read back then, that was it," he said. "You went to work." He was working at highway construction by age 14 and was a skilled concrete finisher by the time he was 18.

"There was this woman there in Kingston who had a kinda hotel," he said. "Black folks wasn't allowed inside, so we just stayed out front on the street. She fixed breakfast for us next morning and carried it out to us on the sidewalk. She knew where we was going. Work groups came in there one right after another, all day long. This woman called somebody and told'em we was there and they sent a truck after us and that's how we got there; just standing and squattin' in the back, holding on. We had to go through some kind of processing thing and then we just sat around waitin' because they didn't have nothing for us to do. And we was getting paid. I got $1.37-½ an hour and that was good. The most I ever made before that was about 75 cents an hour.

40

"I didn't have no idea what was going on. When they first got there, they wasn't nothing but farmers and they was getting them out of there fast. We never could figure out what was going on. They took us to Norris where they used to be a CCC camp and that's where we stayed until they finally put up some huts and then that's where we stayed after that."

Photo by Ed Wescott

Wash day in Black hutments

The hutments were 16'x16' plywood boxes with one door and wooden-shutter windows. Open the shutters in the summertime and invite flies and mosquitoes. Close them and broil. There was no running water, there were no electrical appliances and, for most, no furniture beyond cots, folding chairs and foot lockers. Central bath houses, with four toilets, four wash basins and four shower heads, accommodated 12 hutments, or 48 to 60 people. Four and sometimes five or six workers were assigned to a single hutment, one in each corner and one or two in the center when the coal-burning stove was removed in the summer. Each occupant paid $6 rent monthly.

"The huts was just thin plywood," Williams said, "with big windows and wood shutters that you could close. There wasn't no glass or screens. There was one light bulb hanging down in the middle and that was all the electric we had. Everybody hang clothes on a nail and kinda hang up a blanket for privacy. We had to walk down to the bath house for water and everything.

"But at first, nobody stayed on the site because there wasn't no place. Every morning we'd get up and ride a bus down there at the site. We'd clock in and then we wouldn't do nothing. I clocked in many a day and didn't even go out there where they was working at. They wasn't ready for us yet, but they wanted us there. Many a days I didn't even put a shovel or trowel in my hand. That's just the way it was. But when we started working, it was from 7:30 in the morning 'til 12 o'clock at night."

Williams, still living in Oak Ridge in 2007 at the age of 86, said he was the first concrete finisher at Site X and that he helped build the world's biggest covered building at K-25 and the buildings at X-10. He met his wife, a janitor, at K-25.

"It was kinda hard courtin' then because she lived in the pen [hutments] and men wasn't allowed. And there wasn't no place Black folks could go for entertainment. About two times a week they'd put a screen up on a pole and show movies outside. And we'd play some ball down about where the Kroger store is now. Later on they built a rec center and we had some dances and things there. Sometimes we take a bus to Chattanooga or someplace else. I didn't think nothing of the way we was treated then, because I was used to it. It got better, but not much."

Williams said he was the first African-American to move into a house in the all-Black Scarboro neighborhood and among the first to own a home there. "In 1973," he said, "when the government sold the Scarboro houses, I bought the same house I moved into in 1949 and I'm still living in it."

Williams retired in the Seventies after seeing his two daughters graduate from Oak Ridge High School and attend the University of Tennessee.

Early Oak Ridge Negroes were young, strong, uneducated and mostly single. Some illiterates were given janitor's jobs, purposefully in some cases it is said, so that office paperwork or machinery signs would not be read during cleanup. Like everyone else in the Manhattan Project, janitors were sworn to secrecy about their work. It was OK for them to say they were janitors, but they were not permitted to describe what was being cleaned, what was seen or where.

Unskilled laborers were paid 58 cents an hour, Negroes and whites alike, which was more than most of them had ever earned. Many had worked in fields for a dollar a day and domestics had made as little as two dollars a week. Only about 1,500 Negroes lived in Oak Ridge at one time because living conditions were horrendous, even by Deep South standards. Most rented rooms or houses in Knoxville, which had Negro schools.

"[Oak Ridge] is the first community I have ever seen with slums that were deliberately planned," wrote Enoch Waters, a reporter for The Chicago Defender in a series of stories about Negro living conditions in the 1946 South. A headline read: Negroes Live in Modern 'Hoovervilles' in Atom City."

Negroes were assigned to an isolated section on the edge of town two miles from the nearest white face in an encampment called Scarboro Village. It was a ghetto with guarded gates and a 10 p.m. curfew. Only a few white people ever saw it, or even knew it existed. There were two side-by-side camps, one for males, and one for females. The women were penned inside a five-foot, scrap–wood fence topped by rows of barbed wire.

Women's hutment, aka "The Pen"

Not even husband and wife were permitted to live together until late in the war and then only a few. City police and government guards patrolled the compounds day and night and it was not uncommon for them to pull down a climbing, bleeding male from the fence, thwarting his effort to be with his wife or girl friend. But the number of footprints and leaning chairs on the fence boards suggested that the police didn't always succeed.

"They called the woman's hut area the pen," Hal Williams said. "You could go in there. The only thing about it, you could only stay a few minutes, and there was a guard at the gate to check on you. You'd tell the guard how long you be and where you going and they better not have to come get you."

Women were allowed in the men's hutment area, which was not fenced, but they had to show their marriage licenses and had to be out by 10 p.m. Kattie Strickland, who was married and worked as a janitor at the plants, sometimes got an extra hour or so with her husband; perhaps because of her biscuit-making. She devised a way to brown biscuits using the coal stove in her hutment, and her biscuits softened the hearts of some fence guards.

"Some electricians at the plant made some pans for me," she said, "and the way I cooked the biscuits was that I'd get that big round stove red hot, then prop the biscuits up next to it and let'em brown on the back. Then I'd turn'em around and let'em brown on the front. The FBI man came in and ate biscuits with me. I stayed with my husband at his hut after work and I only cooked for his hut. The guards come around and run the women off at 10 o'clock; except me. They let me stay 'til 11 o'clock."

Hutments and scrap lumber boardwalk

Hutments were the worst of all living quarters in Oak Ridge and they weren't limited to Negroes. Some 2,000 unskilled white workers also lived in hutments, but in White Oak Ridge, close to transportation and stores, and they lived by a different set of rules. White hutment dwellers could go freely about the city day or night, for shopping, restaurants, movies and roller skating. Negroes generally were confined to their compound with its one cafeteria. Feature movies, 16 mm, were shown twice weekly in the hutment recreation hall, which also offered card tables, billiards, board games and a juke box. What the white and Negro hutment camps had in common was violence, bootlegging, prostitution, drunkenness, venereal disease, gambling and thievery. There were rumors of frequent homicides in the hutment areas, but they were never publicly confirmed. Police records were destroyed after the war without review.

In October, 1945, two months after the war, white hutments were dismantled and hauled away. Hutments remained the only Negro housing for more than a year, but with relaxed conditions. By then, some Negro families were allowed to live together and some hutments were connected to create more room for them. Later some moved into "victory cottages," substandard two-family plywood-paneled flattop units used largely by soldiers during the war. The two-room units had a small kitchen, an oil-burning stove, running water, bathroom and a combined living room and bedroom. Six shift-working Negro nurses were assigned to one unit in those post-war days. One slept in the kitchen.

By 1949 a new residential site for Negroes was under construction in a remote area called Gamble Valley that had been a giant wartime trailer park for whites. Fifteen single-family, cinder-block homes, 143 frame duplexes and seven dormitories were built for rental.

A wooded 300-foot ridge separated Gamble Valley from the Y-12 nuclear plants on one side. Nearby on another side was the city dump. Oak Ridge residences have been integrated for decades now, but Gamble Valley still is an all-Negro community, by choice. The Black population of Oak Ridge, about 1,200, has changed little over the years.

The original residential plan for Oak Ridge never included the hutments. In fact, it called for a Negro section on the east end of town with housing comparable to that of whites. But when the population quickly soared to 13,000 (en route to 75,000) the Negro Village plan was aborted. The Army's explanation was that the hutments were a desperation move and although they were unsatisfactory, the arrangement would be temporary and corrected as soon as the housing need for critical and essential workers was satisfied. It never was, not before the war ended.

Five months after the war, Chicago Defender reporter Enoc Waters wrote:

> *If through the work here America has advanced science, it is equally true that in the way it has forced Negroes to live here, America has retarded the cause of democracy. And this is ironical because it was to preserve democracy that this whole [Manhattan] project was brought into being. But Oak Ridge today is the most eloquent testimony that America has not yet been able to deliver itself of all the meanness of which man at his worst is capable. There are few other places in the South where the plight of the Negroes is as wretched as it is here.*

A year after the war, Negro children were allowed in Oak Ridge, but there was no school for them. Following the practices of the segregated south, Oak Ridge schools were for whites only and it would be more than a year before classes for Negro children were arranged. Beneath a Chicago Defender Headline that read: "Negro Kids Can't Go to School at Biggest Brain Center," investigative reporter Waters wrote:

> *This sprawling Tennessee town—home of the awesome atom bomb—is a city of paradoxes. Here at the secret birthplace of the atomic age, some of the nation's greatest brains are engaged in exploiting the unknown future of atomic power but Negro children are denied the right to learn their ABCs.*

In 1946 a makeshift school was established in a government building previously used for agricultural research. Grades five through eight met in one room with one teacher. There were more students attending classes (85) than there were desks. There were no art classes, no music classes, no physical education classes. High school students were bused about 25 miles to Knoxville's all-Negro Austin High. The state of Tennessee observed a so-called "separate but equal" segregation policy, but there wasn't a high school for Negroes in all of Anderson County.

Compounding the post-war plight of Oak Ridge Negroes was a white overseer named C. Carson Ridenour from Clinton, a lawyer and state representative for Anderson and Morgan counties. He gained sweeping power over the Negro hutment area. In 1946 the Ridenour Management Company was awarded a concessions contract for the hutments and authority over all Negro housing. Under the watch of Ridenour, the Negro hutments deteriorated even further with leaking roofs, bare electric wires, garbage-strewn grounds, dirty bath houses and rat infestation. Ridenour charged double rent if payments were a day late. Prices at the Ridenour-operated concessions were 50 to 75 percent higher than those in white Oak Ridge. Passes for out-of-town visitors, issued free to white Oak Ridge residents, cost 25 cents each for Negroes in the Ridenour-managed hutment area, a so-called application fee. Ridenour also represented almost all Negroes in court matters.

For some years, Negroes were unable to buy automobile insurance in Oak Ridge because, insurers said, jurors hearing automobile accident cases in court invariably would decide against Negro drivers.

In the spring of 1950, Bruce Barto, a 16-year-old sophomore at Oak Ridge High, wrote a letter to the local newspaper, *The Oak Ridger,* admonishing the school board for its treatment of Negro students and calling for desegregation of Oak Ridge schools. The letter got him a trip to the principal's office where he was reprimanded for speaking out of school. But the letter was applauded by many of his classmates and by some influen-

48

tial townspeople who sprang to action. By the following fall, high school classes had been set up for Negroes with two full-time teachers, one part-time teacher and a large contingent of highly qualified volunteers from the white community. The curriculum included physics, chemistry, math, music and biology. Meanwhile, in preparation for desegregation that was soon to come, Oak Ridge teachers were stressing in classrooms the importance of tolerance for cultural differences, the injustice of segregation and the danger and sickness of hate and racial prejudice. After the Supreme Court's 1954 landmark decision in Brown vs. The Board of Education mandated the end of segregation across the country, Oak Ridge became the first non-private high school in the deep south to integrate. The municipal swimming pool also was desegregated.

Oak Ridge's mostly southern, pro-segregation blue-collar residents far outnumbered the town's sophisticated, mostly northern liberals; but they were no match in political action. Attempts to derail or sabotage Oak Ridge's desegregation were few, minor and unsuccessful. Negro athletes soon joined varsity teams, but did not play in road games if opponents objected. In 1963, opponents who refused to compete against Negroes were dropped from Oak Ridge schedules.

Two years after the integration of ORHS, neighboring Clinton became Tennessee's first purely public high school to admit Blacks, but with far more difficulty and with worldwide attention. White supremacist maverick John Kasper, 27, a Washington D.C. book store manager from New Jersey, drove down, recruited out-of-town racists and organized street protest mobs. Teachers were threatened, a minister was beaten and Governor Frank Clement called in the Highway Patrol and National Guard troops, who were supported by tanks. Many Clinton residents, including the Clinton High football team, formed a home guard and patrolled the school and the city. A member of the Clinton marching band chased thugs out of the hallway after they had pushed aside a teacher, the principal's wife, looking for trouble. Kasper eventually was arrested, the mobs dispersed and order was restored. Or so everyone thought.

Two years later starting at 4:21 on Sunday morning, October 5, 1958, three separate dynamite explosions, three minutes apart, destroyed Clinton High School; including the science department that had just been outfitted with new teaching equipment and other material for the first time in 25 years.

That incident led to one of the proudest moments in Oak Ridge history. The city invited the Clinton students to use an empty elementary school and three days after the explosion, Clinton High was back in session—in Oak Ridge. Working night and day Oak Ridgers cleaned, painted and equipped previously closed Linden elementary school and then turned out by the hundreds to welcome Clinton students to classes early on Thursday morning, October 8. Standing in a light rain, the Oak Ridge High Band played the Clinton High alma mater as students filed off their buses. The student body president, a farm boy, accepted the key to the school, opened the door and led his schoolmates inside. It was a tight fit for some, sitting in desks designed for 11-year-olds, but they worked it out. For two years Clinton High School was in Oak Ridge while a new Clinton High was being built. No one was ever charged with the school dynamiting.

Oak Ridge would be in for some ugly racial incidents, too; when Blacks, along with some white residents, joined the National Association for the Advancement of Colored People's Civil Rights movement as it gathered momentum across the south in the 1960s.

"We got organized and were having sit-ins at McCrory's 5 and 10," said Kathleen Stephens, "and we were picketing at the movies and the restaurants and the Laundromat. We had to go to the Black theater in Knoxville for a movie, or go to Oliver Springs or to Clinton where they made us sit upstairs in the balcony. After the war when I came from Alabama to live here with my parents, we lived across the street from the drive-in movie. Blacks couldn't drive in, but as children they let us walk in and watch the movie. But we couldn't do much else.

"We couldn't wash our clothes at the Laundromat so we picketed the Laundromat at Jefferson, and the Ku Klux Klan made an appearance, white sheets and all.

"One day I was at a sit-in at McCrory's and some white people were with us. I was sitting in a booth, going through some books, and a guy in the next booth looked over and said, 'How does it feel sitting beside that Nigger?'

"They had a skating rink down on the west side in the Jefferson area and they wouldn't let us skate there except on Sunday. The owner said he would shut down before he integrated his rink." Sure enough, when integration came, the skating rink closed.

By 1963 Oak Ridge was well on its way to becoming a fully integrated city, with a Negro minister at a previously all-white church, with its first Negro policeman and with Negro teachers in its schools. Restaurants served everyone. Negro children were in every Oak Ridge school.

Nobody Liked Us,
Especially in Football

Oak Ridgers weren't liked very well outside the seven security gates that protected us. We especially weren't liked by most of the families forced out of their homes and off their farms because of us. They didn't like the Gestapo-like government agents who served their eviction notices. They didn't like the invasion of fast-talking Yankees who followed, or their smirking references to "Dog Patch," or the young soldiers who ogled their women folks. They didn't like the military brass from Washington, or the science nerds or the overwhelming demands that were placed on their county services—their roads and their limited goods. They didn't like the Oak Ridge construction mud tracked into their stores and offices, or the barbed-wire fences and security gates with gun emplacements that denied them access to their churches and family cemeteries and the crops they left in their fields. They didn't like the traffic that clogged their country roads or the government's special treatment of the newcomers—the new refrigerators and stoves and furniture and books that rolled into Oak Ridge by the trainload almost daily.

Because of Oak Ridge, Anderson and Roane counties together lost 93 square miles of real estate (Anderson lost one-seventh of its land) from their tax rolls. Since all Oak Ridge housing was government rental, no one paid property taxes, including the U.S. government. Neighboring counties were raided for teachers, tradesmen, merchants, clerks and laborers with the promise of better pay and benefits.

Not least on the list of resentments was Oak Ridge's seemingly elitist school system with its highly paid teachers from some 40 states including dozens with PhD and Masters degrees from 162 colleges and universities. Oak Ridge students had new buildings with all new furnishings and new textbooks and cafeterias at a time when some neighboring schools had toilets that didn't always flush, roofs that sometimes leaked and classroom walls with peeling paint.

Oak Ridge schools had gymnasiums with rope climbs, tumbling mats, badminton courts, lockers and showers. They had playgrounds with paddle ball courts and swings and slides and softball fields. There were microscopes and slide projectors, classroom movies, pianos, typewriters, calculators and art rooms with art teachers and music rooms with music teachers, libraries and woodshops and metal shops. Every elementary school had kindergarten and some had pre-school nurseries. There was a school psychologist and a summer tutoring program and adult-education classes.

It was an extraordinary school system, astonishingly put together from scratch in three months by a bright, innovative school superintendent, Dr. Alden Blankenship, 34, a former Washington State football player with a new PhD from Columbia University. Blankenship was interviewed at Columbia on the morning of July 3, 1943, by an Army captain who swore him to secrecy, offered him the job in a location he would not reveal, and then demanded an answer by 4 o'clock that afternoon. The young educator, son of a sheriff dad and a school teacher mom, accepted the assignment at exactly 4 p.m. and was handed his orders: Have Oak Ridge schools open in 90 days with an extraordinary staff and a strong curriculum that will satisfy sophisticated intellectuals whose children will be prominent among those attending. No school building existed in Oak Ridge at the time, and construction had barely begun.

Blankenship had no teachers, no curriculum, no textbooks, no equipment, no supplies, no secretary. He didn't have an office or a telephone and he didn't know the size of his enrollment. The driver scheduled to meet him at the train station in Knoxville failed to show and when the superintendent finally arrived at Site X, he had no place to stay. He slept that night in an unfinished dormitory.

Ninety days later, remarkably, on Friday, October 1, more than 600 students registered and classes began the following Monday at three schools. One of them was Oak Ridge High, which had 87 pupils and a teaching staff of 20. There were only 27 seniors in the first ORHS graduating class and all but six were girls. But in 2½ years, Oak Ridge schools grew from 637 students to more than 8,000 in 12 schools with a teaching staff of almost 400. Classes grew in number almost weekly.

The first high school classes met in an unfinished building that sat high on a hill, 76 boardwalk steps above the town's main shopping center, Jackson Square. Only the wood and metal shop classrooms were completed by opening day. Some classes were held in rooms with no windows and no blackboards and no chairs and with the noise of heavy equipment and banging hammers so loud it often drowned out the teachers' voices. Some classes met beneath shade trees while classroom paint dried. Some students helped to uncrate furniture and more than 3,000 text and library books, which were trucked by the Army to Oak Ridge directly from the publisher in Nashville. Lockers had not been installed when classes began, nor a school bell. The first high school principal, Margie Pritchett, stood in the hall and rang a cowbell to signal class changing time. If she wasn't available, a girls' physical education teacher blew her gym whistle. At Robertsville School, a small two-story brick building predating Oak Ridge, some 400 students showed up in grades 1 to 8. Many of the elementary grade pupils were bused to a nearby dormitory for classes until new classrooms were completed.

Despite the early ugliness and hardships in Oak Ridge, teachers were attracted by extraordinary salaries for the time (about $210 a month compared to $85 to $150 elsewhere), a 200-day work year (four weeks more pay than the standard 180 working days across most of the country), generous benefits and an interesting collection of students from virtually every state, many of whom were the bright, motivated children of bright, motivated parents.

Teachers also were attracted by Dr. Blankenship's promise of a new, progressive, virtually autonomous school system created without concern for restrictive traditions, free from institutional meddling and open to individual ideas and group thinking. Oak Ridge operated independently within the Anderson County School Board and had total jurisdiction over its own policy, personnel and curricula. The county board received funds from the government earmarked specifically for Oak Ridge schools from which Oak Ridge administrators wrote the payroll checks.

After school and during summer vacation, the school grounds became supervised playgrounds offering arts and crafts and box hockey and tether ball and paddle tennis and volleyball and table tennis and dance and dramatics and organized age-group softball and basketball for boys and girls from mites to intermediates who competed in citywide leagues. It was like day camp after school and all day during the summer. All free. During the summers, some parents dropped off their children at a neighborhood playground in the morning with brown-bag lunches and picked them up in the afternoon.

After the war, despite the intentions of many good-spirited county officials, the resentment for Oak Ridgers was especially evident. Those who lost their land to the Oak Ridge project were angered upon learning that, in the process of enriching uranium for the atomic bomb, some of their former farms and streams had been contaminated by toxic waste that might last 100 years or more. Further, Anderson county voters were blistering mad in 1947 when Oak Ridge's liberal majority carried a liquor referendum that made Anderson a wet county for the first time ever, despite heavy rural opposition.

Neighboring county schools and their teams' fans were also irritated by the secret city's closed-gate policy that continued almost four years after the war. It forced motorists to drive around the 96 square-mile town and caused visiting high school teams, their coaches and fans to obtain government clearance passes before being admitted for games. They were stopped at the security gates, scrutinized and subject to search. An armed guard boarded every team bus at the city's border and remained with the team as an escort until it departed.

The umbrage was most apparent at high school football games where neighboring teams tried to take advantage of the neophyte Wildcats up and down the field.

The first Oak Ridge football squad, formed in the first week of October, 1943 after the season was well under way, barely had enough players to fill the 11 positions. Thirteen players reported that first day, some so green they didn't know how to put on their pads. Oak Ridge played four games that first year, all against area varsity B teams, and lost them all.

Ferris Leo Bynum, a 33-year-old graduate of Southeastern State College in Stillwater, Oklahoma, was Oak Ridge's first football head coach, but he was drafted by the Army after the first season and never returned. The school's first athletic director, Ben Martin, took the football job and also coached basketball and track. It was Martin who selected the team's nickname, "Wildcats," in honor of his alma mater, the University of Kentucky. He also chose the colors, cardinal and gray, which his son, Bob, said were borrowed from Kingsport Dobyns-Bennet High, a perennial state athletic power at the time.

There wasn't a blade of grass on the newly bulldozed ORHS football field, no football shoes, no game jerseys, no bleachers, no home games and no fan participation that first season. And no publicity. Government censors prohibited last names of Oak Ridge players from being printed in area newspapers or to be called out over public address systems at games.

"Five-yard run by No. 26," one might hear after a play, or "Oak Ridge tackle by Jack." The intent was to avoid the possibility of attracting attention to last names of notable scientists, engineers or other accomplished Manhattan Project personnel.

The first-year Wildcats practiced in dust when it was dry and in mud when it wasn't. They took their practice uniforms home for mothers to wash, and wore them in their four scheduled games. They drove family cars to the November 10 season opener in Clinton, the Anderson County seat eight miles to the north, then to nearby Maryville High, to the Tennessee School for the Deaf in Knoxville and to Clinton again.

"Nobody beat us real bad," Ray Schubert recalled more than a half-century later. The 5-7, 135 pound Schubert, an 11th-grader from St. Charles, Virginia, was the first Oak Ridge tailback. He didn't score that season, and neither did anyone else.

Schubert dropped out of school his senior year to join the Navy. He returned after the war and became a successful businessman in Oak Ridge for more than 30 years.

"We just didn't have enough players," he said about that first year. "But families were moving in so fast I think we had about 24 players by the end of the season."

About 30 players reported for football in 1944 and the number increased as the season wore on. Oak Ridge High now had all new equipment, new game uniforms, and a new, artfully crowned, green-grass football field with lights. It also had a pep band, cheerleaders, a growing fan base and no more B-team opponents. The Wildcats won their first game ever in the 1944 opener, 13-6, over Harriman. The two touchdowns were scored on runs by Jack Crigger and Dick King. Records are unclear about who scored first. Oak Ridge went on to a 7-1 season, losing only to eighth-ranked Rule High of Knoxville and in 1945, their first 10-game season, the Wildcats finished 7-3, losing only to Knoxville powers Central and Knox High and to Lenoir City.

Coach Ben Martin with 12-man Wildcat squad

With the chaotic post-war drop in population, Oak Ridge had a losing season in 1946 but got its first statewide recognition with a 6-3-1 season in 1947 that ended with a 6-0 post-season upset of state champion Chattanooga Central. The touchdown was scored by little tailback Sammy Hurt, a hard-muscled, 5' 7", 140-pound junior from Kingsport, one of Oak Ridge's first stars recognized across the state. He is now a member of the Oak Ridge Sports Hall of Fame.

By 1949, under the coaching of former University of Tennessee tailback Buist "Buzz" Warren, Oak Ridge had an 8-1-1 year and climbed into the state's top echelon where it would stay for most of the next 60 years. The 1950 team (9-1) had the school's first all-America player, a chubby tailback named Tom McGrew. The 1951 team started the season ranked No. 2 in the state and reached the No.1 spot for the first time during the first month.

Photo by Ed Wescott

Celebrating at Blankenship Field

As the team grew, so did its supporters. Nobody had a bigger Friday night following. Oak Ridgers didn't own an acre of their town, not a single home or building. They still rented government housing and rode government buses and burned government coal and cashed government checks. But it had become their new hometown, and the Wildcats were *their* boys, the cheerleaders and majorettes were *their* girls, and the band was composed of *their* children. It was not unusual for 8,000 to turn out for games in a town whose population had dwindled to about 30,000.

Since the Tennessee Secondary Schools Athletic Association had no classification system and no playoffs in 1951, the state championship was a mythical one decided by two ranking systems, the Associated Press sportswriters' poll and the Litkenhaus Ratings, a formula system devised by Dr. E.E. Litkenhaus, a Vanderbilt math professor. Oak Ridge, with district sprint champion Dave Griffith at tailback and with at least five college scholarship prospects among its starting lineup, was unbeaten against all nine of its Tennessee public school opponents and lost only to Baylor of Chattanooga, a military prep school with older post-graduate players, and to out-of-state Flaget High of Louisville, Kentucky, which featured a future Notre Dame all-American, Heisman Trophy winner and National Football League hall-of-famer, Paul Hornung, at quarterback.

"Two things I remember most about my high school football career," said Wildcat Captain Harry Conner years later, "tackling Hornung and intercepting one of his passes."

Griffith, Oak Ridge's single wing tailback, was the most elusive ball carrier in the state and probably the fastest. (He finished second by inches in the state 100-yard-dash finals.) Griffith stood 6' 1" and weighed about 170 and he had a quick, darting start like a deer. In the 1951 season he had touchdown runs of 100 yards, 97, 77, 75, 69, 65, 59 and 51. In one game he ran for 228 yards in three plays. In a post-season bowl game he ran off-tackle left for 65 yards and a touchdown that was called back on a penalty. He then ran the same play to the right and went 70 yards for a touchdown. Fifty-nine years later his 2,677 yard total still was the ORHS record for a single season.

Oak Ridge finished second in the state football ratings in 1951-52, highest finish ever for the Wildcats at the time. Griffith was named to an all-America team and six teammates were selected to the All-East Tennessee team.

By 2010, Oak Ridge High had won eight state championships, one mythical national championship and had 11 undefeated regular seasons. It also won two boys' basketball state titles, three in girls basketball, five in boys track, three in girls track and three in girls cross country.

Oak Ridge's "Who's Who"

The following list of Oak Ridge's Top 10 most significant personalities was selected, at the editor's request, by Fred Strohl, tour coordinator for the Oak Ridge National Laboratory. He works in the Office of Communications and Community Outreach and has been connected to Oak Ridge for almost 30 years. He either knew or met eight of the top 10. He is a former newspaper and radio journalist.

10 Most Significant Oak Ridgers

1. Eugene Wigner: As the director of technology and later as director of the Oak Ridge National Laboratory, Wigner oversaw the transformation of the lab from a World War II-era facility doing research on the Manhattan Project to a post-war laboratory researching many different areas of science that would attain world-renowned prestige. Wigner also oversaw the first major modernization of ORNL in the 1950s when many of the old 1943-vintage temporary structures were replaced by more permanent brick buildings, providing for a permanent presence.

2. Alvin Weinberg: Twelve years after ORNL was started, Weinberg took over as director, and for the next 20 years oversaw a period of the lab continuing to progress. Not only was Weinberg leading ORNL, but he was also advising presidents on science issues. Long after he left the ORNL directorship, he was still a science authority called on from time to time to address science issues. Weinberg also helped start Oak Ridge Associated Universities, which was a key part of bringing many different institutions of higher learning into partnerships with Oak Ridge.

3. Herman Postma: He was Weinberg's successor as ORNL director. During his tenure, technology transfer—where science is developed in the laboratory and then is licensed to the private sector—became a huge part of the mission at ORNL.

4. Bill Madia: Assuming the ORNL directorship in 2000 after UT-Battelle gained the contract, Madia helped spearhead the massive modernization effort at ORNL. Convincing DOE to go along with the concept of state and third-party financing of many of the new buildings, ORNL's modernization was able to move forward over five years instead of what would have been 30 if only DOE funding had been allowed.

5. Gordon Fee: As director of Lockheed Martin Energy Systems in the mid-1990s, Fee encouraged a more public display of activities taking place at Oak Ridge's DOE operations. That encouragement resulted in a series of community days and the Oak Ridge Public Tour, which have attracted more than 25,000 visitors to Oak Ridge DOE facilities during the past 13 years.

6. Alvin Bissell: As the longtime mayor of Oak Ridge — serving in city government from the late 1940s into the 1980s — Bissell helped bring Oak Ridge into the awareness of the state of Tennessee as he rose to become one of the most influential mayors in the state. Locally, Bissell oversaw the city's incorporation in 1958 and presided over a period when Oak Ridge went from a secret city behind a fence to a public city open to everyone. A city park is named for him.

7. Randy McNally: As a state legislator with strong ties to Gov. Lamar Alexander during the late 1970s and early 1980s, McNally was influential in convincing the governor to place more state investment in the science and technology potential of Oak Ridge. Prior to the Alexander administration, governors and state legislators kept somewhat of a distance from the goings-on in Oak Ridge — considering it strictly a federal town. Alexander, with McNally's help, began recruiting business and industry to Tennessee, pointing out the benefits such new establishments would have with Oak Ridge's technology support in the back yard. McNally was also instrumental in getting the Pellissippi Parkway extension accomplished from West Knoxville to McGhee Tyson Airport, providing a direct link between the airport and Oak Ridge. Many influential forces in West Knox County opposed the parkway extension when it was proposed in 1980, but McNally helped move the proposal to reality.

8. Dick Smyser: He served for almost 40 years as editor of The Oak Ridger, literally starting a daily newspaper out of the dirt. As editor, Dick took many strong editorial positions that were not always popular and didn't always rule the day. However, he ran a newspaper that made people think and served as a conduit for Oak Ridgers to follow the events of the time. Through this effort, The Oak Ridger gained a national reputation as a local newspaper dedicated to spearheading debate of local issues. Dick would eventually serve as president of the American Society of Newspaper Editors and later as president of the Associated Press Managing Editors Association. It was in this role that on Nov. 17, 1973, when asking a question of President Richard Nixon during a news conference in Orlando, Fla., Nixon gave the famous answer that he was not a crook.

9. Eugene Joyce: A distinguished Oak Ridge attorney who served as a strong political influence on the local, state and national levels. Joyce helped bring a new generation of political leadership to Tennessee in the post-World War II era while managing the successful U.S. Senate campaigns of Estes Kefauver in 1948 and Albert Gore Sr. in 1952. Joyce also first defined the concept of the Oak Ridge Technology Corridor, running at first along Pellissippi Parkway, but in the ensuing years branching out in directions toward Chattanooga, the Tri-Cities and

South Central Kentucky. Many new businesses and jobs in the region have been created as a result.

10. William Blankenship: The first superintendent of schools in Oak Ridge, he built the foundation of a strong school system in what was considered a temporary community located in the middle of dirt roads and mud, surrounded by a fence. He brought in a core of individuals who believed in the concept of excellence in education, striving to continue that goal in classrooms all over town. That philosophy helped boost Oak Ridge to one of the highest ranked school systems in Tennessee.

Dr. Eugene Wigner and wife, Mary Annette

Cemesto housing along Outer Drive's "Brain Alley"

Photo by Ed Wescott

66

Book Two

Our Childhood...

Photos by Ed Westcott

67

"Oh, Andy, Take Me Home"

On moving day Andy Rathbone drove into Oak Ridge through the Elza Gate security checkpoint with his wife and three children. It was their first look at their new town—piles of gravel, piles of sand, stacks of sewer pipe, stacks of lumber, half-built structures, bulldozers, Army trucks and Army buses. It was August 13, 1943. Andy, a bus driver from nearby Maryville, had taken a job in Oak Ridge driving a fire truck and was considered an essential employee. Housing was promised.

Nine-year-old Sue Rathbone remembered the day. "We drove to a nice old farmhouse that had no electricity, no running water and a brand new outhouse," she said. "When mother saw it she started to cry: "Oh, Andy, take me home."

But the Rathbones never went home. Andy walked two miles to the firehouse to work and didn't get home until after midnight. The children rode an Army bus to Robertsville School, a two-story red brick building that pre-dated Oak Ridge and was undergoing renovation and expansion. Homework was done by the light of oil lamps. Wild animals roamed around at night and sometimes the cry of a mountain lion would break the silence of the night.

Baths were taken in a No. 2 wash tub and bath water was shared. Sue got the first bath because she was smallest. She got the cleanest water.

Water was drawn from a large canvas reservoir that hung from a metal tripod at the side of their weatherboard house. An Army weapons carrier transported the water from Clinton every day, pulling a 500-gallon tank mounted on a trailer.

"I know it sounds awful," Sue said some 60 years later at the 50th ORHS reunion, "but we children loved it." We live in our memories and the early days of the Secret City. They are wonderful memories that we hope to keep for as long as we live."

But the pioneer living wasn't for everyone. Many less adventurous families turned around and went home once they saw the town and its near-primitive living conditions. Records show that 17 percent of construction workers left within months of their hiring and plant worker defections were almost as high. In addition to the near-primitive living conditions, there were block-long lines for almost everything—at the post office, grocery store, the laundry and even for the bad food at the cafeterias.

Those who remained were a venturesome mix of young families and military personnel with an average adult age between 28 and 32. Only 19 percent of the population was over 40. Nobody was old and nobody was disabled. And until the end of the war, there was no unemployment.

By late 1944, Oak Ridge had employed more than 140,000 from virtually every state and every walk of life; workers who uprooted young families and set out for the hills of East Tennessee without knowing how far back in the sticks they would be, or what they would be doing or how long they would be doing it. The government promised to pay moving costs for many and to pay for the move back home when the project was completed. The government also offered wages higher than most workers had ever earned. Some tripled their pay.

Some 88,000 construction workers would take jobs in Oak Ridge at one time or another. The first arriving swarm placed fences around the 92-square-mile Site X reservation, using barbed wire from the confiscated farms when possible and placing "No Trespassing" signs every few-hundred feet. A bigger swarm of workers arrived in February 1943 when ground was broken for Y-12, code name for the electromagnetic uranium processing plant that would employee 22,000 and provide the explosive material for Little Boy, the Hiroshima bomb. Another swarm was assigned to launch the construction of X-10, home of the now-famous graphite reactor. Thousands more converged on the K-25 site to build the massive gaseous diffusion facility that would feature the world's largest roofed building, a 44-acre, 4-story, U-shaped structure with two half-mile wings; so big that employees used bicycles for inter-department travel. All of the secret plants, purposely built miles away from the town in case of an accident, were enclosed by sturdy eight-foot chain-link fences and patrolled by armed guards. The residential area, which took up 9,000 of the 59,000-acre reservation, also was heavily guarded and crawling with government agents; some in uniform, some not. Residential construction continued right up to the final day of the war, even while the allies were negotiating a peace agreement with Japan.

Of Mice and Men
And Chamber Pots

Louise Hill was 36 when she moved to Oak Ridge from Chatta-
nooga in 1944 with her husband, Freeman, a barber, and son Gene
Pharr, age 11. Early in the war she had been a riveter at a Califor-
nia air base, but quit because the men workers, she said, treated
women like prostitutes. In Oak Ridge her family was assigned a gov-
ernment trailer in the Midtown Trailer Park, part of which was
located where the high school now stands.

All trailer park streets were named for birds. We lived on
Starling Road. They say now that there were 5,000 trailers there
during the war. I never knew how many.

One of about 5,000 Midtown trailers

Our trailer had no running water so we carried water from
the bathhouse, about a block away. You could get hot water at
the bathhouse only at certain times. I left my little white kettle
there one day and went back to get it and saw a lady with it. I
asked her if she found a kettle and she said, "No, that's my ket-

tle." Her husband was right there with her and they both said it was theirs so I didn't make a stink. Anything metal like a kettle was hard to find.

I used that kettle to heat water so I could wash dishes. I washed dishes in a dishpan and threw the dirty water down a pipe that fed into a big bucket beneath the trailer. Trucks came along in the morning and emptied them.

We used an ironing board for a table and cooked on a little oil stove. I was scared of that thing and the fumes gave me a headache. We had a half bed and a couch that sleeps two. You could hear little mice running around at night when it got quiet.

Some of those families we knew at the trailer park had double-wides because they had a gang of children. I don't know how they did it.

We used chamber pots at night and carried them to the bathhouse every morning to empty and to wash out. That was so embarrassing. But we got used to it after awhile and we would stand around down there at the bathhouse—some in bathrobes with hair in curlers—and talk and visit with our chamber pots in our hands.

We were a family of three and we only had one chamber pot so we'd pass it around at night. If two wanted to use it at the same time it went to the one who was hurting the worst.

We were always warm in the winter, but we weren't cool in the summer. If you worked shift work and had to sleep during the day, you almost had to have someone fanning you. You just toughed it out.

It was the same way at the women's dorm where I worked. It was so hot in there, and there was always somebody trying to sleep during the day. One time I was supposed to wake a woman up and when I went to wake her she had a wet rag over her eyes. She looked like she was dead and I screamed. That woke her up all right. She said that's the only way she could sleep.

Freeman, being a barber, heard all the town gossip. Customers would tell him just about everything. He knew the whisky runners and where the prostitutes were. There was a lot of that.

We were still in that trailer when the war ended. I remember people running around the trailer park yelling, "The war is over! The war is over!"

Those were hard times and it was hard living, but despite all that, it was the best place we ever lived in some ways. You were lucky to get any place at all then. There were so many people from somewhere else and they all got lonely. We kind of helped one another like family.

I don't know why I remember so much about that. When you're as old as I am you're lucky to know your name. I got to thinking about how old I am one night and got out of bed to get a calendar to figure it up. I didn't know if I was 78 or 87.

But I'll never forget the trailer park.

--As told to Jay Searcy by Louise Hill at age 87

Home, with a white picket fence

Dr. Wigner and the Paperboy

"For all his genius," said Don Robinson of his Outer Drive, Nobel Prize winning neighbor, Eugene Wigner, "he could never remember his weekly 35-cent paper bill." Don was his paperboy and dealt with the brilliant physicist almost weekly. "Dr. Wigner was a shy little man," Don said, "with an unusually big head and a heavy Hungarian accent and he would answer the door rather meekly on Thursday evenings when I came to collect."

"Collect." Don would say when Dr. Wigner opened the door.

"Collect?" Wigner would ask. "Vot do you collect?"

"Money. For the Sentinel."

"Oh, for da newspaper? How much?"

"Thirty-five cents."

"Tuddy-five cents?"

"Yessir."

Wigner would then withdraw a few feet from the doorway and walk around in a circle in his hallway, slowly counting pennies, nickels and dimes chosen from an old leather coin purse.

Next Thursday, same thing.

"Collect."

"Collect? Vot do you collect?"

Next Thursday, same thing.

It Started in a Saloon

Blake Chambliss, a graduate of the Harvard School of Design, began his architectural practice in Grand Junction, Colorado in 1963 and became a Fellow of the American Institute of Architects in 1984. Later in Denver he transformed his work into assistance to nonprofit organizations and rural nonprofit organizations in 12 western states (and a dozen Native American Tribal groups) to find new alternatives to house and improve the quality of life in their families. He currently writes a weekly newsletter in defense of the poor, the environment and social justice.

The forces that took me and my family to Oak Ridge began with an incident in my father's youth that shaped the trajectory of his life. Dad was born in Dodge City, Kansas where his father was a leading businessman (banker), gambler (poker) and civic leader (he helped establish the first church in Dodge City). It was a time when gambling was seen as a way of life—whether in ranching (wagering cattle and crops against the threats of summer dry or winter cold, rustlers and distant markets) or storekeepers (playing the odds of remote and unreliable suppliers against the price and credit demands of an emerging and shaky local community economy). His family had moved out to the western frontier after the Civil War, or "War Between the States," as they called it in their home in Deep-South Louisiana. Dodge City held the promise of new beginnings, new opportunities.

In his youth, Dad played in the saloon where his dad played cards. He learned how to tell the difference between an in-the-shell hardboiled egg and a raw egg—important distinctions at the bar, where an egg and beer was standard lunch fare (no one wanted fresh yolk down his shirtfront). That example, the basic physics of the nature of matter in its various forms, made a strong impression on him. It awakened in him a fascination and lifelong curiosity about the building blocks of matter. He became an engineer and spent his life as an inventor, tinkering with the mechanics of simple tools, expanding his inquiring mind through a hunger to know how things work, come apart and fit together.

In 1943 Dad was teaching basic courses in physics and engineering to young Army and Air Corps recruits at the University of Missouri in Columbia. They were the raw inductees, embryonic technicians on their way to create the mighty technological colossus that the U.S. Armies were to become in World War II. Always a teacher, he found the work of stimulating their lively imaginations exciting, but he was frustrated by the rigid military discipline and oversight. He was recruited away from teaching there in early 1944 to explore the emerging "Atomic Age's" new challenges.

He went away from home for several months to a secret site for orientation and training for his new job. (We weren't told where and, I suspect, we weren't told it was a "secret" site.) When he returned, he was visibly excited about this new opportunity: to tinker on a grander scale in important new ways (though of course he couldn't tell us why it was so important to him). He told us we would be moving to "some place in Tennessee." We would have to leave all our friends and family behind at the end of the school year.

It was a hard family decision, and it was particularly difficult for my sister June. She had just completed her junior year in high school and was looking forward to being a leader in her class for her senior year. She was devastated; she would have to leave established friendships to go to an unknown, untested school in the backwoods of far-off East Tennessee. My older brother Dee was established in the elite University High School, and was not enthusiastic about leaving the journalism-rich high school academic program in which he excelled. My younger brother Don and I, in the third and fourth grades, on the other hand, thought it would be a lark, and were excited about going to a new place, with new friends, and new yards, woods and countryside to explore. We had no qualms about leaving. We would miss cousins, but there would be new friends and new horizons. At the time I was not paying attention to June's angst and Dee's loss in the move. I was not uncaring; I was just absorbed and caught up in Dad's own excitement.

Dad had not told us much about the place we would be going. Maybe he hadn't had time to look around much. He did tell us that during the months he was there it was very dry—it hadn't rained the whole time he was there. But otherwise, though it was hillier than Columbia, it was similar in its climate, trees and neighborhoods. He was wrong.

We completed the school year, and were packed up by the beginning of June. Mom and Dad arranged for our furniture to be shipped (though Dad had warned us we might not need it all—a great understatement.) We would later learn how little would actually fit in our new home. We had a last-minute crisis when Dad realized that our 1940 DeSoto sedan's balding tires might not take us all the way to Oak Ridge. We would have to buy at least one (there was no way, with gas and tire rationing then, to consider a "set" of tires) plus a good used one for a spare. Moreover, Dad had to hustle up enough extra gas coupons for the 600-mile drive.

After completing all our exiting preparations, we arranged to re-group and spend the night before leaving at my Granny's house. Aunt Rooney, Dad's sister, would go with us to help us get settled (and, I suspect, to help June deal with the adjustment to our new home). In the morning Mother awakened us early to eat a hearty breakfast and help Dad load the car. We had to fit all our gear in for the long journey, and still leave space for the seven of us. Luggage was jammed into every nook and cranny. My father, the tinkerer, had sent his metal lathe with the movers but had forgotten to ship the motor for it, so he stowed it under the hood jammed between the battery and the chassis. June was livid! She had to leave some of her dearest possessions behind, but Dad got to have his "toy."

After saying goodbye to family and curious gathered neighbors, Dad eased the loaded car, springs nearly on the frame, out of the driveway with the bumper scraping the pavement as we left the drive. We all held our breath as the car finally got out onto the smooth pavement and underway.

We began elbowing for personal space and adjusting to what we knew would be cramped quarters for the next two days. To make more space, Don and I took turns lying on the ledge above the rear seat (no seat belt or safety issues then). It was a long, hot and uncomfortable drive, but Don and I were excited about all the new and ever-changing scenery along the way. Mother had packed lunch and snacks for us so we wouldn't have to stop more often than necessary. We spent the night at an auto court near Nashville. It consisted of a group of little cabins marooned in the middle of the sea of its loose gravel driveway. We got an early start the next morning, crunching up onto the pavement and into the early morning sunshine for the final leg of the trip to Oak Ridge. We arrived at the Oliver Springs Gate a little after noon. We were all agog, taking in the activity around the gate: MPs in uniform, cars stopped and searched. One helmeted MP stuck his head in our car window checking each of us out. It was a first hint of what would be a common experience in our new home community. Dad went into the guardhouse and signed for passes for each of us, and got directions to our new home.

In the creation of the town of Oak Ridge barely two years earlier, the planners had rejected the most expedient alternative to provide worker housing—the creation of a typical temporary military camp. To provide for the project's security, it was located inland, away from the ocean and enemy submarine-borne spies, and to gain access to massive power generation capacity of the TVA network, hidden in the mountainous backwoods of rural East Tennessee. There would be no ready access to regional commercial centers for the workers day-to-day goods or services. Therefore, the workers, with their families, would have to be housed in relative isolation for the duration of the War. Thus the master planners made the commitment to intentionally create an integral, entire living community for the workers and their families. Nationally renowned architects, planners and engineers were engaged to create this new self-contained community. The community as conceived, with its imposed mix of public and private functions and services, would manage behind barbed wire security fences for the duration of the war.

The physical planning for the town was creatively conceived. Streets were laid out with sweeping curves, matched to the irregular undulations of the natural topography. Sometimes that created difficult intersections where serpentine streets met at odd junctures. Neighborhoods were carefully orchestrated, composed by grouping homes, arranged in clusters, around the elementary schools, with neighborhood shopping centers close at hand. All new physical facilities were designed to fit into to the natural contours of the East Tennessee landscape. Beyond the physical planning for housing the workers and their families, the town would also have to provide a full range of local government functions, street maintenance, utilities and trash collection, hospitals and health-care, a complete school system and transportation services. The Town Center was developed with entertainment, a movie theater, shops, a department store, municipal offices and other commercial activities. It was positioned at the center of the public bus transportation network. Other facilities and services that would serve the entire community, such as the hospital, doctor's offices, hotel and a single multi-denominational chapel, were located adjacent to it.

It was a great place, as we quickly learned, in which to grow up. It was an environment created to support a "normal" family life for the workers at the cutting edge of a new technologic age, and created to replicate and conform to the acceptable social structure of the Deep South at the time. It was not the same as any community that any of the new residents had come from.

It was easy to live in, but easy to find your way around for the first time, it was not! We arrived at our house, finally, after missing our turns at several obscure intersections. We crossed over town and up East Drive, and finally found our house at 101 Eaton Lane. Turning off the uphill drive we entered a level lane carved out of pinewoods surrounded by a cluster of six cube-shaped prefabricated homes on stilts. Our house was at the corner, above and looking out over East Drive and the houses along the other side of East Drive, which were set below street level as the land dropped away. Out in front of each house was what we at first assumed was a large doghouse. We thought that was peculiar. We didn't have a dog. Was everyone expected to have one? After a debate, Dad laughed and explained that it was a coal bin. Each house was provided with one, out next to the road where the town utilities would deliver coal for heating the house throughout the winter.

Our house was a three-bedroom flattop set up on timber piers, with the front door at the top of a long flight of wooden steps. The entry door opened into the living room with large windows facing out to the south, downhill over the roofs of the houses below. It looked out to an unimpeded view through the trees to the hazy, blue-tinged hills beyond.

I thought the house was cute, and was fascinated by the "tinker toy" technology of building real houses with pre-manufactured parts. June was incensed; she thought it was ugly, without any grace at all, and propped up on spindly stilts, exposing its untidy (and slightly obscene, with its plumbing showing) underside. She was even more disappointed when we went inside and saw the size of the rooms. It had three tiny bedrooms and an undersized kitchen (mother liked to cook and was used to having lots of elbowroom). There was a living room with a pot-bellied, cast-iron stove in the middle and one bath for the six of us (seven with Aunt Rooney). June chose the little bedroom. It was about 6 feet by 8 feet, barely big enough for a bed, which she arranged with a mattress placed on top of a set of bureau drawers. Dee, Don and I opted for the largest bedroom, with just enough space for bunk beds. Don and I took the top bunk, level with the high strip windows along the back of the house, which allowed us an occasional surreptitious exit. Mom and Dad took the mid-sized bedroom. Aunt Rooney slept in the living room until she went back to Columbia a week later. We began to be concerned about the amount of furniture that would be coming in a few days. There seemed to be no way it would all fit in. It didn't. We used what we could and put the rest in storage (Dad's lathe included).

As the rest of the family began to settle in, Don and I ran out to test the depth and extent of the woods. Contrary to Dad's predictions based on his weather experience, it started to rain. It rained every day for the next month. It wasn't a steady frog-strangling downpour, but intermittent showers with quick-moving grey clouds scudding just above the ridge tops. It rained just often enough to create sodden and sloppy mud in all the places not layered over with some form of ground cover. Don and I played out in the rain in the gravel swale alongside the road, acting as engineers, damming the sudden brown streams of water flowing off the road after each downpour. When the water filled to road level, we would break the dams and watch boats constructed of flat wood chips with leaf sails float down the swift-flowing streams. We would come home water-soaked and muddy. Or we would explore the woods, following along the raised wooden plank sidewalks built through the woods back behind the houses. One would be our daily connection directly to Glenwood School where Mom had enrolled us for September.

We explored beyond the barbed wire security fence just across East Drive. There was a special excitement in sneaking through it and dodging the frequent passing of the armed horseback patrol guard. The guards were disarmed after one bored officer reportedly took target practice at a rabbit, shooting just as his horse stumbled, unfortunately into the line of fire. He killed the horse. The rogue rabbit escaped. The horseback patrol was totally abandoned shortly after. The now undefended barbed wire strands were soon loosened and sagged uselessly from our frequent passage through the fence. Just beyond the fence was a tiny stream at the bottom of the hill (full of water bugs, salamanders and crawfish) and up the other side of it where we found a cave. We would stash cigarettes there that we would skulk away to smoke illicitly. A few yards farther we discovered the L&N railroad tracks, along which we were able to extend our explorations, and which challenged our imaginations with further visions of worldwide travels.

In the woods, Don and I discovered an abundant array of large and small, dappled or color-splashed, black and white, blue-backed, red breasted, red and black, brown and gold–flashing birds flitting through the trees. We were thrilled with their color, their carefree flight among tree's limbs and the variety of bird-songs warbling out through the branches. (It would not be until my seventh grade class with Mrs. Walsh that I would begin to put names to most of them from the White Lily Flour bird cards we collected.) That summer I began to expand my awareness of, and a lifetime's appreciation for, the contribution birds have made to the lush affluence of the world environment. Without birds' example, would humans have ever learned to fly, or aspire to float suspended above the earth, or explore beyond our ground-limited horizons? I think not.

It was a new kind of environment for me. It was open and wilder than any of the towns I had visited or lived in. Oak Ridge was not composed of houses with clumps of trees between, but houses inserted into an undulating and rambling forest floor. The clusters of houses were the interlopers in a jumble of trees and undergrowth covering the mounded East Tennessee hillsides. I fell in love with the occasional stands of white-pine trees towering over a soft uninterrupted layer of needles, impermeable to any other undergrowth in the shade under them. I was enthralled with the variability of the sizes and shapes of the hardwood trees: a canopy of oak, hickory, maple and buckeye over a thick undergrowth of sassafras, dogwood, redbud, rhododendrons and azaleas each changing color, many adding bright flowers or an aromatic smell, on its own schedule through the seasons—a carnival of a forest.

The return of daily rainfall had greened the woods—the great canopy of trees above and the thick and verdant undergrowth below, with the occasional delight of a jack-in-the pulpit peeking out from the shrubs and groundcover. Even the birds seemed cheered by the rain, and their minute voices added to the brightness of the atmosphere. I had never experienced "blue ridge mountains"—there was a palpable texture and dimension to the hazy air that I had never experienced before, adding to my enchantment with this new place.

Our first trip to the grocery was a novel experience. The neighborhood shopping centers, which were composed of a grocery and a couple of adjacent shops, were of an almost military utilitarian design with little architectural character from the outside. Nor were they particularly customer-friendly on the inside. All the stores were operated by a single concessionaire, so there was no competition for price or quality of goods or service. The shelves were never full, perhaps due to food rationing, but also due to the store's newness and the management's unfamiliarity with this new amalgam of customers. Residents comprised a mix of families from all states, bringing different eating preferences from a wide variety of food cultures. Foods with other than plain southern cooking ingredients, however, were seldom on the shelves.

Many in the neighboring towns were suspicious of the peculiar goings-on in this interloper, this new gated and vaguely sinister Oak Ridge community. In return, the town's residents often responded with their own brand of paranoia. For instance, this was the time before age-dating of canned goods, and we were warned never to open cans that had begun to bulge at the ends. Some speculated that outdated canned goods were typically sent to Oak Ridge stores. Though it is not likely that ever happened, we were never sure—and the shared suspicions inflamed a continuing source of good gossip.

When a new shipment of scarce rationed goods would appear—butter, oleo, meat, sugar, milk and eggs, soap and toilet paper—rumors of their imminent arrival would have passed from neighbor to neighbor. Families would gather and long lines would be waiting for the goods to be delivered and distributed. Long lines became a part of our new way of life. But it also brought neighborhoods closer together. For instance, Mom's farmer families back in Missouri occasionally sent us bacon and other produce from their farms. A neighbor who had moved from California had family members that sent them big navel oranges, which they shared with us. I had never tasted anything as close to pure sunshine as those were. Mom became friends with a farm family outside Oak Ridge and was able to buy unrationed beef, chickens and fresh eggs, and made them available to neighbors. Neighbors shared in the hardship of scarcity, as well as the isolated but not infrequent instances of abundance from outside sources. Those spontaneous connections bonded neighbors, building relationships into a sense of community that the town's planners had hoped for, but never could have achieved by physical planning and design alone.

Shortly after our arrival, we began looking for a new church home. There was no United Church in Oak Ridge, but we were told we could join a group holding services on Sunday mornings in the gymnasium of the Glenwood School. When we started attending the services we met other youth. They became our closest friends and helped Don and I make the transition to life in Oak Ridge. I had never met another "Blake," but there was one—and he was a twin! The first people I got to know were Blake and Billie Joy Alexander. We became part of a wonderful youth group that became a center of Don's and my social life as long as we lived in Oak Ridge. The Chapel on the Hill was the original multi-denominational church in the town center, serving a large number of congregations until they could build their own homes. As our little congregation expanded and became more established, the leadership requested space in the Chapel on the Hill, and moved its services there. They still worship there.

As we adjusted to Oak Ridge, there was one issue to which Dad could never be reconciled. We had never experienced the separation of the races as we saw it in Tennessee, and condoned in the planning for Oak Ridge. All history of the place was erased, obscured by the imperative to complete the bomb, including the dark memory of this very land's slave plantation past. The planners had separated the living quarters of the white community from the "colored." In our daily activities we remained largely unaware of the presence and injustice done to black workers, past and present. Nothing at all was said of the history of the Gallaher-Stone Plantation's heritage here. Dad was appalled by the Colored/White separate and unequal drinking fountains and toilets in all the public places. The "colored only" facilities were universally maintained in less than sanitary conditions. Dad's outrage at those continuing injustices is a message I have carried with me ever since. We were left with the bitter irony that the legacy of fear and prejudice, from our nation's and this land's slavery past, should shape the community at the leading edge of the race to the Atomic Age's brightly promising future.

Throughout the summer, Don and I expanded our explorations and began to learn our way around town. As September approached, we started to focus on school and the new and expanded universe of friends we would be meeting. They would enable our final transition from our Missouri connections to this new place; we were adding a new set of friends, each of whom would add to the richness of our now Tennessee home. There was something special about meeting new acquaintances, equally displaced persons, each of whom brought with them a specific attitude and point of view, who melded into a wonderfully and richly diverse group of friends. Over the summer we began adding new friends through the youth group and through neighborhood connections. To Blake and Billie Joy, we added Lyle Teague, Mary McCall, Peggy Bugg, Margaret Dykes, Priscilla Savage, Sammie Clinton, Susan Bowman, and a growing list of others who shaped my life in important ways then and, though I moved out of their lives, have never been far from my consciousness.

At the end of our first summer, school began at Glenwood Elementary School with a bang! One of our first learning experiences was an air-raid drill. We were marched into the hallway and instructed to sit in two lines facing each another down the length of the hall with our legs tight against our chests and faces protected with our heads on our knees. Our jokes and jostling stopped when we were lectured about the dangers of enemy bombs. We quickly sobered as we were told of the dangers that lurk in the larger world, and the fear of others who were opposed to our carefree (to us) way of life. Though we weren't to be told the specifics of why we had been brought to Oak Ridge, it was impressed on us that our town would be a potential enemy target. It was the end to a kind of innocence we had brought with us to Oak Ridge. It would be the beginning of our growing up to and with, the enormous promise— and danger— the new Atomic Age would portend for the whole world.

Blake Chambliss

Denver, Colorado

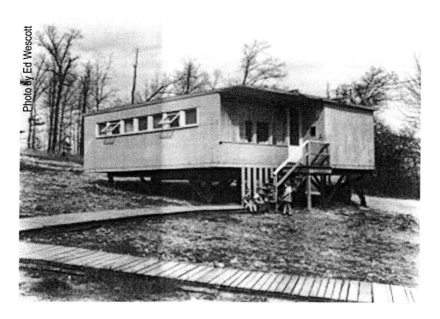

Photo by Ed Wescott

Plywood flat tops were glued to wooden posts
and had canvas tops

No Electricity, No Plumbing

Jimmy Edwards' father arrived in Oak Ridge in early 1943 when construction of the city had just begun, when many area residents were suspicious and resentful.

My father was a construction carpenter and got a job where the secret project had started in 1943. There was virtually no housing for families, so our family of five children moved into an abandoned farmhouse off the government reservation that the owner had declared uninhabitable. But Mother was determined to unite the family with our father, so we lived there through one winter where I completed the third grade at Ball Camp School in the Byington community.

We had no running water and no electricity and no bucket to draw water from the well. Metal buckets and tubs or anything metal could hardly be found in those war years, so we purchased a wood bucket and got a used metal tub with a hole in the bottom. My father plugged the hole with his soldering skill and that met our needs for laundry and bathing. We had an outdoor toilet and got multi-purpose use from catalogs. Kerosene lamps provided light and wood provided heat. Despite those inconveniences, we were happy to have our family together again.

I walked to the school bus stop and for my welcome someone asked where I had moved from. When I said "Virginia", he replied, "We don't like Virginians."

My parents were always looking for a better house and they found a place in Strawberry Plains where we lived one summer before moving to Oak Ridge. My father had been hired to work in the plant and that made us eligible for Oak Ridge housing. We were home at last.

Jimmy Edwards

Cincinnati, Ohio

A Barrel and a Radio

Joan Collins Lane, a rower at the age of 75, was a member of a gold medal-winning women's eight at the National Masters Regatta in 2009.

We moved to Oak Ridge in 1943 from Madison, Wisconsin. I was nine and my sister Carol, was seven, so we adjusted easily as young children do. But for my parents it was an event that completely changed the course of their lives. The catalyst, of course, was World War II.

As great history upheavals go, i.e. the cultural revolution in China or the Noah event, Paul and Burdette Collins' story is small potatoes, but it may be relevant to some of the other 75,000 who were funneled into this secret "pretend" town.

In the years before leaving Wisconsin, my parents were hit particularly hard by the Great Depression. My father came from a large Irish family. His father was a prominent well-to-do businessman in Madison, but his lumber business was totally devastated by the depression, leaving his children unexpectedly scrambling to make a living. My mother was a third generation Norwegian and very culturally tied into her hard working, farming family. I don't think either of them had ever traveled very far outside of their Midwestern environment, although Dad did go to Georgetown University.

I was not privy to their financial difficulties, but it seemed that we moved an extraordinarily number of times in Madison and I would guess that my parents were often unable to come up with rent money. I also know that Dad was declared 4-F in the military draft due to diabetes. The opportunity of finding a job with a construction company in Tennessee was very welcome even if it meant pulling up stakes. Of course, it was temporary, they thought, but actually they remained in Oak Ridge, mostly, for most of the rest of their lives.

My dad's employer was Stone and Webster Construction Co. one of the contractors given the awesome task of building up the area from scratch. Dad later worked for Roane-Anderson, the company in charge of maintaining all of the area homes.

At first, there was no place in Oak Ridge to live, so Dad came down alone. He was housed at the Whittle Springs Country Club in Knoxville. Mom helped out by boarding wives of Air Force men stationed at Truex Field just outside of Madison.

Finally we were able to move down when Dad rented part of a house in Knoxville. His job at Stone and Webster did not qualify him for a house in Oak Ridge, so mother got a job with Tennessee Eastman, eventually landing us a beautiful rare little "H" house on Alabama Circle.

The new home was especially good because life in Knoxville was inhospitable and neighbors were suspicious. Memories include an incident when sister Carol came home in tears one day because she was teased about being a Yankee and told that her belly button was where the Yankees shot her. Another surprisingly enduring impression was of walking through the cold early morning dew to school. The spring chill was a surprising experience for me because, as I understood later, the change in temperature from night to day causes heavy dew. That didn't happen in Wisconsin.

The dew I mentioned before was incorporated in about three feet of mud around our new house. We moved in a few days before Christmas. Besides our clothes, our sole possession consisted of a large barrel packed with kitchen items, which, after emptying, was turned upside down to become a table. Our other piece of furniture was a small dome-shaped radio. Into this humble household we welcomed holiday guests, my dad's sister Dorothy and her husband, Tommy. Tommy was a PhD chemist and later came to work at the Oak Ridge lab. My dad borrowed Army cots somewhere and somehow acquired a dining table and chairs.

Tommy parked his Hudson in front of the house and woke up the next morning to find it sunk in red clay up to its fenders. My resourceful dad went across the street to the Army barracks to enlist the help of six soldiers. They lifted the car and carried it to the more stable main road, all for the price of a six-pack of beer.

At last we started a new life at home in Oak Ridge, happy and content—at least most of us. Mother's thinking remained vested in the temporary refugee status for almost the next 20 years. She had little trust in the local amenities and she would travel back to Madison for the important transactions such as dry cleaning, real Norwegian cooking ingredients and even the "right" color pumpkin (orange, not yellow). For all of us though, the adventures in early Oak Ridge were just beginning.

Joan Collins Lane

Oak Ridge, Tennessee

Movie and a Bus Trip: Two Bits!

I was 10 in 1944 when we lived at 376 West Outer Drive in a two-story duplex called a "K." It was approximately 150 yards from the #17 Highland bus stop at the intersection of West Outer and Waddell Circle, and about 250 yards from a stop for the #2 Pennsylvania bus at the intersection of West Outer Drive, and Pennsylvania Avenue.

Five bus tokens cost 30 cents. On some Saturdays I boarded the #17 Highland bus at around 11 a. m, dropped a token and asked for a transfer. I got off at Grove Center, boarded a #6 Townsite bus and had my transfer punched. At Townsite I went to a movie at either the Ridge or Center theaters. Nine cents. Gene or Roy. Popcorn was a nickel; so was a Coke.

I started home on the No. 2 Pennsylvania bus, handed the driver my transfer and got off at the intersection of Pennsylvania Ave., West Outer Drive and Outer Drive—250 yards to our house.

Not bad for a quarter.

Stanley Finch

Harriman, Tennessee

More than 800 buses ran daily

It was Like Going to Heaven

At the age of 15, Marty Leibowitz, a junior at ORHS, had earned enough credits to graduate and won a fully funded scholarship to the University of Chicago.

When our family moved to Oak Ridge from Baltimore in 1948, where my mother had a job as a sales lady at a department store, we were having tough times. My father, a Russian immigrant, had owned a small men's clothing store in York, PA, where I was born. He died at age 40 when I was four. I was basically raised by my mother and two older sisters.

My sisters, 11 and 9 years older, helped keep the family together. Lucille, the oldest, had just earned a degree in physics at Syracuse University when she took a job in Oak Ridge. She got a "D" house on Damascus Road and Mother and I moved in with her. My other sister, Ann, came down after she finished nursing school at Mount Sinai in Baltimore. Lucille later married a chemist, Howard Heller, whom she met in Oak Ridge.

It was like going to heaven for me in Oak Ridge. My school in Baltimore, PS 49, was hell. The pressure on kids was horrendous. I covered three grades in two years, but I was a misfit and I struggled. PS 49 was incredibly strict and the teachers were overbearing. I shudder to think about it. It was totally different in Oak Ridge. The schools were progressive, and the teachers were nurturing. And the town had a community center—Ping Pong and chess (I became state junior chess champion), and a place to hang out with other kids. Everyone was so open and friendly. It was easy to fit in.

I started in the eighth grade at Jefferson Junior High, but earned enough credits in a special summer school in North Carolina to skip ninth grade, so then on to Oak Ridge High. To earn some spending money, I babysat for 25 cents an hour. Baby-sitting was beneficial in a lot of ways. There were so many interesting families and they had great record collections and books and games. After a while, I decided rather than babysit, I would start a baby-sitting service. I provided the baby-sitters and took a nickel out of every quarter.

When The Oak Ridger came to town, I got a job delivering papers in my neighborhood. To jumpstart their circulation, the paper held a contest with a new bike as the prize to the delivery boy with the highest percentage of subscriptions on his route. I got everybody on my route for 100 percent, then went back and talked some customers into taking a second subscription with the promise that I would give them two months of free baby-sitting. I ended up with 107 percent subscriptions and won the bike.

In my junior year at ORHS, the guidance counselor encouraged me to go to Chattanooga to take a test for a scholarship at the University of Chicago. Miracle of miracles, I learned a few months later that I had actually won full funding. I stuffed everything I owned into a trunk and my family took me to Knoxville and put me on a bus to Chicago. I was 15, and said good-bye to Oak Ridge.

Martin Leibowitz

New York City, New York

Most Likely to Succeed

Melvin Douglas George was voted Most Likely to Succeed at ORHS, earned a math degree at Northwestern while playing piccolo in the marching band, got a PhD in math at Princeton and became president at St. Olaf College and Interim president at the University of Missouri.

There is no doubt that the years I spent in Oak Ridge, 1946-1954, were terrific for me. I arrived in April of 1946, near the end of grade six, which I finished at Pine Valley School. Until then, I had been in about 10 different schools, as my father had moved around a lot in various jobs with the federal government. So I'd been through difficult years of saying goodbye to friends and moving to a strange place to start over–more times than I would have liked.

In 1940, I'd been in Trinidad (then called the British West Indies) in a Catholic school; where punishment was administered by a swat with a ruler across the open palms of a misbehaving student. A couple of years later we lived in Hanford, Washington, in a trailer on the eastern Washington desert, where sand blew through cracks into your mashed potatoes at dinner, and showers were taken in a common facility in a temporary wooden building up on stilts.

Later still, we were in the Los Angeles harbor area, living across the street from an oil well (yes, an oil well) and next to a horse paddock. Most of the evenings in that mild climate I spent out in the neighborhood playing "kick the can" (remember?) with neighbor kids. I remember when our beautiful Persian cat, Minnie, was poisoned (by one of the neighbors we think). And one day a nearby house had all the shades drawn with a sign in the window announcing that the end of the world was coming that day. It didn't. I also remember the shock of an Army fighter plane crashing in the next block. I can still see the charred body of the pilot in the wreckage.

From California, we took the train to New Orleans for the commissioning ceremony for my dad as a second lieutenant in the Army, and then all of us took the train to Knoxville to relocate in Oak Ridge, which – lucky for me – was home for the next six years until I left for college. My father, who was basically an accountant, worked for the Atomic Energy Commission in an office charged with "auditing" the supply of nuclear material, developing statistical tests to try to determine whether a decline in the amount of fissionable material was due to natural decay or theft by the Russians. Many years later, he received an award for the techniques that office developed.

I don't recall our first house in Oak Ridge, but I am pretty sure it was off New York Avenue. Early that first summer, we moved to a "C" house at 400 Michigan, where we stayed put! I recall lots of walks on the boardwalk through the woods, around the Chapel on the Hill, to Jackson Square for a movie or shopping or a soda. After Jefferson Junior High, with vivid memories of Alice Lyman (and her non-gentle habit of beating time on my leg to keep me in rhythm), I went to the old, original high school on Kentucky Avenue until our senior year when we all moved to the new and quite elegant high school. One of my major commitments was to the ORHS band, both marching and concert, and I especially remember the New Year's Day 1952 trip some of us got to take to New Orleans with the UT band. Tennessee was playing in the Sugar Bowl that year, and the UT band wanted to increase its size by adding some high school musicians.

In two summers while I was at Northwestern, I returned to Oak Ridge to work at X-10 in the Mathematics Panel, testing and programming the second scientific computer in the country, Oracle. The machine was in a large air-conditioned room (to dissipate the heat from the vacuum tubes) at X-10, had 1,024 words of memory, and the input/output mechanism was a paper tape reader and printer. The programming was done in hexadecimal machine language, operation by operation. My main job the first summer was to calculate cross-sections on a Marchant calculator, then do the same on the computer, to check that the computer was working properly. Sometimes, I had to go to X-10 after midnight to run on Oracle–quite an adventure. Later (perhaps 1957?), I worked at Bendix in Mishawaka, Indiana on mathematics problems involved in the design and construction of a missile they were developing for Navy ships.

After graduation I completed graduate work at Princeton and was working on a fellowship research project at the University of Maryland when I was offered a position as assistant professor of mathematics at the University of Missouri–for the princely salary of $6,200 per school year. I accepted and eventually became associate chairman of the department. I left Missouri twice but returned both times, and I never left the world of academics.

Mel George

Columbia, Missouri

Boy in Boat Nabbed by Guards

Norman Oliver Pleasant was into boating, golf and fishing, played chess, ran track, flew radio-controlled planes, scuba dived, was a photographer and studied when he was in high school. He does many of the same things today.

I remember doing some things that happened about 1946 or 1947 that caused a bit of commotion, and created a problem for my father.

I decided to go fishing on Popular Creek down near the K-25 plant. I got a fishing pole and some bait, caught a bus at the old Jefferson Terminal and headed for the K-25 area. I got off the bus just before I got to the old Wheat Community and walked north a mile or so through an old farming community until I got to Popular Creek. I fished some as I moved westward toward the K-25 plant and came upon a small fishing boat made of scrap lumber that had one oar. I got in it and continued fishing, drifting down stream until I could see the off-limits K-25 buildings. I had not intended to go that far, so I rowed back up the creek. When I was some distance from the K-25 plant a security patrol, four of five armed guards, caught up with me, ordered me ashore, destroyed the boat and took me into custody.

I had done two things wrong: I got too close to the plant, and didn't have my resident badge with me. At security headquarters they traced down where Dad worked and had him come to indentify me. Dad was not amused.

Norman Pleasant

Hilltop Lakes, Texas

Ouch! Barefoot on the Boardwalks

David Hobson played trombone in the marching band and in the orchestra and ran track. He worked 43 years as a metallurgical engineer at Oak Ridge National Lab.

In April, 1944, Dad told us that he had gotten a house and that we could finally move to Oak Ridge. All of our furniture had been put in storage when we moved from Memphis to New Albany, Mississippi, so he arranged to have it moved to Oak Ridge.

He came to get us and we got on a train for the trip to Knoxville. The train was crowded and we didn't have a seat. So we sat on our suitcases in the vestibule, over the couplings. One of the suitcases was made of thin metal and crackled with every movement. It was a really strange trip.

From Knoxville we rode a bus to Oak Ridge and eventually crossed a big bridge to a wooden building placed across the road at Solway with a lot of soldiers around it. It was getting a lot more interesting and just a little scary.

Two soldiers got on the bus looking at badges and pieces of paper. Dad had his badge and papers for Mother and me. Next we stopped at Townsite in front of the post office. I looked out at a sea of khaki uniforms. The place was crowded and dusty. The bus continued Tennessee Avenue, to Pennsylvania Avenue and onto Hunter Circle, which was a gravel road. We walked to our new home at 109 Hunter Place on what was to become very familiar in the coming years – a boardwalk.

Today it's not a particularly nice neighborhood, but then it was splendid. The house was brand new, with traces of sawdust still on the floor. After living as boarders for the previous three years, it felt good. The house was a Type T duplex with a single door at each end of the building. It was the second-to-the last house on a dead-end street and was a perfect place for a young boy to play. The house was built on 8-by-8 posts and was far enough off the sloping ground to provide play room underneath. From that vantage point, I could look out on the backyard, which was red dirt, and beyond that was a line of trees and a wonderful grapevine swing.

Directly out of our front door was a boardwalk that climbed through a field to Waddell Circle. The type L and K duplexes were just being built, so there were great adventures to be had around them. My good friend, Jimmy Waters, from the other end of our duplex, and I spent many hours playing all over the hill and in the woods. Incidentally, those boardwalks were a real menace to us when we were barefoot. It was routine to pick up a splinter or cut a foot on a nail head sticking up a little. The really bad thing was to run along and trip on a board that had warped and risen unevenly. Band-Aids on the big toe were a common remedy for lost skin.

I started school in the fifth grade at Highland View Elementary. I walked up the boardwalk to Waddell Circle, up Wabash Lane to West Outer Drive and crossed Highland Avenue to get there. I think Rollin McKeehan was the principal. At recess we would stridently yell at each other about voting for either Franklin Roosevelt or Thomas Dewey, reflecting our parents' political viewpoints.

One day a minister came to visit us at home. He was Dr. Bertram Larson, a Presbyterian minister out of Knoxville, whom Dad had met while attending the Chapel on the Hill above Jackson Square. He invited us to attend as a family. We joined the church in April, 1945. The chapel was a standard military church building designed for many faiths. It had a cabinet for the Torah for the Jewish congregation, an altar and kneeling benches for the Catholic congregation and a pulpit and lectern for the Protestants. The Catholics held an early Sunday mass and the priest and nuns would be leaving as we arrived for our service.

One lasting impression for me, in a quite literal sense, was formed by the pews. These were constructed out of five 2-by-4s, two forming the back and three forming the seat. The catch was that the three seat boards had one-inch gaps between them! Even though the edges were rounded, one couldn't sit still very long without gradually having one's bottom conform to those gaps. Watching closely, I could see everyone in the congregation surreptitiously shifting back and forth to bring a new area to bear. I was always grateful when we stood for a hymn.

There was seldom a service when someone didn't accidentally pull one of the kneeling benches over with a great bang. They were hinged to the pew in front and people invariably put their feet up on the edge.

The following interaction, interesting in the context of the time, happened at the United Church, probably in the late 40s. Dad was serving a term as head usher. One Sunday morning an African-American gentleman showed up at the church door for the service. The ushers at the door were astonished and called Dad over for advice. Dad hurriedly conferred with the minister, then and told an usher to seat the gentleman.

I have often wondered what went through Dad's mind at that time – whether he made the decision to seat the man and just alerted the minister, or whether the minister made the decision. Dad grew up in Mississippi and was subject to the mores of that region from birth. Yet I never saw him or heard him demonstrate racial dislike toward Black persons. I will never know the answer. Incidentally, the congregation welcomed the gentleman that Sunday.

David Hobson

Oak Ridge, Tennessee

The 69-Year-Old Virgin

Donald West Robinson received a B.S. degree in interior design at the University of Cincinnati College of Applied Arts, and had a successful business for more than three decades in the Cincinnati area until his retirement in 1996.

Mother was a student at the University of Minnesota when she was 15, completed eight years of studies in seven years including medical school, and was a doctor at age 22. She was Anne West, one of 14 children who grew up in Minneapolis. All the children were home schooled by their mother, a graduate teacher, and their father, Willis Mason West, a professor at the University of Minnesota. He also wrote textbooks. The kitchen table was the classroom and school was basically 365 days a year. I'm the 15th generation and they have all stressed health and education. They've been living in Minnesota since the war of Jamestown, whenever that was.

My father grew up on a farm in Kansas and met Mother while he was studying engineering at Minnesota. She wouldn't marry him until she was through college because hers took longer than his. He ended up with two degrees, mechanical and electrical engineering, while he was waiting for her. I don't know how bright my father was. I think it was just diligence. He was a terrible bigot and no one in the family understood why Mom married him.

Mother was not prejudiced at all; she grew up in a family of flaming liberals. Mother came from a family with a lot of money and felt we never needed to work while we were in school. I did carry a paper route, but little else. My father resented the fact that she spent a lot of money on us. If there was something we wanted and she felt it improved the quality of our lives, we got it. Trips and things. Not just to spoil us, but because she had been given much as a child in the way of theater, concerts, etc.

She was given a nice growing up period where she didn't have to work summers. Summers were for fun.

Dad was always cutting his dirty looks or something if he thought we had too much. He grew up on a farm where everybody had to work 365 days a year.

So rather than have arguments, Mom and Dad just separated, but that was well after the war. It was not a legal separation, they just lived separately. I was glad he was out of the house. He was not a nice guy and he seemed particularly to dislike me. Mom spent her vacations with him and he spent Christmas with us. They got back together when all the kids were out of the house and they lived the last 16 years with me. He had mellowed by then.

Mom always reminded us that we were very privileged and because of that we had a great responsibility. "Never prejudice anyone," she reminded us, "and never judge."

After becoming a doctor, Mom stayed home for years while she was having five babies. I was the fourth and my sister, Betsy, was last. We were both mistakes. Mom returned to her practice when the war came along and tried to join the Army so she could work at the Oak Ridge hospital. She was refused because she had three children at home under the age of 14. So she became an industrial physician at X-10 and Y-12, code names for two of Oak Ridge's nuclear plants. Dad, meanwhile, was one of the first 50 engineers hired to go to Berkeley, California to study the secret calutrons. He then returned to Oak Ridge and helped build the first reactor at X-10. So both of my parents knew what was going on, but I never heard them say a word about it. I don't think they ever did.

My parents played a lot of bridge and they had a bridge game at our house every week. There was a couple from the neighborhood playing with them one night and the radio was tuned to some news broadcaster named Hale. Suddenly he blurted out something about a secret town somewhere in Tennessee that was making some kind of new weapon. Mom and Dad just looked at each other, and then at their guests and continued playing without a remark.

Dad was restricted to certain portions of the plants that were directly related to his work. Mom had more access at the plants than almost anyone. Her color-coded badge allowed her in the most secret places because in case of a major catastrophe, she would have to be able to get to people, and to know what to treat them for. Actually, there were eight or 10 doctors on the payroll and they had a large complement of nurses who worked around the clock. They kept some patients in the dispensary rather than put them in a public hospital if their sickness or injury was related to radioactivity. Doctors would have to know the nature of their problems. Dr. Robinson did know and was trained how to treat radiation problems. Patients with no radiation problems also would be sent to the plant dispensary if they knew too much. They might divulge something under drugs, they reasoned.

I loved my days in Oak Ridge. I was nine when we got there and I could go most anywhere on my own; me and my Chow dog, Mogi. I had my perimeters set. I couldn't go beyond Grove Center, which was the middle of town, because Mom said it was rough beyond that point on the west end of town.

My world expanded when I became a teen-ager. I ran around with a little older crowd for a while, and I got to know all the hookers that used to work at the T and C Café and that one high-priced one at a magazine shop in Jackson Square. And I knew all the bootleggers because I was getting all my booze from them.

I was just 16 then. There were all these older people I knew, 18, 19, a couple in their 20s. One of them was a call girl. Well, not really a call girl. I think she just liked sex. Giving her cash would be an insult, but she got nice gifts and she liked that.

Funny story: There was this prostitute case in court one day and my brother, Ted, who worked at the plants, was on the jury. Time passed and one day Ted's wife Dee ran an ad in the paper looking for a housekeeper and that prostitute answered the ad. When Ted came home from work that day, Dee said, "Oh, Ted, I found the most marvelous woman to work for us and live in. She's good with kids and everything." It was that prostitute who had served her time. Ted never told Dee about her until after she left a couple of years later. He didn't care as long as she treated the kids well and did her job, and she did. Besides, all restaurant workers and people who worked in homes had to have a health card then.

There was a whole pack of people who used to hang out at the Ridge Rec Hall. I started drinking when I was 15 and by age 16 it was a major thing every week with me. I always took Thursday off from school because I was hung over from Wednesday night down at the Jefferson Rec Hall, where I wasn't supposed to be. If you look back on my high school record I bet I missed 30 Thursdays in 36 weeks of school. Everybody at school knew, but nobody could do anything about it because my mother always wrote me an excuse on a prescription pad: "Please excuse Don Robinson from school yesterday. He was ill." That's all she would say and she would sign it A.W. Robinson, M.D. and what could they do, argue with a doctor? Mom would rather have me home and with an excused absence. It was fine with her as long as I kept my grades up. And I did. She wished I didn't drink, but she wasn't going to stop me. I just had to agree to stay in the house all day Thursday. I couldn't be seen anywhere.

Did Mom worry? Sure she did. But when you're 16 you don't worry about what your parents worry about. You're out to have fun. And I did. Patsy Miracle was my closest friend. She was a pretty classmate. We used to get bombed. Her mother loved me when we were taking Latin in the ninth grade. She hated me by the time I was a junior in high school, because I led her daughter down the garden path.

I liked to get drunk because you could say anything, do anything and it didn't matter. It relieved the inhibitions. We would drink at the Jefferson Rec Hall, or on a boat when we went fishing or at somebody's house. Patsy and I used to drink out in the football stadium at the old high school. We'd do it at lunch time. I'd stop and pick up a loaf of unsliced pumpernickel bread, she would bring a cheese thing and put it in her locker the day before so it got nice and ripe and stinky. And we'd take a pint and go out there and sit and eat and drink. There was never anybody around. You just did things you weren't supposed to do because you weren't supposed to.

Some of the older guys we hung out with were having sex but I remained a virgin. I still am. Just having good friends was enough. I have gone through life this way and I'm 69. I have such a low libido my fist has taken care of me all my life. Safest sex you can have. Now at this point—overweight, diabetic and with neuropathy–I couldn't get it up if I had to. When Viagra first came out I asked my doctor for some samples. I've been going to this guy for 36 years. He said, "What do you want this for?" I said, "Well, I still have my right hand."

My life hasn't been perfect but I remind myself how lucky I have been. I don't believe in God per se, but I believe in some source of Supreme Being and I just thank him that he has allowed me to have as much fun in life as I've had. The older I get the more I realize that I'm probably one of the luckiest people on earth and so happy with life in general. I don't miss not having children. I realize that they do add a lot to your life in some cases. I think sometimes it would have been nice. But then I think my kids would have been more rotten than I was and I would have thrown them out of the house and never had any contact with them. So it's probably just as well.

I was privileged in that I was taught early on the worth of knowledge. The more you know about how the world works and how people react, the better you can interact and the more friendships you find. I know people from all walks of life and I enjoy them equally. And it's never a case of judging someone based on social or economic status or racial background. It's just having this wonderful collection of different people and their differences are wonderful to know about. It makes you aware that you are responsible to do intelligent things. You have to put something back. And I've done that for years. It's part of being a decent, civilized human being. You owe your fellow man something.

Mom told us about responsibility. She always reminded us that we were privileged and that if you can ever help somebody, do it. When you get involved in a small way, it makes you realize that you're needed and that you have to give back. She gave us good values and what a gift you get when you have values.

Don Robinson

1934-2004

Graduation

We met in grammar school and junior high, most of us, 60 to 65 years ago —strangers in a secret town, classmates in brand new schools. We were from Everywhere and we lived in Nowhere. And then one night we graduated from high school.

On a beautiful East Tennessee evening on May 29, 1952, members of the Oak Ridge High School senior class were together for the last time: Graduation. We were assembled in alphabetical order on an auditorium stage in six crescent rows of metal folding chairs. We wore rented light gray caps and gowns over white shirt and tie, white dresses and blouses. The girls wore heels and held facial tissues, many of them, for the tears that were sure to come with our last singing of the alma mater. Our shoes were clean and shined, our hair was cut and brushed and our dress slacks had sharp creases. Our moms and dads and uncles and aunts and siblings filled most of the 1,000–plus auditorium seats and they lit up the place with flashbulb cameras.

Our handsome, ever-smiling principal, Donald S. Roe, sat upstage with his back to us, along with the superintendent of schools, the officious, bespectacled Wellington G. Fordyce. Father Francis H. McRedmond sat alongside.

It was a brand new school near the center of town, a $3 million state-of-the-art complex. It was considered one of the best-staffed, most attractive schools in the south at the time. We, the Class of 1952, were the first to graduate there.

Ours would have been a graduation exercise like most others – long, somber and a little dull, but we had something else going on. One of our class clowns, a football player named Jimmie Woullard, was planning to pull off a daring farewell prank during the ceremonies. And, unknown to anyone at the time, we would also witness a rather colorful, unscheduled walk-on performance by Don Robinson, a roly-poly classmate who was sitting unsteadily on the back row. He was drunker than Cooter Brown.

Our class president, lanky Richard "Footsie" Reece, got the evening started on a shaky note when he forgot the opening lines of the speech he had been working on for weeks. He stared blankly at the audience for what seemed a minute or two before collecting himself.

"I'll begin," he said finally, "just as soon as my knees stop shaking."

There were 240 of us on the graduation list. It was a record number for ORHS at the time. Three years after our graduation, Oak Ridge would become the first desegregated public high school in Tennessee, but in 1952 it was an all-white commencement.

Having gathered from 28 states and two foreign countries in the Forties, we were about to strike out on our own and scatter once more around the country. We were eager for our diplomas and, for some of us, eager to discover what it would be like living on "The Outside" in a normal, everyday town. But immediately, we were more eager to witness the bedlam that was about to take place on stage when Principal Roe called prankster Jimmie Woullard forward to receive his diploma. But before the principal would get to the Ws, as in Woullard, on his alphabetical list of names, he would have go through the Rs, as in Robinson, the drunken, red-eyed Donald Robinson, who was trying to will himself sober enough to walk across the stage in a straight line. How did he get so drunk *before* graduation? Some 50 years later he explained.

"I didn't want to attend graduation," he said, "because it was going to be a long, boring evening. So, I tried to convince my mother to let me stay home. She said no and she wouldn't budge, so I devised a plan. I knew that if I got drunk, she wouldn't dare let me out of the house."

110

His mother, a prominent medical doctor at Y-12, one of the nuclear plants, left her office early on graduation day to prepare a special dinner for Don and to accompany her son to the ceremonies. She refused to consider Don's stay-home pleas throughout dinner.

So when it was time to get dressed, Don smuggled a pint of I.W. Harper into the shower with him and drained it. Some 45 minutes later, with his mother banging on the bathroom door, Don and I.W. Harper emerged as one.

"Sorry, mom," Don mumbled as he stumbled out, "I've had a snoot full. Guess I can't attend graduation."

"Guess again," said his irate mother. "You are walking across that stage tonight and receiving your diploma like the rest of your classmates, drunk or sober. Get dressed."

Don got dressed but never stopped pleading, even as Dr. Robinson drove him to the auditorium.

"Mom," Don begged as the high school came into view, "I think I'm getting sick."

"You're walking across that stage and I'm going to be there to watch you," she said. She parked, escorted her unsteady son to the auditorium, then took a seat near the front of the auditorium next to a family friend, Margaret Barnes, the school's prim and proper old-maid guidance counselor.

"Margaret," Dr. Robinson leaned toward Ms. Barnes and whispered, "I must tell you something. Donald is drunk."

"He's what?" Ms. Barnes whispered back. She stood quickly and looked for the quickest route to backstage.

"Sit down, Margaret," said Dr. Robinson. "It's too late."

On stage Don sat quietly, acknowledging nothing and no one—head back, eyes closed, weaving perilously now and then in his slippery metal chair.

When the last speaker sat down and Principal Roe stood to begin the long diploma procession, classmates began peeking across the stage in the direction of Jimmie Woullard, the prankster to be. Woullard sat alphabetically on the back row, next to last on the diploma list. After all the speakers had finished, the diploma call began.

"James Martin Adams," Principal Roe announced the first graduate's name. Adams, a lanky freckle-faced pole-vaulter and cheerleader, rose and walked to center stage, accepted his diploma from the nodding superintendent, shook hands, flipped his cardinal red sash to the left of his mortar cap and circled back to his seat.

"Billie Joy Alexander . . . Gilbert Blake Alexander, Jr. ... " the principal continued the diploma call.

It had been almost two hours since Don's last swallow of I.W. Harper and his condition had improved enough that he was no longer in danger of falling out of his chair. But could he walk a straight line?

". . . John Robert Carver . . . Johnnie Faye Clayton . . . Sammie Dale Clinton . . ."

Ron Roseberry, sitting to Robinson's left and having recognized his problem, tried to encourage him.

"You can do it," Roseberry whispered. "See that red fire extinguisher hanging on the wall?" he asked, nodding toward the left wing of the stage. "Concentrate on that fire extinguisher as you start your walk. Don't take your eyes off it. OK?"

Don rolled his eyes in that direction and nodded uncertainly.

"Pearlie Elizabeth Eads . . . Carol Patton Easler . . . Jimmy Carroll Edwards . . ."

Meanwhile, back in the Ws, Jimmie Woullard was getting a little nervous —and feeling a little guilty. Nervous because word had gotten around that the school board could withhold his diploma for disciplinary reasons if it so chose. Students simply did not challenge authority in the Fifties as Woullard was about to do. Also, Woullard found out just before he walked on stage that those ribboned scrolls being handed out by the superintendent

112

weren't really diplomas. They were certificates of some kind indicating that the student had completed the required courses for graduation. The actual diploma was to be handed out after commencement in some room in the music department.

The reason for Woullard's guilt was sitting next to him in the very last chair—little Jane Wright, a shy, dark-eyed pixie who rarely opened her mouth except to sing soprano with the school chorus. If Woullard's prank caused a serious commotion, would little Jane ever get to walk across the stage and shake the superintendent's hand? Would her parents be denied that once-in-a-lifetime scrapbook graduation picture?

"Sammy Henry Kilgore . . . James Edward Kitchin . . . Jewel Evelyn Kite . . . "

As the procession continued, Woullard turned and whispered to Jane. "Do you know what I'm about to do?"

"I've heard," she whispered back.

"I'm really sorry," he said. "I hope this doesn't cause a problem for you."

Jane shrugged. "It's OK".

". . . James Lazenby Nicholson . . . Mary Carol Norton . . . Delores Butcher Okes . . ."

Woullard had not thought about little Jane when he was booking bets. What started as a $5 dare by football teammate Herrell Akers had snowballed and Woullard had collected bets all over school totaling more than $300. Most of the bets were with classmates, but some teachers, who remain anonymous to this day, also had bet he wouldn't take the dare. Woullard's bet sheet was four pages long by graduation day. Three-hundred-dollars represented almost a month's wages for many of our parents in 1952. Woullard couldn't afford to back out.

As Principal Roe reached the Ps on his name list, the back row got the signal to stand and follow the line. As they shuffled closer to the front of the line, Roseberry squeezed Don's hand.

"Listen. I'll be right behind you," he whispered. "Keep your eye on that fire extinguisher."

"... Karen Ann Reynolds. . . Douglas Hardy Roach . . ."

"Here we go. Don, Get ready," Roseberry whispered.

". . . Betty Lou Roberts . . ."

"This is it, Don. You're next."

"...Donald West Robinson . . ."

Don stiffened his back with his first step, stuck his nose in the air deliberately like an English butler, fixed his bloodshot eyes on the red fire extinguisher on the opposite side of the stage and began his perilous journey. He paused briefly after each step for sure footing until he found a rhythm. It was a calculated high step, as if he were walking on a mattress, and it was accented by perfect posture and an exaggerated look of mock sophistication. He walked straight as a string and accepted the superintendent's handout without stopping, without shaking hands and without taking his eyes off the red fire extinguisher. Instead of returning to his seat, he thinks he remembers wandering off stage and getting sick.

"...Wade Cothran Smith . . . James B. Spalding Jr. ... Betty Jo Stinson," the procession continued.

We cut our eyes for a glimpse of Jimmie Woullard as Principal Roe droned through the essses. Woullard stood in line unflinching, looking straight ahead.

"... Fredrick Gene Tate . . . Lyle Thompson Teague ... Daniel Lloyd Terry . . . "

Woullard was one of the more handsome boys in the senior class, with locks of wavy brown hair, flashing brown eyes, broad, muscled shoulders and a trim waist. He seemed always relaxed and confidently in control. He was a starting left end on our football team, lettered in basketball, track and baseball and served as vice president of the Letterman's Club. And for a little extra-curricular balance, he was a member of the Latin Club.

"… Peggy Ann Williams . . . Mary Jane Wilson … Jimmie Lee Woullard."

Some two hundred grinning classmates trained their eyes on Woullard as he strode boldly to center stage, accepted the so-called diploma and shook the superintendent's hand. But instead of walking back to his seat, he turned toward the audience, threw his mortar cap into the air, raised both arms in a grand salute as if he were the Pope, and released a high-pitched, pulse-pounding scream that sent shock waves through the unsuspecting crowd. It was shrill at first, like a Tarzan bellow; then more thunderous like a gathering storm, echoing back and forth from wall to auditorium wall. It lasted only a few seconds, but it seemed much longer.

The crowd exploded into near hysteria. They laughed and clapped and slapped their knees and stomped the floor. Gowned classmates jumped up and down on stage and punched the air. Soon, almost everybody was standing and began to applaud, louder and louder, laughing and cheering.

Everybody, that is, except Principal Roe and Superintendent Fordyce. They stood stoned-faced, in shocked silence. It was as if the ceiling had collapsed around them.

"Sit down," Principal Roe turned and shouted to us, threatening with a pointed finger. "Sit down and be quiet or you will never graduate from this school."

"We just did!" Leland Stanford Hollingsworth shouted back, waving what he thought was his diploma.

Woullard was practically mugged by congratulating classmates. They shook his hand, slapped his back, and hugged him. But not for long. When Woullard spotted Principal Roe storming toward him, he slipped quickly off stage and hurried down a hallway. The crowd eventually tired and quieted itself and a measure of order was restored.

And there, standing on the side of the stage, was little Jane Wright, the last on the list of graduates. She had been waiting patiently, quietly, wondering if she had been forgotten. With everyone back in place except Robinson and Woullard, her name was called. As she began her walk, the audience rewarded her with stirring applause.

When it was over we wandered off stage to find our parents, posed for more photographs, then turned in our caps and gowns and disappeared into the night and into our future.

Book Three
Moms and Dads...

Patriot Thomas E. Lane

There Should Be a Monument

There is no grand monument in Oak Ridge to honor Thomas E. Lane. There is hardly a mention of his name in the city's early history. There is no epitaph on his bronze grave marker to indicate what a pillar he was. "Thomas E. Lane, 1904—1971," it reads. It could also read: "Perhaps no one ever worked so hard for a town, or loved it so much."

Before there were fences around Site X, before there were nuclear plants or a place to live or an office or a desk, there was Tom Lane. His job was to provide the necessary personnel for the K-25 gaseous diffusion plant, largest of Oak Ridge's wartime nuclear compounds. K-25 was only a code name on a blueprint when Lane began recruiting workers for it. And once they began arriving, he continued to expedite the flow of workers. Meanwhile he kept peace with labor and its unions. He was an engine that never quit chugging, even long after the war.

His first workplace was a room—his room— in the Andrew Johnson Hotel in Knoxville. From there he began locating skilled workers across the country by the thousands, coaxed them to Oak Ridge in swarms, and he supplied replacements when they quit and went home. About one in four wartime Oak Ridge workers did quit and go home because of stress or the bad cafeteria food, or poor housing or homesickness. From those who remained Lane got pledges not to strike or attempt to organize during the war, and they kept their word for the most part. He convinced them with sincerity, patriotism and good wages.

"I hadn't the foggiest notion about what Dad did at the plants," said Don Lane, one of his six children. "He never volunteered to tell us and we never asked, but we knew it was important and we knew he had come a long way from his roots."

He grew up dirt poor in the tenements of Irish Catholic East Boston, one of 12 children. In his teens he worked as a boilermaker's assistant in the Boston Navy Yards. Later he tried to work his way through Massachusetts State College, but had to leave short of graduation because of finances. But while he was there he met and married Jean Campbell of Cambridge, a transfer from fashionable Radcliff College. He went to work with Lever Brothers, a soap company, operating a machine on the midnight shift, filling boxes with Rinso laundry powder. But he was soon promoted to the front office handling labor relations, a field in which he became an expert.

By 1942 he had moved on to Brunswick Corporation as a special consultant in industrial relations and soon after he was recruited by Union Carbide to join the top-secret Manhattan Project. It was after the war before the family knew he was head of industrial relations at K-25. Lane's responsibility, in addition to hiring personnel to run the giant nuclear facility, was to keep workers on the job under discordant wartime conditions. One of his greatest contributions was solving squabbles and keeping labor unions on the job during the tension-filled war years

Many of his recruits made Oak Ridge home after the war, negotiated with him at the bargaining table when the unions organized, and paid their respects at his funeral in 1971. His funeral at St. Mary's Catholic Church was standing room only—company presidents from across the country, union bosses, federal mediators, blue collar workers and civic leaders

"I think it's a token to my dad that he was respected by both sides," said Don Lane. "A union official told me that Dad was the most fair-minded negotiator he had ever dealt with. He said that Dad knew what we needed and what we didn't need. He could wash the baloney out real quick. If there was a way to blow something by the company that would help us, by god he'd blow it by them. Sometimes he stuck his neck way out for the union.

"I remember years after the war, 1954, when I was on liberty from the Navy, Dad was in negotiations with labor leaders and he had invited some men to our house to take a break. They were all sitting around the dining room table and the phone rang. It was the White House. The Cold War was on and the Big Red Bear was rattling swords and President Eisenhower didn't want the weapons stream to shut down. I don't know who was on the other end of the line, but I heard Dad say, 'The union agrees not to strike. Call the company.' "

He was as effective in the post-war development of Oak Ridge as he was in his wartime work at the plants. Some 45,000 Oak Ridgers went back home when the war ended. Tom Lane stayed and made it home. He was founder, first president and board chairman of the town's first bank. He started the town's first Boy Scout troop. He was instrumental in the formation or operation of the Red Cross, the Chamber of Commerce, Rotary, the Elks Club, and other organizations for mental health, race relations and AARP, not to mention numerous charities.

"He never said a lot to us as children," Don said, "but when he did say something, you'd better listen because it was something you would need to know."

Since 1971, Don Lane's father has rested on the eastern side of Oak Ridge Memorial Park, a 120-acre cemetery he helped develop a half century ago.

"There should be a monument for Dad," Don said.

They Locked Dad in a Jail Cell

Classmate Bill Cromer was a lieutenant in the Signal Corp, and worked in engineering and management in a career that included stints at General Electric, Hoover, and Emerson Electric. He shares a U.S. patent with a deceased co-worker.

My dad, a farmer's son from Marshall, Oklahoma, was a natural mechanic. Back in the Twenties, not a lot of farmers had a flair for keeping tractors and other equipment running. Dad could fix almost anything. He once broke an arm cranking a tractor when it backfired and pushed the crank back at him. It is said that he built the first radio in Logan County.

Sylvan Cromer, engineer

His name was Sylvan Joseph Cromer. He married Ruby LaFevers. They both graduated from Oklahoma University and Dad then taught mechanical engineering there. Later he received his Masters degree in petroleum engineering. We moved to Baton Rouge where he taught petroleum engineering at LSU. That's probably how the government found his name after World War II broke out.

He was recruited for the Manhattan Project in 1943 and was assigned to Columbia University in New York where he became an essential player in the making of the atomic bomb. We moved to a house in nearby Teaneck, New Jersey while he was there, then on to Oak Ridge.

Years later, Dad told us about his first days at Columbia where they locked him in a jail cell with classified documents he needed to read in order to know what his boss and few fellow workers knew. I am quite certain Mother did not know what he did other than that it was for the "war effort."

As the K-25 project neared startup, we moved to Evans Lane in Oak Ridge, in November 1944. The K-25 project managed to produce enough "product" to support one of the two atomic bombs that was dropped on Japan to end the war.

After the war, Dad was requisitioned by Los Alamos National Laboratory, in New Mexico, to go there on loan from Union Carbide for one year, to help keep the program alive while dozens of physicists departed to resume their scientific careers. Later, when he probably could have told us what that was all about, we failed to ask. Anyway, we lived in Los Alamos for 10 months beginning in early 1946.

It was a wonderful place for the family, Dad and my sisters Jean and Sylvia, but not so much for Mother, who had to cook in a tiny, inadequate kitchen. We lived in a four-family government building with plans to later move into a very nice new government house. For the most part, the accommodations for a family were fine. Because we returned to Oak Ridge before our year was up, we never got to see the finished new house. Carbide called Dad back because we had learned the Russians also had a bomb.

My personal life was never better than the time we were in Los Alamos. The Army post built a "Scout house" near our apartment and started a Boy Scout troop. Army officers took us in army trucks to several camping locations in the mountains with all the food and equipment furnished by the U.S. government. Los Alamos was specifically selected as a "hideout" for the work on the bomb. But it was a wonderland for a 12-year-old boy.

Upon our return to Oak Ridge, on Everest Circle, Dad was the chief engineer of all future gaseous diffusion plants at Oak Ridge, Paducah, Kentucky and Portsmouth, Ohio during the nuclear arms race with the Soviet Union. We now know he worked on all aspects of both physical hardware and instrumentation to be used in all future scaled-up versions of the original K-25 plant in Oak Ridge

When the gaseous diffusion plants shut down, Union Carbide promoted Dad to vice president of its nuclear and ore division in New York City.

He spent his career in nuclear power, beginning in 1943 at Columbia. Dad's nuclear specialty was gaseous diffusion, which was the ultimate source for all later nuclear weapons and peacetime nuclear reactors. He moved seven times and retired in Oak Ridge in 1971.

He died in 1987 at the age of 80 and is buried in Oak Ridge Memorial Park.

Bill Cromer

Punta Gorda, Florida

Mom, Dad and the Corrugated Box

A year after mother's death in 1994, a package the size of a shoebox arrived in the mail from the U.S. Department of Energy, postmarked Richmond, Washington. It was accompanied by a letter.

"We are grateful for all your mother did for our research and for our country," it read in part. It was signed: Ronald Kathren, director, U.S. Transuranium and Uranium Registries. The corrugated box contained mother's ashes.

Long before her death the Department of Energy had asked for and received mother's pledge to donate her body to nuclear research. She outlived many of the doctors who were eager to study her remains, and when she died at age 86, the DOE wasted not a moment in getting her body into their laboratory. Just hours after her death, she was on a plane with an escort to Washington State.

Mother (Dovie Ryan Searcy), a widow for more than 30 years, had lived alone in a three bedroom, wartime "C" cemesto on Meadow Road, in Oak Ridge. It was her home and the family base for 47 years. She was painting kitchen cabinets at 5 a.m. when she suffered an acute cerebral hemorrhage—a stroke. She managed to activate a medical alert device that hung from her neck. They found her on the kitchen floor, a paint brush in her hand. "Oh, what a headache," she managed to say when she arrived at the emergency room. Those were her final words. She died that afternoon, 27 years after retirement from a classified job in a radiation-hot building at Y-12 where she was a process operator. She never told anyone details of her work. "I signed an oath of secrecy the day I went to work there," she explained, "and I signed another one the day I retired."

What she did there, what she touched there, what she was exposed to there and what she inhaled there were the reasons

DOE researchers wanted her body. Hers was an unusual case. After the war, after the Oak Ridge secret was known around the world, mother was rushed home from work one day accompanied by two medical officers who instructed her to gather some things she might need during a period of isolation in an undisclosed medical facility. The officers waited outside in a government car while she packed a small suitcase. She couldn't say why she was being hospitalized and she didn't know where.

Within an hour she was admitted to a remote ward somewhere within the Oak Ridge Institute of Nuclear Studies' complex under the code name Y-1, along with four fellow workers with code names Y-2 through Y-5—four women and a man. They were quarantined until further notice. No names. No visitors. No publicity.

Mother, a workplace body-count device had disclosed, was registering one of the highest radiation readings ever recorded at Y-12; two times higher than the so-called safe level established by health physics experts. The other four hospitalized workers also had body counts far beyond the safe level. Doctors and health physicists were as mystified as they were concerned. The five workers had little in common. They had different jobs in different buildings and worked with different materials, yet had similar high readings within days of one another.

Where had they been? What had they been exposed to? And why weren't their body counts falling within the normal range? Once a day the family was allowed to talk to Mother on the telephone, but details of her isolation could not be discussed. She didn't feel sick, she didn't sound sick and she showed no fear of whatever health physicists might find in her body. "There is a reason for everything," she told us years later after she had agreed to donate her body to research. "Maybe this is what I was put on this earth for, to benefit others who come after me."

Mother, a pretty Irish lady with a pretty Irish name, Dovie Mae Ryan, went to work in Oak Ridge in 1944 when she was a

37-year-old mother of three, when World War II was raging and when hardly anyone knew that the town or the plants existed. She was the oldest of Isaac and Jeppie Ryan's eight children, born in 1907 in Dutton, Alabama, a tiny farm community atop Sand Mountain in the northeast corner of the state. Dutton was named for her maternal grandfather, Marion Dutton, who was its first postmaster.

As a teen-ager, mother was a housekeeper and caretaker of her younger siblings—changing diapers, cooking for 10 on a wood stove, drawing water with a rope and bucket from a well, washing clothes in a boiling pot over a fire in the back yard, hoeing and picking cotton with her brothers in the field. She was the first in her family to attend college and, even before she earned her teaching certificate at Jacksonville (Alabama) State, she taught six grades in a one-room mountain school near Trenton, Alabama; riding a borrowed mule bareback from a farmhouse where she rented a room. It was a large frame house with a yard full of kids and a large storage shed that was always locked and smelled of apples year round. One day after school she rode into the yard just as two men were handcuffing her two landlords.

"Dovie," the woman called out as she was taken away, "please watch the children until I can get back. We've been arrested." The two strangers in the yard were revenuers who had discovered a stash of bootleg apple jack in the storage shed, along with stacks of sugar bags and bushels of apples.

Later that year at the little school, the usually shy Miss Ryan stood up to one of the older boys who arrived drunk and sent him home. Word spread quickly across the mountain because the boy's daddy was an unpredictable roughneck with a terrible temper. Later that day, during recess, the boy and his burly, shotgun-toting father walked onto the school yard. "You're takin' my boy back in that schoolhouse," he demanded, "or there's going to be trouble."

127

"Well then there's going to be trouble," Miss Ryan replied, "because I'm not having drunk children in my classes."

Just as she said that, several mountain men whose children were in school stepped out of the nearby woods, each carrying a shotgun.

"Now you jist git on back home," one of them said, "and let this young lady teach our young'uns a thang or two."

She met my father one Sunday afternoon after he outbid his older brother and others for a coconut crème pie she made for a school fund-raising auction. For a $2 bid (equal to about $25 in 2010), he got to share the pie with the shy, auburn-haired teacher, and got to walk her home.

After their marriage and a baby, mother returned for her final year at Jacksonville State and took daughter Mary Glenn with her. At the Thanksgiving break she gathered her few coins and carried the baby and a suitcase to the train station for the trip home.

"I'm sorry ma'am," the ticket agent told her when she got there. "You're a quarter short for a ticket to Scottsboro."

She took a seat in the waiting room with little Mary Glenn in her arms and wondered what to do, where to go. The campus had shut down. Before she could decide, the ticket agent, who had been watching her, walked out from his window with a ticket in his hand. "Here's your ticket home," he said. "Have a nice Thanksgiving." He wouldn't take her few coins.

Mother told that story many times at Thanksgiving, and she used that experience as her guide for giving for the rest of her life. She was generous to a fault, and would do without in order to give. When we lived in Stevenson, she never turned away a hungry hobo from the nearby rail yards who begged at our back door during the depression years. "Wait here on the porch," she would say, and then she would go find something for him to eat.

Mother was a 50-cents-an-hour spinner in a cotton mill and Dad was foreman in the shipping room when they left Stevenson for jobs in Oak Ridge in the summer of 1944. They worked round-the-clock, 8-10-12-hour shifts from the beginning; sometimes 60 hours a week, rarely on the same rotating schedule, riding work buses to and from. We had no car. Not many did. We kids learned to keep house, to iron, to cook, to shop. At 14, Mary Glenn was cooking dinner in their absence and I was making cornbread at age 11.

My father, Harley Johnson Searcy Jr. (everyone called him H.J.) was small at 5'7", 130 pounds, an inch shorter than Mother. He was a smart, tough, playfully creative man with little formal education. He was taken out of high school after the 10th grade to work on the family farm in Long Island, Alabama, and later learned carpentry and cabinet making from a book. Growing up on a farm with six siblings, he learned to doctor sick animals like his self-made veterinarian father, who used him as an assistant—to wrestle down and rope cattle and mules and sheep so he could treat them.

When Dad was a grade-school boy, his father would sometimes position him at one end of a barn hallway with instructions to wave his arms and stop the charging horned cattle that would be rustled into the opposite end and corralled. Dad always held his ground and the cattle always stopped. Once he brought a 750-pound boar to his knees. His father had been hired to cut the tusks from the unruly hog and after it had been roped, Dad crawled into the pen to help hold it still. Suddenly the boar jerked his head, snipped the rope cleanly with his razor-like tusks and charged. Dad sidestepped and grabbed the hog's ears as he went past and held on. While the boar dragged him around the pen, Dad bit down on an ear and ground his teeth into the tender gristle. The boar squealed, his knees locked and he quit.

At Oak Ridge he was a service mechanic during the war and later a chemical operator in a number of buildings including Mother's 9212, but they never worked together. We never knew, even after the war, that Dad worked around radiation-emitting material and equipment. He never told us that his radiation readings were routinely higher than the plant's safe limit for years, or that body counts showed his elimination to be slow. Maybe he didn't know. Specific radiation-count data were not included in his medical records requested by the family some 40 years after his death. But a letter dated May 9, 1963 from J. D. McClendon to Dad's supervisor, M.F. Schwenn, concerning radiation safety, stated: "On the basis of in-vitro measurements and the slow elimination rate, it is recommended that Mr. Searcy be assigned to a non-uranium area. It is requested that this work restriction remain in effect until notification is given that his estimated quarterly exposure rate is less than 25 percent of that specified in radiation protection guides."

Too late. Dad died September 24, 1963. He was 57.

Buried among the hundreds of pages of his medical notes was this one: "His exposure was probably of the acute nature and due to slow elimination of the activity via urinalysis and/or the digestive tract, the assignments at locations which offer the least exposure liability did not help, i.e. for the time period involved since he currently meets the plant's removal criteria." Another report indicated that he probably had "inhaled some insoluble material... at the metal burning operation since the extraction process is of a wet nature." Still another report stated that an exhaust pipe had blown out in his face and that he was exposed to an "unknown substance."

Included in the voluminous medical records were four inserts from the Department of Energy declaring that certain pages had been omitted because they "contain classified information."

The cause of death was listed simply as "oat cell carcinoma of the right lung." The autopsy was more revealing: "Bronchogenic carcinoma of the right lung with extension to the mediastinum, left lung, pluras, bones, liver, pancreas, left adrenal, left kidney, tracheobronchial and lumbo aortic lymph nodes and stomach."

The number of similar radiation-causing deaths at Oak Ridge is unknown.

Mother worked in Y-12's hottest building, code named Beta 9212, the last stop for the enriched uranium processing. It was a four-wing building, designed so that accidents in one wing would be less damaging to other departments. Army guards stood in doorways between rooms. Mother and other women wore men's white coveralls and worked alongside men in a room where temperatures reached 112 degrees. They handled uranium in its various forms, in various ways, enriched and depleted, under the direction of physicists and engineers. She was told when and how to do, but never what or why. She would find out on August 6, 1945 when the first uranium bomb detonated over Hiroshima.

Mother's first thought, she said when she learned of the bomb, was that the war will now end. Her second thought was the horror of the destruction, the tens of thousands of workaday civilians like her and her family, killed by a weapon she had helped create—birds ignited in the sky, vegetation and pets and fish evaporated for miles and, oh my God, all those little children; disintegrated in temperatures of more than 5,400 degrees. She thought of the scorched bodies of our American boys at Pearl Harbor and the Bataan death march and the kamikaze bombers. She thought of her brothers. "I had two brothers who fought in Europe," she said, "and they likely would have been part of the Japan invasion forces. The bomb may have saved their lives, along with hundreds of thousands on both sides. I guess we did what we had to do."

When mother died, we never expected to learn more about her work. We heard nothing from the researchers at the Uranium Registry for a year. Then one morning in 1995 the box of ashes arrived, along with a separate package containing more than 500 pages of research notes and some details about her job that she was never allowed to tell.

"Your mother was handling 93 percent U-235," said C.M. "Hap" West, a health physicist who studied her case and published research papers about it. "At the same time, they enriched U-234 in her building and that has much higher specific activity. By that I mean it takes less U-234 weight-wise to give the same amount of radiation. (U-234 is an isotope extracted from pure plutonium 238 and has a half life of 246,000 years.) Consequently, the stuff they were handling was about 100 times more radioactive than normal." Some material was so sensitive that a drop of sweat could have set off a reaction strong enough to blow up the building.

Mother was handling enriched uranium in a form called green salt when her extremely high body count was detected. Green salt was packaged in building 9212 during the war and sent by secret courier to Los Alamos, New Mexico, Site Y, where it was tooled for the first uranium bomb. During the Cold War of the 60s it was stockpiled for use in nuclear weapons.

"They put green salt in a cylinder made of something very substantial that wasn't subject to much corrosion," West said, "along with some lithium or some other chemical, I'm not sure what now. But they heated that in a furnace until it reached a certain temperature and you got uranium in a metal form. They took off the top of the cylinder and knocked the metal button out and into a dry box and cleaned it. It was melted and cast into the shape they wanted, then transferred to the machining division where it was machined to the exact size they wanted. The machinists' drills left little burrs of uranium that were cleaned by a power wire brush. The airborne uranium caused by the brush was sucked into a special elephant snout ventilation system similar to a vacuum cleaner. "Somebody used it to dispose of a Kleenex," West said, "and it caused it to stop up. So then a machinist started grinding that stuff and it was throwing it right back in his face."

Researchers never knew when or how Mother and the four others under study got over-exposed. All they knew was that all five had been running relatively normal body counts and urine tests and suddenly their body counts shot up. There was only one body counter for the entire building, so not everyone was tested. "The body counters used for internal radiation were so time-consuming and expensive, you could only do one about every 30 minutes," West said, "so we just used them for those workers who had the greatest potential for the greatest exposure—like your mother. We used urine tests for other workers and had them wear a radiation-sensitive film on their badges to test for exterior exposure."

Every microscopic bit of uranium was accounted for. If there were spills, operators had to mop them up and save the mop water for extraction. One of Mother's co-workers once was handling a "batch of something" and got some of it in her hair. She was rushed to a shower, stripped and scrubbed. Her bath water was saved for processing and she was instructed to save her shampoo water at home and take it to work for processing.

At the end of every shift, workers' gloves, hats, shoes and protective clothing were tested. Contaminated items were sent to a special laundry for decontamination. If contamination still existed, the items were either burned or stored until all traces of uranium diminished by radioactive decay. Paper was placed on floors like rugs in some rooms and burned daily. A gadget called "sneezy" measured radioactive dust in the air. Warning devices triggered a siren alarm when a radioactive worker drew near or when there was inadvertent criticality. At X-10, rabbits and rats were placed in strategic locations to determine the dangers of long, extended exposure.

Radiation sickness was not common, but when it happened, there was always a threat of death or permanent damage. "What happens," said West, "is that cells in the blood that fight off infection get pretty well depleted. If they are depleted enough, you die. It's kind of like AIDS. It usually takes about six weeks or so for the blood to get as bad as it's going to get. Either you die, or you begin to recover. If you get a large dose and it gets into the gastrointestinal system, it just takes you apart and you hemorrhage to death. In cases of extremely high dosage, it attacks the central nervous system and those people may die in a matter of days or hours."

There were no short-term deaths caused by radiation sickness in building 9212 in Mother's time, but there were some scary incidents. In one of the most chilling—but not in Mother's workplace—a uranium solution was pumped through a "safe pipe" to an overhead tank after it had been cleaned and flushed with water. The uranium solution was mistaken for water by operators on the next shift. When the tank was drained into a 55-gallon drum, an operator was supposed to be watching the drum but failed to notice that the liquid was as yellow as urine and was not water. When the drum got about one-third full, it began to boil and went critical.

"The solution continued to drain into the drum," West said, "and the detectors and sirens went off and people scattered. I think the guy who was doing the draining realized just before it happened what it was doing and jumped back and ran as the alarms went off." Some radiation sickness followed, but there were no deaths.

There were two radiation deaths at Los Alamos, both prominent physicists who were exposed in different experiments. On August 21, 1945, a week after the war ended, Harry Daghlian, working alone, dropped some material on a nuclear assembly that started a chain reaction, exposing him to immense amounts of radiation. He died within a month. The following May, Louis Slotin was standing next to two pieces of plutonium propped apart by a screwdriver. The screwdriver slipped, the two pieces fell together and the room filled immediately with ghostly blue, warm radiation. Slotin heroically knocked the pieces apart, saving the lives of seven others. He died in nine days.

Mother's high dosage was not her biggest problem. While the radiation readings of the man in the study (Y-4) fell at a fairly normal rate, the women's readings remained mysteriously high.

"Your mother's biological half life was extremely long," West said. "Half life is the time it takes half of the uranium in the lungs to leave the body—in urine and feces. The next half life is the time it takes half of the remaining uranium to be excreted, and so on. If the slow excretion rate continues, then these people are probably going to be exposed for the rest of their lives."

The normal half life in Y-12 incidents was considered to be about 120 days. The women's half lives were 400 days and up. Mother's was more than two years. After a week in the hospital, she was instructed to remain home until further notice and to leave urine and feces specimens on her porch periodically for medical officers to pick up and test. Weeks later when she returned to work she was transferred to a non-uranium building where she remained until her retirement in 1971.

Y-12 assigned a high-level scientist to find what the five exposed workers had been exposed to and after a detailed six-month study, several materials were suspect. "We took those materials and did an in-vitro study and put some of them in testing for simulated blood and kept them warm and shook them to see how fast uranium would dissolve into that fluid," West said. "At Hanford, some of that material was put in dogs and it just didn't stay in dogs the way it stayed in those women. The dog had a 300-day half life. We never found out what the exposed material was. There had never been anybody with half lives like those four women. It's hard to understand why it would happen, then never happen again. And it never did."

Two years after the puzzling exposure, Mother was diagnosed with squamous cell skin cancer on her face and suffered from kidney problems the rest of her life. Traces of breast and lung cancer were found by DOE researchers after her death. She was still registering a body count the day she died.

She died at 1:36 on a Sunday afternoon with brother Charles and Mary Glenn at her side while I was racing through Virginia from Philadelphia. Within minutes of her death, DOE officials took charge of her body and saw that it was properly prepared and labeled for shipment to researchers in Hanford, Washington. I arrived at the Methodist Medical Center just as a hearse was backing up to a loading dock to pick up her body. I ran to the morgue and was permitted to see her quickly. Her shrunken body was lying on a cold sheet of metal in a near fetal position. Her body was the last of her many gifts.

Someone came for her, packaged her in a blue corduroy body bag and rolled her down a hallway to the loading dock in a silver Ziegler casket. I followed and stood back as she was lifted into the hearse.

"May I help you, sir?" an attendant asked.

"That's my mother," I said.

"Oh, I'm so sorry." He paused to look at some papers. "I see here that she's a full-body donor. There aren't many who do that."

"There aren't many like her," I said.

Someone closed the doors and the black hearse rolled slowly down the driveway onto Tennessee Avenue. I watched it until it became a dark speck and out of sight. It would turn left at the traffic light on New York Avenue, then cross the Turnpike onto Lafayette Road toward Y-12. It was the route mother took to work for more than a quarter-century, passing through the old wartime security gate entrance where she showed her badge thousands of times. But on this trip she would go south on Illi-

nois Avenue toward Knoxville and to the airport. Mother loved
to fly.

Mom and Dad at Jay's 1956 wedding

Dad Signed the Checks
That Paid for Oak Ridge

Charles Franz VandenBulck, a star student in ORHS's Class of 1952, arrived in Oak Ridge from Hoboken, N.J. in 1943, months after his father had cleared the way for the city and its nuclear plants.

It was May 25, 1963 and I was at a dedication ceremony for the new Charles VandenBulck Bridge, which is where the old Whitewing Bridge (pontoon style) once stood. It crosses the Clinch River on Highway 95 on the western outskirts of Oak Ridge.

Senator Albert Gore Sr., and Senator Howard Baker Sr. were there as speakers. S.R. Sapirie, head of Oak Ridge Operations, was there, and the state highway commissioner and the general manager of TVA, plus the Oak Ridge mayor, R.A. McNees, and county and state officials. Local newspapers, six radio stations and a TV station covered the proceedings. And on the water there was a huge flotilla of cabin cruisers, some of them 56-footers.

They were there to honor my father, Colonel Charles VandenBulck. Until that day, I never quite realized just how much my father had done in his work in Oak Ridge for the Manhattan Project.

Governor Frank Clement signed a joint resolution of the Tennessee Legislature to officially name the new bridge. My mother, Gertrude, and I represented my father. Mother was 53 and I, the only child, was 29. Dad died seven months before the bridge was finished at the age of 58.

The flotilla was headed by the TVA towboat, Pellissippi, and as the flotilla followed it slowly beneath the bridge, Mom aimed a "magic wand," which disintegrated a ribbon suspended from the bridge. There was a loud cheer for Dad. It brought tears to my eyes. I knew that Dad had won the Atomic Energy Commission's Distinguished Service Award, the commission's highest honor, and that he had won the War Department's Legion of Merit Award for his service to the Manhattan Engineering District. I remember when he was traveling so much, 150,000 miles in about two years, before jet airplanes; travel he couldn't talk about. It was very mysterious.

He was the chief administrative officer at the beginning of the Manhattan Engineering District; and he had a blank check fed directly by the U.S. Treasury. He bought $2.6 million worth of East Tennessee land and paid for the removal of about 3,000 persons from their homes. That land became Oak Ridge. He financed the construction and improvement of 55 miles of railroads and 300 miles of roads. He bought raw uranium from Canada, the Belgian Congo and from the Colorado Plateau.

He started writing checks in 1942, before the United States was fully mobilized into World War II. By the end of the war, he had written checks for approximately $1.6 billion dollars. He was the disbursing officer; and he operated under such cover that the Inspector General's Office had trouble finding him. When the Inspector finally found him and called on him, he told Col. VandenBulck that he must fill out certain forms and papers as was required by law.

Dad filled out the required paper work, and the Inspector took it and started to leave the office with it.

"I'm sorry, Inspector," Dad said. "But you can't take those papers. They have to stay in Oak Ridge." The Inspector said he had to take them and would not leave without them. It took several telephone calls to convince the Inspector, who finally left town. The papers remained in Oak Ridge in a safe.

Normal accounting practices were suspended so the usual practice of check-and-balance could not be followed. At one time Dad was Contracting Officer, with unlimited authority, and was also serving as Certifying and Disbursing Officer, which violates all concepts of proper checks and balances. But, as Dad said, "Such practice would not be tolerated in any good organization, but the Manhattan Engineering District had a job to do, and this type of assignment helped get it done."

In all, my father spent 36 years in service as a civilian employee and as a commissioned officer until his retirement. He came to America from Antwerp, Belgium as a 9-year-old and he grew up in New Jersey. America never had a more loyal patriot. I am proud that there is a bridge named for such a good man, a man who loved the town he helped to create.

I've had many memorable moments when a friend or stranger has asked me about the VandenBulck Bridge, which they crossed over in East Tennessee.

Charles VandenBulck

Savannah, Georgia

Col. Charles VandenBulck

Whatever happened to...

Book Four

Class of '52

The Class Poll:
Politics, Religion and Sex

By Joel Anne Morris Lambert

OK, a few of us in the Class of 1952 smoked a little marijuana, but not while we were in high school. And a few of us were arrested at some point in our lifetime, and some even spent a night or two in jail. Or so we confess in a reunion survey that was circulated among the class months before the 2010 reunion in June.

The survey, conducted by me (prodded by Jay Searcy) was an attempt to discover who we were in the 1950s, and who we are now, 58 years later. Together we formed a slice of "American Pie" during a fascinating period in history. Oak Ridge was and is a uniquely interesting town (*the Secret City*) and we landed there quite by chance from other parts of the U.S. as impressionable pioneer children.

So how did we turn out? What are our politics? Our religion? How's our health, what's our lifestyle? And, of course, did we or did we not smoke marijuana, go to jail and have sex into our seventies?

Of particular interest is the section about our sex lives, or the lack thereof. Mostly, we just wanted to know if we were still doing it at age 75 and 76, and if so, what? What we learned from the survey is that it's none of our business, or anyone else's.

It was clearly explained that the survey was anonymous and that all questions were optional. But that didn't stop some from mounting an anti-survey, name-calling campaign with threats of boycotting the reunion. The issue was especially sensitive, understandably, to those who had lost spouses. And we apologized for that. But apologies didn't stop an exchange of scathing e-mails that heated up the Internet for almost a month. God was called in to testify more than once before reunion planners finally stepped in and threw out the sex section, and promised that results of the sex poll would not be reported at the reunion. And they weren't. But there were no promises that the results wouldn't be available elsewhere. Like this book.

What we learned from those who didn't mind addressing the sex issue is that, yes, many if not most of us still do it, or something closely related to it. Nobody said what, exactly. A few of us, mostly guys, admitted to doing it first in high school. Three were initiated in junior high and one precocious funny guy said he started doing it the day he was born.

Back to marijuana. Most of us didn't even know what a joint was until we were in our late 20s. The 60s generation had to show us how. That was William Jefferson Clinton's generation, remember; and we all know that he didn't inhale.

But we did.

Only a small percentage of us ever touched the stuff and those who did never tried anything heavier. Or so we say in the survey. But one did admit to sniffing cocaine just once, out of curiosity.

We outgrew weed as we got older and forgot about it, except for a couple of grandpas, maybe, who keep a little around for medicinal purposes (and for a little euphoria, as Norman Mailer liked to say). There may be others who keep a stash, because only 60 out of the 168 living classmates responded to the questionnaire, and some of those didn't answer the weed question. Anyhow, we didn't smell any pot at the reunion.

The survey offered a few other surprises. For instance, the majority of us voted for George W. Bush. Not once but twice. And we weren't smoking anything. Yet on another line in the questionnaire, a clear majority named Bush the worst president in our lifetime (followed by Jimmy Carter and Barack Obama, who had been in office just 18 months at polling time). Curi-

144

ously, only two of us gave this ranking to Richard Nixon, the only president ever forced to resign for misconduct in office.

There are other such goodies hidden in the complete survey report that follows. Interestingly, two thirds of the responses were from men, about the same ratio as the attendance at the reunion. Although the survey was meant to be anonymous, about half of us identified ourselves.

Personal Statistics

The large majority of us arrived in Oak Ridge from 1943 to 1946, entering grades 4, 5, 6, and spent an average of 7 ½ years in the school system.

Three of every four graduates attended college, earning 31 bachelor's degrees, 12 master's, and five doctorates—two MDs and three PhDs. Fifteen reported receiving honors of one sort or another.

About half of us lived in Oak Ridge for awhile following graduation, but only nine lived there more than five years. One person, Herrell Akers, has lived there 66 consecutive years.

Three-quarters of us had parents who worked at one of the plants, mostly in blue collar and white collar jobs. We lived in all kinds of housing, the largest number in flattops, followed by duplexes and cemestos.

Almost all of us married—a large majority only one time, about 20 percent twice, and a handful three times. The youngest to marry were 17, some waited until they were 33. More than half of us married someone we met in Oak Ridge. Now in our 70s, widows outnumber widowers 2 to 1. Divorces among men, however, outnumbered those among women by more than 3 to 1. We can take pride in the fact that the rate of divorce, 10 out of 60, is remarkably lower than the national average of 50 percent.

The 60 respondents have a total of 165 children, substantially higher than the population replacement rate. Eleven of the 60 have had a child who died. We have 318 grandchildren, one family reporting 17, and 25 of us have great-grandchildren.

The Oak Ridge Experience

All but two of us rated the Oak Ridge experience a good one, more than half saying it was one of the best periods of their lives. About 40 percent of us felt "special" when representing ORHS outside of Oak Ridge, primarily as participants in musical events, chorus, band and orchestra festivals, or sports events.

Oak Ridge was created in secrecy starting in 1942, a rudimentary pioneer town, but about half of us felt either positive or OK about the mud-and-boardwalk conditions when we arrived. The majority felt safer in Oak Ridge than we might have elsewhere.

Most of us did not wonder why there were so few blacks in evidence in Oak Ridge, yet a majority remember seeing where they lived or went to school at some point or other. On the other hand, a large majority of us were OK with the integration of the public swimming pool when that happened later (but very much ahead of the rest of the South), and so were most of our parents. A very few objected strongly.

Most of us were living in Oak Ridge when the first atomic bomb was dropped. Several mentioned the "ending of war, and returning of loved ones" as being the cause of celebration rather than the bomb itself. Only about 20 percent of us reported having heard scary things about atomic energy at the time. Specific recollections included hearing that a chain reaction could get out of hand, that radiation is insidious and potentially fatal, and that it causes cancer.

A large majority of us thought then, and still do, that the decision to use the bomb was correct. Similarly, most of us trust nuclear energy as a power source and would favor making it a major source of energy for the country.

We are of divided opinion as to whether there will be a nuclear war someday. Only a handful thinks a nuclear war is likely in our lifetime or that of our children. But, two to one, we think that a nuclear war, should one happen, will spell the end of life as we know it.

Young Adulthood and Beyond

Upon leaving high school, our career ambitions were all over the place: from minister or nurse to architect or truck driver. A surprising 50 percent of us did what we set out to do! The careers we actually followed were too numerous to list, but jobs associated with education, from kindergarten teacher to college president, were most numerous. Next came military, clerical, industrial, plant work, sales, church-related work, scientific, and medical, but no lawyers! Most of the women were both mothers and career women. About a quarter of us are still working, at least part-time.

Culture and Lifestyle

To the question, "What are your main pleasures?" our answers were ordinary—reading, travel, family, gardening, sports, socializing, church activities, and music. A few listed hunting and fishing. One person mentioned Civil War reenactments.

Surprisingly, classical tops our favorite music list, followed by country. Less than half of us still dance, although more than half say they used to.

If we were to write a book, our top subjects would be memoirs, history and social issues.

All but a few of us are computer literate, at least as far as using e-mail. About a fifth of us are on Facebook. Only one of us Tweets.

What makes us happiest? Family and friends.

Six of us admitted to having been arrested at least once, mostly for traffic offenses, including DUI. Rowdy behavior and a fraternity prank accounted for the others. Four of the six spent a night in jail.

Health and Nutrition

We have a long list of illnesses and a longer list of medicines we're taking, but most say they are in good or excellent health. "Hey, I'm still here, aren't I?"

Not surprisingly, diseases associated with aging are dominant: diabetes, high blood pressure, heart disease, cancer, glaucoma. About 10 percent say nothing at all is amiss. Similarly, we report very few missing body parts, and only a handful use a cane, walker, or wheelchair.

In the habits department, only two of us smoke , although a majority used to. But a large number of us admit to being overweight, and we are not so great when it comes to fitness. Almost a third of us never exercise.

Most of us drink, but quantities admitted to are for the most part modest and only one admits to past overindulgence.

The great majority of us are happy with Medicare. The most frequently mentioned improvement suggested by the few who commented would be to make it universal.

Religion, Or Not

Eighty percent of us consider ourselves religious, half of those strongly religious. But fewer than half feel that religion is good in the world. The number becomes a clear majority if you add in the "it depends" group. For these, presumably, it depends on whose religion you are talking about. About a third of us feel that religion can be either harmful or both good and bad for the world.

Not surprisingly, four fifths of us are Christians, Baptists being the most numerous. A couple of us switched from Christianity to Buddhism or Mormonism.

The majority of respondents believe in Evolution and about a third do not or are unsure. About a quarter of us believe in Intelligent Design.

Most of us consider ourselves "saved." A large majority of us pray. Most attend church or temple regularly, and the number is only slightly lower today than when we were in high school.

As for whether God causes everything that happens, most of us think not. And while less than half expressed an opinion as to why God allows bad things to happen, most of those who did are inclined to let Him off easy, ascribing this outcome to human free will, the nature of life, and, for at least one of us, the Devil. We think "end times" are coming by a 2 to 1 margin, but only a couple thinks it will be anytime soon. One of us said it is a dangerous belief because it fatalistically encourages people to ignore the problems of our world instead of trying to fix them.

Not very many of us ventured to describe heaven and hell, but to be in the presence of God or to be excluded from it is a recurring theme among the answers.

Some of us look within to find heaven in one's state of mind, or in knowing that one has a purpose and that one is acting upon it. A handful of us dismiss the whole notion of heaven and hell, or consider them to be symbolic notions.

Although nearly a third of us avow that God has spoken to them, this appears mostly an internal event, "a still, small voice," "an angel on my shoulder," and "a comforting awareness." Some feel the presence of God in the words of the Bible, others in the beauty of nature.

About a third of us meditate, more than half believe that the mind has healing powers, more than a third think that one's mind or spirit can attract good things into one's life.

As for secrets of life, suggestions included: Follow the Boy Scout creed, keep a positive outlook, love and serve God all your days, do your best, let the rest go and follow the Golden Rule.

Our Older Years

Good news. More than half of us expected to live as long as we have, and a similar proportion does not feel as old as we are. The same happy outlook is expressed by the half of us who expect to live between 5 and 20-plus years longer. As for "bucket wishes," (things we would like to do before we kick it) a goodly number of us would be happy to keep on doing the things we already enjoy. Others would like to do something new, like ride in a balloon or play the piano. Still others yearn for higher goals, like serving God better, seeing the world at peace, or, at a more modest level, "leaving my stuff neat and orderly."

Very few are afraid of dying, although the prospect of dying alone stirred a bit more concern. Far more are distressed by the thought of living alone.

Half want to be buried, the other half cremated. Some have a funeral ceremony planned and some even named the music they want played: *Amazing Grace, Ode to Joy, How Great Thou Art, If You Could See Me Now* and *So Long, It's Been Good to Know You.*

US and World Concerns

Our local newspapers are the print media most often named as our principal source of news. The New York Times is the most often cited national publication. Our radio and TV preferences are predominantly local affiliates of the traditional national broadcast networks. PBS and NPR get a fair number of mentions. Among cable sources, CNN is named most often.

There is no consensus on preferred commentators. Favorites range from Rush Limbaugh to Bill Maher. Bill O'Reilly is mentioned slightly more than anyone else.

We regard education as the top national priority, followed by energy independence, controlling health-care costs, and scientific research.

Politics

Half of us rated ourselves as politically conservative, with liberals and neutrals splitting the other half. On the other hand, those of us identifying ourselves as Democrats outnumbered Republicans, and a sizable number say they are Independents.

Ronald Reagan was the most often-named president we considered the best of our lifetime, with Franklin Roosevelt only slightly behind. Next in order were Truman, Clinton, and Kennedy.

We would be OK with a woman president, but we consider Sarah Palin to be unqualified. By 2 to 1, Hillary Clinton is seen to be qualified.

We favor changing the presidential election to a popular vote and most of us think the tax system is unfair. A like number is concerned about the growing income inequality in the United States. A big majority disagrees with the Supreme Court's decision allowing unlimited funding by corporations and labor unions of candidates for electoral office. Most of us feel our democracy is eroding, and more than half think we are in danger of losing superpower status.

Almost all of us say we vote regularly, and at all levels of government.

Top government concerns are ineffectiveness and stalemate, overspending, pork-barrel spending, excess campaign financing, corruption and overregulation. Advice for the president was divided between those who want him to be more assertive and those who would like him to resign.

Social Issues and Attitudes

We are pro-choice by a margin of two to one. We favor gun control by about the same margin. We favor legalizing the medical use of marijuana.

We are mostly pleased with the progress of race relations in the country, and we are not concerned by the fact that whites will soon no longer account for a majority of our population.

Most believe that homosexuality is genetically determined and not a choice, while opposing gay marriage and adoption of children. A clear majority favors allowing gays to serve openly in the military.

We are virtually unanimous in our concern over the growing sexualization of children in our culture. The media and parents are both blamed about equally for this trend, while others find fault with the schools, advertising, and "society." In line with these sentiments, a majority of us approves of sex education for children, with half of these in favor of starting at pre-teen ages. Half of us do not believe that "abstinence only" works, and far fewer favor the distribution of birth control devices to children.

Only one person out of the more than 30 responding thinks that today's children are receiving good moral, social, and civic values.

Our Generation

Not many people commented on how our generation compares with the "honored" 40s generation and the "boomer" 60s; but those who did said essentially, " Hey, we are OK, too." Several people said "We are the BEST!"

As one person wrote: "We were a generation of servers, givers to the world around us. We had a sense of civic duty and community concern." Others said we were the innocent generation; we had a fresh-eyed ability to find life new and exciting!

One person pointed out that since Tom Brokaw's "greatest generation" brought us up, the apple didn't fall very far from the tree, and that in raising our successful boomers, we must have instilled in them some of the "save the world" values they had.

All about Sex

When did we first have sex? About two-thirds of those responding waited until our college years, engagement, or marriage. A few, especially boys, had their first sexual experience in high school. Three boys claim it was junior high (and rumor has it there was one precocious one-year-old among us!)

Happily, two thirds of those responding say we are still having sex at our age! Most strongly disagree that "sex is for young people" and would like to have sex weekly or more often.

Sadly, a substantial number of us are having trouble with our equipment. Some of us are coping with this by means of work-arounds, making special dates for sex, and aids like Viagra, lubricants, and sex toys.

No one will be surprised to learn that some of the men feel that foreplay takes too long, and that not a single woman agrees with them! Men and women are much more in accord about hugging and kissing, with a strong majority of both sexes expressing a fondness for these activities. A couple of people pointed out the "life-giving" quality of big hugs!

There is even stronger agreement among those answering the questions about sexual interest in or activity with members of one's own sex. Denials are unanimous and often vigorous, and there were some who replied this way to these questions who answered no others!

Men and women were sharply divided about how much we think about sex. Where a substantial number of men confessed to daily, and even hourly, thoughts, only two women admitted to having them more than seldom!

Finally, a near unanimous chorus of voices, men and women alike, endorsed the notion that love is the key to sex, and that it has either everything, or almost everything, to do with it!

Joan and Roy: Colonels Together

Joan and Roy Loudermilk were Oak Ridge High sweethearts from the 10th grade. She was the beautiful Miss Oak Ridge High. He was the clean-cut saxophone player in the band. They were stars in school, and they became stars in the highly competitive, walk-the-line U.S. Army officer corps. Only one in 100 second lieutenants ever rises to the rank of colonel. Roy was one. They were a military family for most of 30 years. This is their story. It starts at the end.

Colonel Roy Loudermilk bent over the hospital bed to listen. His wife Joan wasn't breathing. She had been lying unconscious for 20 days from a massive stroke. She wanted the stroke and, by refusing to take her prescribed medications, asked for it. She chose a stroke over a cancerous brain tumor that was killing her a little each day.

She was wearing a light rose lipstick. A blonde wig hid her bald head and the bandaged wounds from brain surgery. Someone had folded her hands over her sunken stomach and they rested motionless on a white sheet. Her fingernails were plum red, carefully painted by Roy's mother.

There were no protruding tubes, no dangling IV lines, no straps or wires around her body, no blinking monitors. She didn't want life supports, and Roy promised there would be none.

An Army chaplain, one of Joan's best friends, said a prayer. It was 3 o'clock on a Sunday afternoon, room 316 at St. Joseph's Hospital in Tampa, Florida, September 14, 1986, the 30th anniversary year for the Colonel and Joan Merle Upchurch Loudermilk, age 51.

There were no tears. They had been used up long ago. Now there was numbness, the end of a wondrous, often turbulent and sometimes mysterious adventure.

Before the cancer and before the stroke, Joan inherited a peculiar family gene, a biological flaw that had stalked her mother's family for generations. Some say it was caused by an intra-family marriage somewhere down the family line in rural Kentucky. Others said it was just some kind of bio-chemical imbalance. Whatever the cause, mental problems and suicides were common among the Stocktons. Joan didn't learn about them until she was in her mid-30s.

- o -

For years Joan was a near-perfect military wife, cleverly filling a tactical supporting role in her husband's distinguished career. They climbed the Army ranks as a team. In Lexington, Kentucky in 1958 she stood at ceremonious attention next to him, on his left side, the side closest to his heart, and pinned the silver bar of a first lieutenant on his left shoulder, his first promotion. He rose to captain in Turkey, and to major in Thailand. Joan was at his side again at the Pentagon, in 1971, pinning on the silver leaf of lieutenant colonel. Then in 1979, she and General Bill Hilsman decorated him with the silver eagle of a colonel at Fort Gordon, Georgia.

No one in the Loudermilk family had ever accomplished so much, risen so high, been so respected. Roy gained command of two companies by the time he was 30. From a pool of 90 Signal Corps colonels in 1979, he was one of only five to receive a brigade command. And he was among an elite few selected to study at the Army War College in Carlisle, Pennsylvania. He was the exemplary officer—loyal, resourceful, accountable—and she was the patriot wife—delightful, ambitious and tactful. She organized fundraisers and art shows, planned parties, directed golf tournaments and bowling leagues. She taught etiquette, charm and modeling to officers' wives and daughters. It was military protocol that wives of superior officers be addressed as "Mrs," never by first name. But not with Joan. "Hi, I'm Joan Loudermilk," she would introduce herself, which was an invitation to call her "Joan." The wives loved her for it. She was so much a part of the military, Roy affectionately referred to her as "The Colonel" in appreciation. They were, he said often, colonels together: "She was such a fighter. She knew which buttons to push and whom to cow-tow to. She knew who the boss was, who the boss's wife was and how to get inside them. She was good at it."

What no one knew was that she also was good at hiding certain things—her thoughts, her tricks, her addictions.

- o -

Someone covered Joan with a sheet, and rolled her away on a gurney—down a hallway, around a corner, onto an elevator. It was the last time Roy would see her.

Everything had been done according to Joan's requests in a living will, which she had arranged months earlier. Roy saw that she got everything she asked for, everything except one last cigarette and one last visit from her mother.

In her final lucid days, after her brain surgery and before the stroke, she had begged for both. She had smoked like a brush fire since she was 14 and despite a lifetime of doctors' warnings and family pleas, she could never quit, or wouldn't. She smoked Benson & Hedges longs, two or more packs a day.

"Oh, Sylvia, please," she begged her longtime smoking buddy Sylvia Laubecher on her last hospital visit. "Just slip a couple of cigarettes under the mattress before you leave, Stick one in my drawer. Please?"

As much as Sylvia wanted to, she didn't. It wouldn't have made any difference, she reasoned later, but at the time she was optimistic about Joan's recovery. "Nobody thought she would die so quickly and I thought the cigarettes would hurt her chances. And Roy had been on her for years about quitting, so I didn't leave cigarettes for her. But now I know what pleasure it would have given her."

When it became apparent that she would not survive, Joan telephoned her mother in Nashville several times, urging her to visit. "I want to see you, mother," she pleaded. "Please."

From the time Joan was old enough to talk, she had been making that same request, because they seemed always to have been separated for one reason or another, even when she was a baby. The answer more times than not was no.

"I just can't do it right now, Joanie," her mother would say, and there would always be a reason. So many missed birthdays, so many absent Christmases. She missed Joan's wedding. She would miss her funeral.

In Joan's final summer her mother was a frail and confused little gray-haired lady in her late 60s. She had been married four times and wore the dry, lifeless expression of a woman tormented by a lifetime of mental problems. Her memory slipped in and out so she wasn't always rational, but it didn't matter to Joan. This was her mother, she was her only child. Joan never quit asking to see her.

Joan's funeral service almost filled the United Methodist Church on Fletcher Street adjacent to Joan and Roy's backyard in North Tampa's Lake Magdalene Estates. The Loudermilks were church members and Roy, a strong Christian and biblical scholar, taught Sunday school there.

It was difficult for Roy to believe that this once-beautiful, bright and loving wife was lying inside that bronze coffin. It had been a roller coaster ride and "Oh, what a ride it was," Roy said, "from the time I first met her that summer night in Oak Ridge."

They met one night at the Wildcat Den, a teen recreation center named for the high school mascot. Roy, a tall clean-cut carpenter's son from McCaysville, Georgia, stopped his pool game when he saw Joan walk in. He leaned on his que stick and admired her from across the room. She seemed to glow—corn silk hair, sparkling blue eyes, peach-red cheeks and physically mature beyond her 14 years.

The Wildcat Den was an after-school and summertime gathering spot, a place to play games and dance, to flirt and make dates. The girls wore saddle oxfords and bobby socks and their daddies' white dress shirts with the shirttails hanging out and over rolled-up jeans. The boys wore creased jeans or dress slacks, collared shirts, penny loafers, and had their hair cut in ducktails or flattops, some bleached blond with peroxide.

It wasn't unusual to see new faces at the Den, but not many were as strikingly attractive as Joan.

On a dare, Roy walked across the Den floor and introduced himself. Neither Joan nor Roy remembered what he said to her that evening, but he came away with her phone number and an invitation to call. With her beauty and wit, Joan could have had virtually any guy in school as a boyfriend. She chose Roy almost immediately. No one was more surprised than Roy.

Within weeks they were going steady, which meant they withdrew from the open dating pool and declared loyalty to each other. They would argue and break up and date others from time to time during three years of high school courtship, but those interruptions were brief, obvious attempts to make each other jealous.

"Looking back," Roy said, "I would have to rank myself a complete and consummate failure at that time. I never achieved anything worth bragging about. I was always just hanging around. I remember in the seventh grade my teacher wrote on my report card something to the effect that I would never amount to a thing. I was so dumb. A lousy student. I didn't apply myself."

He did enroll in a band class in junior high, learned to play the saxophone and clarinet and as a sophomore he was a member of the ORHS marching band.

"What threatened me," Roy said about those times, "was that I didn't come from a cosmopolitan family, and I use that word out of respect for those I thought were cosmopolitan.

There were so many in Oak Ridge who were so intelligent, so talented. It was just full of accomplished families and I didn't measure up."

His father, Roy Lee Sr., a former copper miner and deputy sheriff, had an eighth-grade education. He was a carpenter for TVA during the wartime construction of Fontana Dam in North Carolina, then moved his family to Oak Ridge in 1945 shortly before the war ended to work at the secret K-25 plant where weapons-grade uranium was enriched. With three children then, the Loudermilks lived from payday to payday. For spending money young Roy delivered The Knoxville News-Sentinel after school.

Joan appeared to be one of the cosmopolitan set that intimidated Roy so. She had advanced two grades in a year in Kentucky schools and appeared confident and poised, socially aware. The only unladylike thing about her was a bellowing horse laugh, but it was honest and spontaneous and it fit her unfailing good humor exactly.

But, as Roy would learn, Joan was an actress. Beneath that facade she was hiding an unhappy childhood and a head full of varying apprehensions. She didn't know it then, but she was carrying that strange, Stockton family gene.

For most of her 14 years, Joan had been a virtual orphan in Kentucky to her twice-married, twice-divorced parents, who clashed and squabbled throughout a turbulent, long-distance relationship that had no place for a child. Her home had always been in someone else's house, mostly with her kind but strangely frugal paternal grandparents in Monticello. The Upchurches were affluent tobacco farmers, among the richest families in Wayne County, but lived as sparingly as the poor. Their home was a modest, two-story frame house with a tin roof and no indoor plumbing. Long after rural electricity was available in the county they burned oil lamps for light and wood for heat. They drew their water from a well, drank from a bucket with a dipper and washed clothes by hand outdoors on a rub board with a bar of Octagon soap. They walked down a long path to a two-seat outhouse. About their only concession to luxury was their automobile, one of the few in the community. Much later they wired the house for electricity, but used it only for lights and a refrigerator.

As a baby, Joan lived there with her parents in an upstairs room heated by a pot-bellied stove. Whenever her parents separated she was left in that house, sometimes with her father and sometimes not. Or she was sent to live with her mother's parents in nearby Burkesville.

Joan's mother, Mary Helen Stockton, was from a prosperous farm family that cultivated rich river-bottom land in nearby Cumberland County. Helen, as she was called, had three sisters, one a twin, and all of them were well-educated and schooled in etiquette, dress and charm. By the time she left home, Helen was already a cultured lady—bright, independent and strong willed. She was a 16-year-old freshman at Lindsey Wilson College, and later completed studies at Vanderbilt University training school in Columbia, Kentucky. There she met and married Joan's father, Chester "Check" Upchurch, an 18-year-old sophomore from Monticello. Joan was born there in 1935, the first year of that marriage.

Check Upchurch was a spoiled child, partly because he was an only child for eight years and partly because he was sickly. A life-threatening kidney infection set him back a full year in elementary school.

Check was tall and handsome and was a popular and well-groomed college student when he met Helen. And he had an automobile on campus.

"He always wore suits and was always driving a new car," said his sister Vesta. "He had cars when nobody else had one. He would use Daddy's or Daddy would buy him one. I can remember him walking down to the barn to ask Daddy for the car keys when he was still in high school, going out on a date. I don't ever remember him working on the farm or anything like that. He was 11 years older than me, so I don't remember much about him until he was in college. Then he became my elementary school teacher."

Helen and Check divorced and remarried before Joan was school age. Check graduated from Lindsey Wilson and taught at Old Glory Elementary, a tiny, two-room country school in the nearby Suzy community. He lived with his parents, and with Joan, taught four grades and served as principal. His sister Vesta was in his fourth-grade class.

Joan's mother, meanwhile, bright, resourceful and ambitious, left Joan and Check while she earned a BS degree at Western Kentucky College in Bowling Green. Then she enrolled at Columbia University in New York and added a Masters degree in chemistry.

"They were very much in love," said Joan's aunt Vesta, who was nine when Joan was born, "but they got interference from outside. If they had just had someone sort of backing them they might have stayed together all their lives. You know, Joan's mother kinda stepped out on Check, but I know they cared for each other desperately."

By 1943, Helen and Check had divorced a second time and, not long afterward, Helen married a classmate at Columbia University—Milus Skidmore—a chemical engineering student and recreational pilot from Harlan, Kentucky. They got jobs in Oak Ridge and moved to the secluded Tennessee town during the final months of World War II.

Joan had visited her mother in New York and longed to live with her full time. So she was ecstatic two years later when she was invited to move to Oak Ridge to live with her mother and stepfather Milus, whom Joan had never met.

They lived on Orchard Lane, a long, rolling street that ran high atop a woody ridge on the town's northern border. It was known as a "B" house, among the best but smallest of some 6,000 wartime government owned rentals—two little bedrooms, a little kitchen, a little bath, a fireplace and a sitting porch. It had less than 1,000 feet of living space, but it seemed like a mansion compared to the cold, bleak Upchurch farm house in Kentucky.

But as always, it didn't last long for Joan. She was sent back to the farm without explanation, but the reason was apparent. Her stepfather, a brooding, unsmiling, impatient man, was intolerant of her, looked upon her as an intruding nuisance and became verbally abusive.

His attitude had not changed in 1949 when Joan was again invited to live with them, but no matter how awkward or how stressful the situation, she was determined to endure her stepfather's behavior because it would be her last chance, she thought, to live with her mother. By 1949, she had skipped eighth grade and had completed her freshman year of high school in Kentucky.

Joan was quick to fit into the ORHS Class of '52. She was smart, daring and engagingly impulsive. She learned to play just enough trombone to get in the band but, as she had planned, was soon elected band sponsor, which meant she was featured in front of her marching teammates carrying a bouquet of flowers trimmed with ribbons of cardinal and gray, the school colors. She starred in intramural sports (there were no varsity sports for girls then), volunteered for Red Cross work, served on the yearbook staff, and skillfully painted in oils and chalk and water colors. She made the Honor Roll, played in *Peter Pan* and served on the student council. (She also led skinny-dipping adventures in the midnight shadows of Norris Lake, and puffed on Benson & Hedges when the opportunity arose.) In her senior year she was voted *Miss Oak Ridge High*. Next to Joan's senior picture in the 1952 yearbook was this rhyming tribute: *"To find another like Joanie would be rare; with her personality plus and lovely blonde hair.*" She would earn an art scholarship to the Wesleyan Conservatory in Macon, Georgia.

But while she was achieving at school, her family was crumbling around her. Back in Monticello her father, distressed by his twice-failed marriage, lost himself in Kentucky moonshine and in 1950, the year after Joan went to live in Oak Ridge, he stuck the barrel of a .22 caliber rifle into his mouth and pulled the trigger. He was found unconscious on the floor of the little upstairs room he once shared with Helen and baby Joan at his parents' Monticello home. The bullet blew away part of his brain, but didn't kill him.

He had taken Valium that day, doctors said, along with his moonshine. He was flown to a Lexington hospital where a specialist from Chicago was rushed in to treat him. He would live with the mentality of a six-year-old in the care of his parents until his death in 1970.

In Oak Ridge Milus Skidmore's intolerance of Joan, his unwanted stepdaughter, had worsened and now Helen's third marriage was falling apart. She worked as an elementary teacher in order to buy clothes and things for Joan because Milus would not.

As Joan entered her senior year in high school, she became puzzled by the increasingly bizarre behavior of her mother, who sometimes wandered away without apparent reason, and drifted into nonsensical conversation. Still no one had told Joan about the peculiar Stockton gene that so many family members carried.

Meanwhile, Joan and Roy had become a poster couple for high school sweethearts. Joan was so pretty, so vivacious and friendly, some guy was always making a play for her. Sam Mumford, for instance. Sam, an upperclassman, had a yellow convertible and Joan loved taking rides in it, much to Roy's chagrin. Sometimes Roy was invited and sometimes not; but either way it was an irritating experience for him, especially when Joan sat in front with Sam, and Roy was relegated to the back seat. "He was trying to make out with my girl, using that car," Roy said, "and I couldn't counter that. I'd get so mad I'd want to scream." But the ride, it turned out, was all Joan was after.

She became a shining member of the Penguins, an exclusive girls' social club at ORHS. Every spring the Penguins spent a week in the cabins at Big Ridge State Park on Norris Lake. They sunned on the beach by day and danced to jukebox music at an outdoor pavilion at night, with boys who drove in from schools all around, and with the good-looking, tanned lifeguards who flirted with them day and night. Joan, a natural flirt, was among their main targets. There was, for instance, Bob Huber, also a natural flirt, a rich man's son from a Knoxville high school who drove his father's luxury car, wore expensive clothes and danced like Fred Astaire. One moonlit night at the pavilion, Huber smothered Joan with such attention that Roy, a non drinker, got drunk and was bent on fighting the debonair intruder. But his more sober friends, who knew that Roy couldn't fight any better than he held his liquor, wisely discouraged him.

Joan enjoyed the attention of her many flattering suitors, but Roy never really had a serious challenger. And neither did Joan. They fell in love in the 10th grade and that never changed. Not ever.

"Some nights I would take a bus to see her in her little house on Orchard Lane," Roy said. "We would close the door and smooch in the furnace room and then she would walk me to the bus stop and wait with me until the bus came. She was such a fun person, always fun to be around."

One Easter morning, after the Penguin Club's annual dance, they attended sunrise services at the high school football field. Joan wore a gray suit with a pink hat and a light pink blouse. "She was the prettiest thing I had ever seen," Roy said. "I can see her now." They would marry someday, they promised, but only after they finished college.

By the time they graduated from ORHS in 1952, Joan's confused mother had divorced for a third time and was living with her parents, who had moved from Kentucky to a 500-acre corn-and-cattle farm near Gallatin, Tennessee. The Stockton gene, that biochemical imbalance, had her on a disturbing downward spiral toward a cheerless and sometimes bizarre existence. She was committed to Central State Hospital in Madison, Tennessee by her parents and she would be in and out of mental hospitals for much of the rest of her life, as would her twin sister, Hilda. Three of the four Stockton sisters would spend time in psychiatric hospitals at one time or another; all would experience at least one divorce and all would attempt suicide. Geneva, so smart many thought her to be a genius, was haunted by flower vases and other such objects that, she said, talked to her. Once she tried to bleed herself to death by piercing her wrists with her fingernails.

When Joan's mother was in her 50s, she flew to California to rescue her twin, Hilda, from a psychiatric hospital. They lived together for a time and took care of each other until one day Helen decided that Hilda needed to go to heaven to visit their late father, Papa Stockton.

"Hilda, I'm going to take you home to see Daddy," Helen told her. She grabbed Hilda by the hair of her head and tried to cut her throat.

Papa Willie Stockton, Joan's grandpa, never showed signs of the peculiar gene, but when his health began to fail in his early 60s he blew his head off with a shotgun on the back steps of his house in Gallatin one evening while Mama Stockton was at the barn, milking.

Geneva's son, Doug Lewis, said that of the four sisters, only Eulena, the oldest, showed no sign of the bad gene. "My mother had several shock treatments," he said "and it was a crude, terrible thing. It was like torture. There were a whole bunch of them in the family messed up. But it wasn't all on the Stockton side of the family. Grandma Robbie Stockton had a sister who killed herself by swallowing carbolic acid or something like that, and another sister spent a lot of her life in some kind of institution. But Grandma Robbie was OK. She and Grandpa Stockton were prosperous for the times, but they worked liked dogs. Grandma Robbie had three kids in diapers at the same time, Joan's mother and her twin and my mother. If she had to get out to the garden or something, she would pick up the bed and sit it on their dress tails so they couldn't go anywhere. She didn't have anybody to look after them."

When Joan and Roy were high school seniors, Roy drove her back to her southwestern Kentucky roots, over rutted gravel roads and through creek beds to the remote tobacco farm where Joan spent much of her first 12 years. Roy met the extended Upchurch family, saw the plain board farm house Joan once lived in, the feather bed she slept in and the potbellied stove that once warmed her. There was an old truck out front and, by then, a television set in the front room, which the family watched on Saturday nights—professional wrestling out of Nashville, the only picture they could get. Theirs was one of the few television sets in the county. Mae and Ben Upchurch invited their tenant farmers to watch TV with them on Saturday nights and they did, sprawled out on the floor.

Heat still came from the fireplace in the Upchurch house, and from the wood stoves. Baths still were taken with dampened sponges or in a washtub in the kitchen with water heated on the wood-burning kitchen stove. Feet still were washed nightly in a wash pan. Grandma Mae, a shy, kind, loveable, mousy little woman, still rose every day before dawn, built a fire and cooked breakfast for the family and dinner for up to 8 or 10 sharecroppers.

Drinking water still was drawn from a backyard well and the old two-seater outhouse was still in use, along with a Sears Roebuck catalogue. The four Upchurch children never knew there was such a thing as toilet tissue until they were almost grown.

Grandpa Ben, a tall, stout, ambling man whose dress was loose-fitting overalls, high-top work shoes and a large, sweat-stained straw hat, had only a fourth grade education but he deftly supervised his tobacco operation. He raised and sold livestock and was a shrewd trader. His barnyard sometimes resembled a zoo with its rotating collection of cows and horses, sheep and goats, turkeys and guineas and any other animal of trading value he might find on his frequent livestock trips to Lexington and Cincinnati. He was one of the few in the county who managed to save money during the Great Depression. He worked long and hard for his money and he didn't let go of it easily.

"Daddy was so tight-fisted," said daughter Vesta, "if he lost a nickel he would spend all day looking for it." He spent little on himself, his wife or the house, and saved virtually everything of potential value—from string to cardboard.

"But you know," said Vesta, "he would loan money to his friends so they could buy things. Once he loaned our family doctor money to buy new furniture and later when the doctor came out on a house call, he was surprised to see that we hardly had any. We had furniture, but it was old and plain and we didn't have much. I don't ever remember having a sofa."

The Upchurches reared Joan without complaint, loving her and, some would say, spoiling her. But it was a life that Joan later described as both privileged and abusive. They fed her, clothed her and dutifully and properly provided her with birthday gifts and Christmas toys. She was cute and clever and could persuade Grandpa Upchurch to buy her most anything. "She got a bicycle once just for asking," said her aunt Vesta, who was a teen-ager when Joan was born. "I never got one when I was younger. For a long time Joan was the only grandchild, so she was quite special, always special, such a beautiful little girl. And she was raised to be a lady."

Joan could have anything, it seemed, except the thing she wanted most—her mother and a home of her own.

Roy had grown up quite differently in a stable blue-collar home with a strong religious influence from his mother, Helgia. His regret is that there was virtually no scholarly stimulation beyond the daily newspaper, the Knoxville News-Sentinel, and his homework. His father, whose ancestry was Cherokee Indian, was not socially cultured or formally educated, but he was a hardworking family man with mechanical skills and common sense far greater than his eighth-grade education would suggest. He became a supervisor at the K-25 plant.

"Dad's personality didn't foster a close father-son relationship," Roy said. "Mother was an active church member. Dad was not. While all that may sound negative, those conditions molded my values and enabled me to face life's challenges, be competitive, have a work ethic, pursue educational opportunities and galvanize my faith in God.

"Mother had a lot of love and compassion for Dad. His health went sour in the mid-50s with several heart attacks and the amputation of both legs. Despite his wheelchair he remained active, modifying a riding lawnmower for his use and building swing sets in his workshop. It hurt Mother to see him struggling. "Poor ol' Roy," she would say over and over, so much that I began to wonder if Poor Ol' Roy was his name."

Roy Jr. didn't accomplish much of anything, he said, until his junior year at Tennessee Tech in Cookeville. "My freshman year I was on academic probation because I was so damn dumb. I was a junior before I learned how to work within the academic system. I think the feeling of inadequacy in those early days caused me to drive a little bit harder later on."

Joan and Roy as ORHS seniors

That, and a constant push from Joan, would lead him to a distinguished military career and leave him just one promotion from becoming a general.

Joan began nudging Roy forward after her transfer to Tennessee Tech in her sophomore year, suggesting goals for him and boosting his confidence to achieve them. She was largely responsible for his nomination as junior class president at Tech, and headed his winning campaign. The next year she managed his successful run for student body president.

By then Roy's grades were up and he was a captain in the ROTC, for which he was paid $28 a month. He earned about $15 a month playing with the college's popular dance band, the *Tech Troubadours*, and he worked part-time at a local hospital. For all that, he was recognized by Who's Who in American Colleges and Universities. There was hardly a more accomplished, more popular Tech student than Roy Loudermilk. And no coed was more popular than Joan, a cheerleader for the Golden Eagles and the coveted campus superlative, May Queen. If only her mother could see her now. But she couldn't. She was back in a mental hospital.

Again, Joan had no home to go to for the holidays or semester breaks and, as usual, was rescued by relatives. Sometimes she went home with Roy. Joan had little money—her mother sent her $15 now and then when she was able—so Roy, whose parents could barely pay his tuition, shared his cafeteria meal tickets with her, tickets he bought with money from his part-time jobs.

At 9 a.m. on June 1, 1956, in the library at Tennessee Tech in Cookeville, Roy Loudermilk was commissioned into the U.S. Army as a second lieutenant. At 11 a.m., in the gymnasium, he graduated with Joan, and at 2 p.m. they were married at the Cookeville United Methodist Church

They were a perfect match, they thought. Roy had rescued Joan from a dysfunctional home and Joan had awakened Roy from his once lethargic self. Joan, still with no home, longed to establish her own. Roy, now full of purpose, was eager for success. He fulfilled his two-year ROTC obligation, left the Army for a year to teach biology at Oak Ridge High, then returned to active duty at the request of the Army.

"In the Army you get a chance to learn a lot of things on your own," Roy said, "and if you do that it shows you are a team player and that is very important. It was apparent to me that if you wanted to succeed, you had to be a team player, for the success and morale of the organization. You do it as a natural thing rather than something you feel you have to do. I bought into that. It's contagious because once you receive a certain rank, you expect your subordinates to be team players, too. I was a team player from the beginning. You learn to capitalize on your talents and abilities and to minimize your weaknesses."

Eleven of his 30 Army years were spent in school, enough to make him a PhD many times over. He earned a Masters degree in public administration at Shippensburg State in Pennsylvania, became a communications specialist and an expert in the Thai language, a complex language with an alphabet of 72 characters, no punctuation and some 4,000 words.

For most of their marriage, Joan was a shining asset in her husband's career—responsible mother, loyal friend, ready volunteer, organizer, promoter, teacher. They lived in 13 states, never longer than three years anywhere. Laura, the second oldest child, was in a different school every year from the ninth grade until she graduated from high school. "Discipline for military kids is severe," Roy said. "They are subject to military rules and regulations. If a kid gets caught shoplifting at one of the base exchanges, for instance, his ID card is pulled. He must go before a disciplinary officer and face his wrath. If a kid gets caught speeding on the post, he is sent to Federal court. My daughter, Kim, and her boyfriend were caught in a car smooching one night and the Military Police picked them up and took them home."

Roy was sometimes separated from the family for long periods, once for 30 months during the Vietnam War. Joan took charge at home. She was a master at persuasion when she needed something, or just when she wanted something badly enough. Roy discovered just how cajoling she could be in the first months of their marriage, when she was teaching high school physical education in Oliver Springs, Tennessee and Roy was completing basic training at Fort Monmouth, New Jersey. One day she telephoned him.

"Guess what, Roy? We bought a new car!"

"We did what? What kind of new car did we buy?"

"Oh, Roy, we bought a 1956 black Ford convertible with a white top and a Thunderbird engine."

"You're kidding, Joan. Tell me you're kidding."

"Oh, no, Roy. It's the prettiest convertible you've ever seen. And, oh, Roy the payments are only $200 a month."

"Dammit, Joan. I only make $220 a month. How are we going to pay for it?"

"Oh, we'll figure out a way, Roy."

During the Vietnam War Roy was twice ordered to Thailand, first for 13 months, then back for another year that included an assignment in Vietnam. He left the family in Oceanport, New Jersey but soon received a letter in Thailand from Joan.

"She wrote that she had decided to move to Hawaii because a lot of military wives were living there while their husbands were in Vietnam," Roy recalled. "She said she knew how to manipulate the system to get there. She could get free airfare for herself and for the kids."

There was no more correspondence for seven weeks. Meanwhile Roy was ordered to Vietnam, so now they were both in transit and neither knew the whereabouts of the other. Eventually Roy got a note from Joan with an address in Honolulu. She had rented a furnished house on a golf course and bought a car. The kids were in school and she was playing golf almost every day, going to the beach, drinking beer. She was there 11 months at a cost of about $25,000 (the equivalent of about $165,000 in 2010 dollars). "I always tried to do whatever made Joan happy," Roy said, "if it made her feel good. Maybe that was the wrong thing to do. Maybe I should have been more controlling. But I was gone so much and it was difficult for her."

In 30 years they never took a vacation, not a real traditional, time-off family vacation. Moving from one base to another was the closest thing. Sometimes, when the move required a drive of four or five days, they would stop and do some sightseeing, but the moves were always stressful.

"If you live in military housing, the house had to be perfectly clean when you moved out," Roy said, "and it is inspected. Inspectors will take a stove apart looking for grease. They will take a refrigerator apart looking for mildew. In most cases it's best to pay a cleaning team to do it. In Arizona we had an 18-room house and it cost us $500 to have it cleaned."

The packers would come one day and pack and the movers would come next day with a van. It was a hassle to get four children, a cat, a dog and two adults into a station wagon. Once when they were packing to leave, the cat urinated in a suitcase full of clothes.

Wherever they lived, they made friends and Joan made their house a home. At Fort Lewis in Tacoma, Washington and at Fort Bliss in El Paso Texas, they lived in beautiful old and historic houses on officers' row.

"Joan loved those places," Roy said. "She was a loving, considerate mother and wife. She was the centerpiece of the family while I was away doing military things. She attended to every need of the children, put braces on their teeth, never let them look unkempt. She was their greatest and proudest supporter in Little League, cheerleading, football, swimming and the like."

And she was good at virtually everything she attempted, which was a lot. She carried a 225 league bowling average and scored in the 80s in golf. She danced and played tennis and painted and sculpted and drew. But she could do nothing in moderation, it seemed. Whatever she did, it was with a passion. She submerged herself into painting and chalk work, producing piece after piece. Much of her work today hangs on the walls and rests on the tables of her four children. It all seemed therapeutic for her, especially the nights of league bowling. Bowling was a great time to be with friends and to drink beer. She didn't drink beer in moderation, either.

No one ever saw Joan stagger drunkenly. She didn't weave as she walked and she was never giddy or unusually noisy. She always looked composed, in public at least, with her wonderful natural grace, remarkable alertness and control. Roy can't remember exactly when he began noticing the change in her. Maybe it was as early as 1965 when he was a captain and in school at the Defense Language Institute in Monterey, California. She became moody there and her eyes often appeared dilated. She seemed troubled, haunted by some deep preoccupation. She was drinking too much and too often, Roy thought.

Then in 1969, after finishing a two-year assignment in Thailand and Vietnam, Roy returned home and noticed a distinct change in Joan. He had been assigned to a year-long army school in Fort Leavenworth, Kansas and was looking forward to being reunited with the family. Joan left Hawaii with the children and joined him in Kansas. But instead of a warm reunion, Roy got a cold shock. Joan not only was drinking too much, but she was also hooked on tranquilizers, three very strong sedating chemicals that caused wide mood swings, frenzied activity and panic attacks. She acquired the pills through friendships with Army doctors and their wives. Once again, she could get most anything she wanted. When Roy confronted her, she bristled and denied any problem. "You're wrong," she snapped. "It's your problem." Soon she began having alarming, imaginary illnesses.

"I'm having a heart attack!"

"I can't breathe!"

"My arms are numb!"

"I can't stand up!"

But whenever Roy took her for treatment, the doctors could find nothing physically wrong with her, and she would walk away with more or different tranquilizer prescriptions. And so the strange behavior continued—one moment coy and full of energy and the next moment moody and helpless.

For a long time Joan hid the addictions from friends. "I would come home and she'd be sick or down in the dumps and her eyes would be dilated and two hours later we would go to dinner and she seemed perfectly normal," Roy said. "I don't know how she did it. It was part of her cleverness. For the longest time nobody knew she had a problem."

Then, sometime during those turbulent days when Joan was in her mid-30s, her irrational behavior grew worse, sometimes uncontrollably violent. On several occasions she was taken, kicking and screaming, into a psychiatric ward.

Roy thought he knew everything about Joan by then. But he didn't know about the troubling Stockton gene, because no one had talked about it. Then he learned that Joan's mother had it. Her aunts. An uncle. Her grandfather. Suicides and suicide attempts.

After Leavenworth, when Major Loudermilk was assigned to the Pentagon (and became a lieutenant colonel), a psychiatrist suggested—and Joan reluctantly consented to—electro-shock therapy. It didn't help. Every day continued to be a new adventure for the family. Some days Joan was a vivacious lady with good humor, charming the Army brass, playing golf, hosting socials. But some days she was a veritable storm.

Moving from Tacoma to El Paso the family had plans for sightseeing stopovers at Yellowstone Park and Mount Rushmore, but Joan's panic attacks forced cancellation. She became terrified by the mountains and tried to hide from them in the floor of the car. Another time, at a cocktail party when Roy was a lieutenant colonel, she verbally assaulted the wife of a colonel who was Roy's immediate superior. It is something of a miracle that he made colonel after that.

Fortunately, Roy's superior officers were sympathetic, and neither Joan's erratic behavior nor Roy's frequent family-related absences from duty disqualified him from promotional competition. He was selected to command a Signal Battalion of 550 soldiers at Fort Lewis and later he was one of seven Signal officers chosen to attend the Army War College at Carlisle Barracks, Pennsylvania. At Fort Gordon he was promoted to full colonel and assigned to command the 11th brigade at Fort Huachuca, Arizona, the highest priority independent signal brigade in the Army. Col. Loudermilk had now punched all the tickets and jumped through all the required hoops. One more promotion would make him a general.

But at Fort Gordon, Joan was an uncontrollable alcoholic and, at the insistence of Roy's boss and family friend, a major general, she was sent to the Navy's Alcoholic Rehabilitation Center in Long Beach, California.

"We had this intervention in the general's office," Roy recalled. "The children, some neighbors and friends were there, too. I had to get some movies to show the kids how an intervention works. They were in high school and junior high then, and they were in on it. Joan didn't know any of this. I had purchased airline tickets and had our suitcases packed. Joan was livid when she found out what we were doing.

"You sonofabitch," she shouted at Roy. "You're not taking me anywhere on a plane."

But they were in the air 90 minutes later. Roy sat quietly next to his fuming wife en route to California. He would stay near Joan throughout her therapy and they would attend some rehab classes as a couple. "I have thought many times how fortunate I was to have a boss like the general," he said. "What boss would let you go for eight weeks from your job to be with your troubled wife? He did it for Joan because he loved her dearly and wanted to help her."

Joan walked out of the hospital after two months and never had another drink for the rest of her life. But she was soon back on tranquilizers, convincing her doctors that she needed them for stability, and it wasn't long before her life was in another tailspin. It was worse this time. There were times when Roy didn't know what to do.

"We were a totally dysfunctional family," Roy said. "I would get the kids out of the way and say, 'God, help me through this.' I guess I could have said, 'I give up. I can't live this way.' But I knew Joan was sick and I just couldn't abandon her. I had a deep love for her and you can't abandon someone you love that much. She was out of control but not because she wanted to be. She couldn't help it."

They were at Fort Hauchuca in Arizona by now and for the first time in Roy's military career, he was having major conflicts with a superior; a former contemporary who had been promoted to brigadier general and who showed no sympathy for Roy's plight and, in fact, talked down to him as if he were some hapless hillbilly in uniform. Joan felt the tension and, in one of her more combative moods, lured the general's wife into her kitchen for coffee one day and unleashed a scathing verbal blast upon her. When Roy returned home that evening she told him. "I really gave her a piece of my mind. I blessed her out for the way they have been treating us."

When Roy reproved Joan, she turned on him. "You just let people run all over you! You have no backbone! I'm not going to put up with it."

"As much of a help in my career as she was in the beginning," Roy said, "she hurt it just as much toward the end. But she couldn't help it, didn't know it."

The next night when Roy got home from work, Joan and the family car were gone. He found a note under his pillow when he went to bed. "You will find the car in Benson behind the bus station," it read. For five weeks Roy didn't know where she was. She had driven to Benson, about 25 miles away, and taken a bus to Phoenix, where she boarded a flight to Dayton, Ohio, to visit aunt Vesta.

"I knew something must be wrong when she called and said she was coming," Vesta said. "She said she just had to get away, so I didn't ask. I was always glad to see her. I remember meeting her at the airport. She was dressed so beautifully, a beige dress, and she was carrying her shoes, walking down the terminal hallway with the pilot. Her feet hurt her so she was walking in her bare feet. We had a good time. She went shopping and bought some nice lingerie, hoping, I guess, that Roy would appreciate her when she went home."

After five weeks, Joan called Roy. "I want to come home," she said. Roy wired airfare.

Meanwhile Roy, needing advice, confided in a long-time contemporary, a colonel who was the command chief of staff at Fort Hauchuca, someone Roy thought he could trust. But instead of helping, the colonel spread word about Roy's family problems to all the base bosses. Roy's military career was effectively over. The attitude of the base generals was that, if an officer cannot control his family, he cannot effective lead and be exemplary to his subordinates.

Compounding the family problems now was Lisa, the oldest daughter who had graduated with honors at the University of Texas, El Paso, with a degree in chemistry and a minor in statistics. She was smart, smart, smart, but she had become rebellious and involved with a religious cult. She held a job for a time with a shale oil company in El Paso, but her behavior became erratic and soon she was hearing voices; voices directing her to do things, to destroy things—to kill herself.

"She called me one day while we were in Arizona," Roy said, and was rambling around so badly I jumped in the car and drove 300 miles to El Paso. I saw the problem immediately, because I had seen similar conduct in her mother."

It was the destructive Stockton gene. Lisa, just 22, was sobbing and wailing and threatening, totally out of control and incapable of taking care of herself. Roy packed her clothes and her furniture and drove her back home to Arizona. Joan, still battling her demons, was devastated. She took Lisa to her psychiatrist for guidance and placed her in therapy. But the voices continued to haunt Lisa and those voices made her angry. She chopped her mother's clothes into rags and burned family photographs and cut pictures out of school yearbooks and wrote angry messages.

In 1982, Colonel Loudermilk was re-assigned to a unified command at MacDill Air Force Base near Tampa, Florida. Lisa, brooding, angry and suicidal, moved with the family, and Joan continued to seek help for her in Florida and Virginia. In the next three months, Lisa was committed three times to mental hospitals and underwent electro-shock therapy. At home she swallowed 100 Excedrin tablets in a suicide attempt and later broke into a drug cabinet at a rehab facility and swallowed a double handful of unidentified pills. Lisa would spend three years in a mental hospital in Virginia before being stabilized and released to state supervision

While she was in a Virginia hospital, she met a fellow patient and after they were discharged, they married. That relationship ended in an attempted double suicide. Both were committed to state institutions once more.

In 1984, still at MacDill, Joan continued to honor her no-drinking pledge but became increasingly agitated and combative. During one psychiatric session she was so argumentative and threatening that her psychiatrist called for police help. Again Joan was admitted to a psychiatric ward. The same psychiatrist, a woman who became a good family friend, eventually found a drug for Joan—Lithium. It controlled manic depression, and it turned her life around. At last, Joan began to experience some degree of peace. She wasn't drinking, she wasn't zapped on tranquilizers and she was full of life once more. In many ways, the next two years were the best years for Joan and Roy since high school.

One day Joan discovered a small lump on the right side of her neck, a slightly protruding knot about the size of a nickel. It didn't hurt and her family doctor wasn't alarmed by it. He prescribed an antibiotic and predicted that it would go away. It didn't. A biopsy weeks later revealed why.

"It's cancer," she was told, "and we're afraid it's gotten into the lymphatic system." It had.

Joan now endured the radiation treatments, three six-week sessions, six days a week without getting sick. Just to show her strength, she continued to play golf and took a job at a boutique. When her hair fell out she bought two wigs. She did everything she could to maintain her dignity and poise. But in time she began to lose her appetite and her weight fell rapidly. She began falling. "Hey, I promise, I haven't had a drink," she would say, laughing.

A neurologist found the tumor. It was on the right side of her skull, just above her ear. A large cancerous mass had formed quickly, unnoticed while she was receiving radiation treatments for the lymph glands. It was May, 1985. An operation was performed immediately.

Joan never told Roy, but just before the surgery she told her closest friend she hoped to die during the operation. She was disappointed when she regained consciousness in the recovery room. When she was released from the hospital weeks later, she weighed 90 pounds, a shriveled portion of her once beautiful self. There was a bandaged hole in her skull. She could hardly walk and she couldn't bathe herself. She was at high risk for a stroke. "You must take your medications or you are certain to have a stroke," her doctor warned her.

Joan never considered taking a single pill. She refused. Enough was enough, she decided. She wanted to die.

At about 5 a.m. on August 25, she had a massive stroke. Roy didn't take time to call 911. He wrapped her immediately in a blanket, folded her unconscious body into the passenger seat of the family Pontiac and sped the six miles to St. Joseph's Hospital. It was their last trip together. Joan had spoken her last word.

For the next 20 days Roy was at her side every possible waking moment, looking at her withered gray face, watching her die hour-by-hour, mindless, oblivious. Every breath was more labored than the previous one, weaker and smaller, like a dying flame.

"I don't think Joan's breathing," he said that September Sunday, Joan's last day.

In the days immediately following Joan's death, Roy returned to work and tried to tell himself that things were better now for Joan, that she no longer was tormented by her demons. The thought made him feel better. But now he was reminded of her at every turn, their house on Moran Drive that seemed so quiet, so empty; the sight of their church that sat adjacent to their back yard, the cemetery, just five blocks away, where she was buried. The scent of her was everywhere, it seemed, in her closets, in her gorgeous clothes, in her jewelry boxes, her chests; in the very fiber of the house. She was in the shower, at the breakfast table, in the backyard pool where they swam together.

"Joan still is very much in my mind," he said 24 years later. "The greatest regret is that here I am, blessed with a great retirement, financially secure, playing golf, no worries about anything. I am just sorry that Joan is missing all this. She worked for it and she isn't here to enjoy it. She could have been here with me."

Roy, center, and Joan at first promotion

When Lightning Strikes Home

Lucille Hart and Bill Russell, a graduate of Karns High in Knoxville, TN, have been married 57 years and worked together many of those years in Lucille's Beauty Shop; both as hairdressers.

It was June, 1967, Owosso, Michigan. We had just finished remodeling the house next door, which we had bought and turned into a beauty shop. Until that week, Lucille's Beauty Shop had been in our house. We finished remodeling and had moved equipment and furniture in on Tuesday and now it was Friday morning, June 16. I had just put color on one of my customer's hair and another one, a nurse, was sitting under a dryer. It looked like a storm coming up. Dark. My husband, Bill, who was an inspector for Buick at that time, hadn't left for work.

We had picked up Mother and Dad in Toledo a few days earlier and they were staying with us for the summer in an apartment behind the shop. When our girls, Monica, 11, and Velda, 13, ran into the shop, Bill looked next door and told them that their windows were open and that they should close them before the rain comes. It looked really dark out, but there had been no rain, no thunder. It was just very dark. "OK, Dad," they said, and ran to the house.

My Dad was outside when they were running across the yard back to the shop and all of a sudden there was this loud cracking sound and Dad was knocked back against the side of the shop. Mother was inside with me. It was a lightning strike, a huge thunderclap at the very same time the lightning struck. Bill went to the door to look. Velda was on the ground, not moving, and Monica had been knocked 21 feet from Velda. Monica was getting up, but Velda wasn't moving.

Bill ran outside shouting. "Call an ambulance!" The nurse under the hair dryer ran out and tried to revive Velda with CPR, but to no avail. A neighbor ran over and Bill told him not to let me come outside. It took the ambulance 18 minutes to get there and we were only 1½ miles away.

As we drove to the hospital I knew what was happening but I couldn't say anything. I couldn't think. They brought a wheelchair to me at the hospital and took me inside to a bed in the emergency room. Bill had gone in where the ambulance went. Then Bill walked in.

"Is she all right?" I asked him.

"Lucille," he answered, "The Lord was good to us. He left us Monica."

Velda was dead. I could hardly believe what had happened. A neighbor, Gail Adams, was standing at the foot of the bed. I don't know why, but I looked at him and asked, "If this had been you, Gail Adams, where would you spend eternity? Just then someone came in and asked us to move our car and Gail went out to move it. And right there in the car he slumped over the steering wheel and asked the Lord to save him."

For me, it was like I couldn't breathe. I couldn't think or talk. Bill wouldn't leave me alone for three days. Now it has been over 40 years, but it seems like yesterday. I'll never get over it. For the longest I couldn't talk about it. To this day I can't stand lightning or thunder storms. I close the drapes. I can't stand to see it. And it was hard, after that, to let Monica do anything by herself. We were so protective of her. Even after she was married, I had a fear that something was going to happen to her.

Velda was a wonderful girl, a pretty brunette. Everybody said she was the spitting image of me. She was serious about her grades. If she got a B in a class she would go talk to the teacher and ask about it. She was forever reading. I can see her to this day vacuuming the floor, the vacuum in one hand, a book in the other, reading as she vacuumed. She had just graduated from the seventh grade when it happened. She played the flute in the school band.

We didn't know this until later, but on the Sunday before, when we drove to Toledo to pick up my parents, Velda said something very strange to Monica. "Monica," she said, "when I die I want to be buried in a pink formal." It must have been a premonition. We drove all over trying to find a pink formal for her funeral, and we finally found one..

For the longest I couldn't go into her room.

I couldn't look at her clothes or the pictures on her walls. And I couldn't stand to see anyone play the flute. I closed the shop for two weeks.

Monica grew up and got married and had three daughters. The oldest is a lawyer, one is an RN and anesthesiologist and the youngest is an Ohio State student.

Now my husband, Bill, has been fighting intestinal cancer. They took part of his small intestine three years ago and got the cancer, but they said it would come back in the liver within five years. He started getting sick last week. He's in the hospital now. I just left him. We've been married 57 years.

Lucille Hart Russell

Owosso, Michigan

He Took His Father's Face
In His Hands and Kissed Him

There have been only a handful of four-sport athletes at Oak Ridge High. Gene Pharr, a trailer park kid from Chattanooga, was one of the first, and the first ORHS graduate to sign a professional sports contract.

He was the starting wingback, a starting defensive back and the best tackler on the football team. He was a left-handed pitcher and first baseman in baseball. He struck out a school-record 13 batters in a seven-inning district tournament game against Farragut High his junior year and he had a .401 batting average as the team's cleanup hitter. He lettered in basketball as a reserve guard and ran the low hurdles and 880-relay in track until the baseball schedule caused conflicts. He was an undefeated boxer in three years of tournaments in junior high, became a 2-handicap golfer as an adult and he could run the table in a game of pool. As a senior, he stood about 6-feet tall and weighed 160 pounds. He was not the biggest or the fastest, but he was one of the toughest and he could do everything well in athletics.

He was among the first wave of extraordinary post-war athletes who helped move Oak Ridge into the ranks of state high school football powers. Before graduating he accepted a football scholarship to the University of Tennessee, extended by legendary Coach Robert Neyland; and was within days of reporting to the UT campus when he was offered, and accepted, a bonus contract with the Philadelphia Phillies to play professional baseball.

He was popular, unpretentious, good looking, friendly, funny, artistic—and a playful daredevil. One summer night he swung barehanded from the Clinton railroad trestle some 90 feet above the Clinch River. Once he got caught in a rural railroad tunnel facing an oncoming train and survived by hugging the muddy rail bed just inches from the passing freight. More spectacularly, he high-hurdled out of a bedroom window of a classmate one spring afternoon when her parents drove up unexpectedly.

One of his rare athletic defeats came on a spring night in his senior year when he strolled through a graveyard with a pretty, athletic classmate. They began wrestling playfully in the darkness and after a few minutes of jostling about, the pretty coed strode triumphantly from the cemetery alone, grinning and brushing off her clothes. Then came Gene, walking slowly, head down, hair tousled, clothes disheveled.

"Strongest woman I ever saw," he said meekly.

Gene's parents divorced when he was three years old and he moved to Oak Ridge from Chattanooga with his mother, Louise, and stepfather, Freeman Hill, in the summer of 1944 when he was 11. New roads were being bulldozed in every direction and red clay mud was so thick and gooey after a rain it sometimes would suck a shoe right off a foot. With some 5,000 people moving into the area almost every month, there was hardly a vacancy within 25 miles in any direction. The town that originally was planned for 13,000 residents had 20,000 in less than a year and hit 60,000 after two years. By 1945 the town's 75,000 residents almost doubled the population of Anderson County.

Gene's family was offered a rental in a bustling trailer park in the Middletown section of town, where thousands of look-alike trailers lined the landscape, packed tightly like kernels on a cob of corn. The trailers were little more than drab wooden boxes. No running water. Oil stoves provided heat. They were living there the day the war ended.

Gene hawked nickel newspapers on the street that day for up to $1 a copy, faster than they could be trucked in from Knoxville. The Journal put out a pink-covered "extra" edition and paperboys all over town were rolling in cash. "People were giving me a quarter, 50 cents, a dollar for them," Gene said. "I was handing out papers as fast as I could get them out of the wrappers. I had money stuffed in all my pockets"

"War Ends" the huge, black-lettered Knoxville Journal headline read, and people held them over their heads and danced with them. "The war's over! The war's over!" they chanted.

On that very night, Oak Ridge began to undergo a dramatic change. Nothing much had changed at the plants nine days earlier after the first atomic bomb exploded over Hiroshima, or three days after that when the second bomb detonated above Nagasaki. The explosion of those two bombs, Little Boy and Fat Man, had cut deeply into the United States' supply of weapons-grade uranium, so the Oak Ridge plants continued to run full bore around the clock.

But now with the war over production demands relaxed almost immediately. By the time the shouting and the street dancing ended across America, thousands of Oak Ridgers were making plans to pack up and go home. Home was virtually every state in the union for the 75,000 residents and most of the 40,000 off-area commuters.

Three months after the Japanese surrender, plant employment dropped by some 31,000. Within 10 months only 2,000 of 47,000 construction workers remained and residents were leaving town at a rate of about 2,500 a month. By June of 1946 the population was down by a third to about 50,000 and falling. Empty prefab houses dotted the landscape as occupants left town or upgraded to the choice cemesto houses that were becoming available daily. The ugly, crude, plywood hutments were knocked down and hauled away. The Midtown Trailer Park where Gene Pharr lived quickly became a ghost town. Gene's family, with nothing to go home to in Chattanooga, upgraded to a two-bedroom duplex called a TDU (temporary dwelling unit) so that Gene could continue in Oak Ridge schools.

By Gene's senior year, 1951, fewer than 30,000 residents remained in Oak Ridge, the security gates had been opened to the public and just over 1,100 students moved into a new $3 million state-of-the art high school. Many members of its first senior class were products of the new, progressive school system from its 1943 beginning, and perhaps the most diverse environment in U.S. in history. Nobody was rich, nobody was on welfare and there was no unemployment. It was as close to a classless society as America will likely see.

After graduation, most of the Class of 1952 scattered. Some who remained went to work at the plants, witnessed the mysterious nuclear buildings from the inside for the first time and stayed there until retirement.

Perhaps no post graduation departure was more exciting than that of Gene Pharr, who was on his way to the University of Tennessee on a football scholarship. But just days before he was to report, he caught the attention of two Philadelphia Phillies scouts at a national amateur baseball tournament in Battle Creek, Michigan. Gene hit .570 for the tournament and got four hits in the final game. The Phillies offered him a minor league contract.

"They were giving me $50 for breakfast, $50 for lunch, $50 for this and that" Gene said. "I'd never seen so much money flying around. I'm not exaggerating. They said 'We want to sign you,' and I said, 'I can't do that. I've already signed a football scholarship with the University of Tennessee.

"And they said, 'How much is that?'

"I didn't know how much it was worth, so I said $8,000. I had never seen that much money. They said OK. Since I was a minor, they sent Mother a telegram getting her permission. She had to sign the contract, too. They gave me $2,000 cash to begin with and the middle of next season they gave me another check for $6,000." (Eight-thousand 1952 dollars is the equivalent of about $30,000 in the year 2010.)

"I didn't know about having money," Gene said. "I didn't even know about paying taxes until the end of the year because they didn't take federal or state tax or nothing out of that. It was up to me. I remember I bought sweaters and tee-shirts and jeans and penny loafers. I had probably every color that was made in a sweater. Mother came down and I gave her a $500 check. When I found out I had to pay taxes I said, 'but I don't have enough money to pay taxes.' But I paid."

Gene was an 18-year-old kid chasing a major league dream, willing to play in dinky class-D ballparks and sleep two-to-a-bed in dingy hotels in little nowhere towns and ride breakdown buses and exist on a skimpy $5-a-day meal allowance. It was a three-year journey that took him to a lot of places, but never to the big leagues.

"I took a bus to Bennettsville, South Carolina to my first spring training," he remembered years later, "and that's where I had an experience I never had in my life. It brought me out into what I call the real world. This was 1953 and on a weekend, the small downtown was so crowded, so many people you almost couldn't walk, and it was full of Blacks. All of a sudden a horn sounded, really loud, like a siren. You could hear it all over. The first time I heard it I didn't know what it was, but after the horn blew, about an hour before sundown, there was not a Black person left in all of downtown. That was their curfew. They could not be caught downtown after dark. I'm just sitting around talking with the ballplayers—there were no Blacks in the Phillies organization at that time—and we didn't know what to say. But it happened every day."

There were surprises at the training camp, too. "I didn't know what to expect, he said. "I thought I knew everything about baseball and I didn't know nothing. I mean I didn't know nothing. I learned a lot real fast, but not everybody did. I remember this kid who wouldn't pay attention to anybody; a big, strong kid. They brought me over to show him how to slide, but the kid wouldn't do it right. There was this man standing there watching us. He had on khaki pants and an old wrinkled shirt and he said to the kid, 'Why don't you do what he said?' and the big kid jumped up and said. 'Who the hell are you, smuck?' He was Ruly Carpenter, owner of the Phillies. The big kid was gone the next day.

"I didn't know what to expect in the pros, but I saw a lot of people who could do a lot. I was a pretty good hitter and good at fielding. I hardly ever missed one playing fungos and other guys told me they wished they could field like that. So I felt pretty quickly that I belonged. There were about 50 of us from everywhere and I was one of the better ones at that time. We had drills about eight hours a day for six weeks. I loved it.

"At the end of training, nobody knew where they would go. They sorted us out: Double A prospects, A prospects, D prospects, etc. Unless you were a phenom, you started out in class D.

"The season started in May. I remember catching a bus going to Mattoon. Illinois. Class D. They had boarding rooms all set up for us. No air conditioning. Before the summer was over I bought an oscillating fan and placed a bucket of ice in front of the fan and let it blow cool air on me.

"Mattoon was very small and had railroad tracks running through the middle of town. It was a farming area, corn mostly, and the team was in the Missouri-Ohio Valley League. One of the teams we played was Hannibal, Mark Twain's hometown, the buggiest town I ever saw. That summer the locusts were so bad in Hannibal they had to get snow plows and push them off the bridge so traffic could cross. People don't believe that, but it's true. It was the seven-year locusts or something.

"Our uniforms were pinstriped with 'Phillies' spelled out across the front in red letters, just like the major league uniform. But the first one we put on was the road uniform with just a red 'P' on front, an old wool thing. Hot. They used wool then because it held the moisture of your body and helped keep you from dehydration.

"It sounds funny, but one of the things you have to learn is how to put on a professional baseball uniform. It's not easy. There are two pairs of socks. First you put on your white nylon stockings. Then you put your stirrup stockings on over that and get both pair straight and even. Your pant legs have elastic at the bottom, so you put on your pants next and pull the elastic up to your knees, then you drop your pants down, inside out, and take your stockings and fold them over the elastic of each pant leg. Then you pull your pants up. You can wear you pant legs high, just below your knees, or all the way down. Talk about embarrassment, The Cleveland Indians asked me to go to Knoxville to a talent camp when I was still in high school. They wanted me to hit some and see how fast I was and I was supposed to run against this guy. They gave me a Cleveland uniform to wear and I couldn't make the stockings stay up. I walked out on the field and my stockings kept falling down. It was embarrassing.

"In Mattoon, we dressed in the clubhouse under the old stadium bleachers. It was like a high school field with a wooden fence with advertising signs. It was the same wherever we went. The ground was so hard and rocky grass wouldn't grow. We went to one ballpark and the groundskeeper was digging holes to put the bases in.

"Hannibal was the worst. It was a four- or five-hour bus ride through St. Louis. Everybody on the team got food poisoning there one time and we had to stay in this old hotel, two players to a bed, and during the night everybody starting shitting. I got up to go to the bathroom and didn't make it and shit in the floor. Then I started to get back in bed but my roommate had shit the bed, so I had to sleep on the floor. We all had to play next day, sick as dogs.

"We dressed in a Quonset hut in Hannibal. We played one game there in 107-degree heat, so hot that our two catchers dropped over from dehydration. The manager came over to me and said, 'Have you ever caught before?' and I said, No way I'm getting behind that plate.

"We rode in an old yellow school bus and one of our players, Bob McGee, was paid $5 for driving it. We're coming back from Hannibal one time and he was driving through cornfield country and came up behind a farmer on a tractor. As McGee started around him, he clipped the back wheel of the tractor and the tire exploded and shot the farmer into the air and into the cornfield. Nobody believes these stories but they happened."

Gene had a good first year in the minor leagues. He was a top fielder on the Mattoon team in the Missouri-Ohio League and led the Appalachian League the next season in stolen bases. He felt good about his future.

"My second year was in Pulaski, Virginia, Class D," he said, "and we had a playing manager named George Triandas, a big hairy 260-pounder. His brother Gus was a big leaguer. George came into the clubhouse one night and said, 'Look what I got, a plastic cup! It's something new, lighter than the aluminum cups.' He was so proud of that thing. He placed it carefully over his genitals and got dressed.

"That very night George gets hit with a foul tip right in the groin and it doubled him over. He could barely get his breath he was in such pain. We all gathered around him and somebody loosened his pants and you could see that his new plastic cup had split and had caught one of his nuts in the split. Somebody said, 'Hey, somebody reach down and get his nut out of that thing,' and everybody just looked down and said, 'Not me.' Nobody wanted to touch it. George was so big nobody could carry him, so he had to crawl back to our dugout on his hands and knees, moaning and groaning.

"We had a little shortstop on that team, a Mormon fellow from Utah, and he had a penis on him this long. I don't know how big it was because nobody ever measured it. But it was the biggest on the team, and maybe the biggest in the league. Every-body just stayed away from him. Every time he got in the shower somebody would yell 'Don't anybody drop the soap! The shortstop's in the shower.' Every time Big George walked by the little shortstop's locker he would look down at him, shake his head and say, 'It ain't fair. It just ain't fair.'

"My last year of ball was in Three Rivers, Canada, Class C. There was a foot of snow when we got there in May. We didn't see the sun for a month. I drove up in a Henry J with the top cut off. I had the top covered with plastic and had all my clothes in it and somebody got in there and stole all my clothes.

"Our manager on that Three Rivers team, Al Barillari, had a monkey. He took that thing on the bus all the time and we all hated it. It was so mean, we wanted to kill it. We were sitting around a big table in a family-style Italian restaurant one night, about 10 of us after a game, and in comes the manager with that red-assed monkey on his shoulder. Our waiter sat this big bowl of pasta in the middle of our table and when the monkey saw it he leaped right in the middle of the bowl and starts slinging spa-ghetti all over the place.

"But that's not the worst. Barillari had trained that monkey so that every time he saw a beautiful blonde woman the monkey would start masturbating. It was embarrassing. We wouldn't even walk with that guy. We hated that monkey.

"Once on a road trip we had a long wait for a ferry to cross the river, so we got out of the bus. There was a big park there. Then we hear the manager yelling. 'My monkey got away and I can't find him!' He made us go through the park and look for it, so we all pretended to look for the monkey, but nobody really did. Nobody wanted to find it except the manager. We never did find the monkey and when the ferry came, we left without him."

After the first month at Three Rivers, Gene was leading the league in hitting with a .481 batting average. Then the Phillies signed a kid for $20,000, a first baseman like Gene, and sent instructions to play him every day. Gene was relegated to the bench as a pinch-hitter.

"Some of the players were saying they never heard of benching anybody who was leading the league in hitting," Gene said. "The manager started playing me in centerfield and said I was his regular centerfielder. But then the first baseman with our class D team in Bradford, Pennsylvania broke his leg and they needed someone to fill out the season there, so I did. I had a good year there, but separated my shoulder in the last game on a double steal in a collision with the catcher. He ended up with broken ribs. They put us in the same ambulance going to the hospital side by side and he was groaning and moaning and I was so pissed at him I yelled, 'Oh, shut up!'

"That was it, my baseball career. I didn't go back for the next season, although I really didn't start to mature until that third year. One of my managers told me a baseball player doesn't reach full maturity until he's about 26, and he's probably right because I played a lot of [amateur] ball after that and got stronger.

"Shortly after I left pro ball I was playing with a team in Raleigh, North Carolina and we go play a team in Central Prison. I was pitching. I'm doing pretty good and I brush this one guy back at the plate and he starts walking toward me. 'Oh God,' I thought. 'This is a prisoner inside the prison walls with prisoners all around us and he was walking toward me with a bat in his hand. He gets almost to the mound and stops. 'Hey,' he said. 'Aren't you the Gene Pharr that played with the Philadelphia Phillies?' I nodded, and he said, 'Well, I'm so- and- so—whatever his name was—and I took spring training with you in 1953.' And then he said, 'Why don't you catch 10 and come in and play ball with us?'

"In mid-season of my first year at Mattoon, I got married. I married Pat Sutton, a girl I dated in high school, and we soon had a daughter, Paula. Then my third year we had a son, Gene, so I needed to do something. It was hard making it on a minor league salary. I was making $375 a month then. We lived in Raleigh in the off season and I drove a fork lift in a warehouse and worked part-time in a pool hall for $12 a night.

"I was a good dad and I liked being married. But Pat wanted a divorce, so we separated and I went to live at the YMCA. I never would have divorced."

Not long after the divorce was final, Gene was drafted into the Army and spent two years as a military policeman. While he was away, Pat re-married and moved away. After his discharge, attempts to see his two children failed. He remained in Raleigh, remarried, became a motorcycle cop (he once had a loaded-and-cocked, double-barrel shotgun stuck in his face), then a sporting goods salesman, and an insurance adjuster.

One afternoon when he was getting dressed to play a softball game in Raleigh, the phone rang and his second wife, Evelyn, answered.

"Gene," she said. "It's for you. It's your dad."

"Freeman," Gene thought, his stepfather.

"It's not your stepfather," Evelyn said. "It's your real dad."

Gene was startled. His hands began to shake and his mind began to spin. He was three years old when he last saw or heard from his father and he remembered nothing about him. Gene was now 30. Why would he be calling?

"It was an awkward situation," Gene said, "but a happy situation. I knew a little bit about him by then because mother had kept in touch with his sisters. I had wondered about him all my life. Everything I ever heard about him was good. Mother had never said one bad thing about him. He had remarried and had two sons, Larry and Don Pharr, my stepbrothers. I knew that he lived in Chattanooga and was a foreman at a foundry, and that's about all."

"Gene, this is your dad," he said. "I've been wanting to talk to you."

Tears began rolling down Gene's cheeks as he listened. Ten years earlier after his first pro baseball season, he had driven to Chattanooga to see his mother and stepfather, who had moved from Oak Ridge. While he was there, he decided to find his father and introduce himself. Gene was 8 when his mother married Freeman and Gene loved and respected him from the start.

"There wasn't a nicer person in the world," he said. "I never heard that man raise his voice or say a bad word about another person. But I always wanted to see my real dad. Did he know about me? Did he know where I was and what I was doing? Was he at the game the time we played Chattanooga Central there in high school? I just thought that here I am in the same town with my real dad and if I was ever going to meet him, this was the time."

He drove his 1950 yellow Ford convertible downtown and parked a few blocks from the foundry and walked across the Market Street Bridge over the Tennessee River. He stopped just before he reached the end, when the building first came into view, and looked down at the Samuel Foundry, the tool and die plant where his father worked.

"What if his reaction is cold and uninviting?" Gene wondered. "What do I say then, what do I do? What do I call him?"

He gazed down at the river below and tried to rehearse.

"Hello. My name is Gene Pharr and ."

"Hi, I'm your son."

"Mr. Pharr? I'm Gene ."

He stood at the end of the bridge until he began to chill, an hour or so, peering across the street at the plant, then down at the river, trying to muster the nerve to walk across the street and introduce himself. But his feet moved slowly backward, step by step until he finally turned and walked back to his convertible and drove away. He decided that if his father wanted to see him, he would do it.

And now, after all those years, his dad was on the phone, wanting to talk.

"I was holding the phone and listening, shaking all over," Gene said. "I didn't know what to say."

"I've kept up with you over the years," his dad continued. "I know about your ball playing and all that. I've talked to your mother. I wonder if you could come down to Chattanooga so we could talk?"

"Yes sir," Gene said. "I'll come see you."

His father apologized for not getting in touch but never said why, and Gene didn't ask.

"Thank you for calling," Gene managed to say. Then he put down the phone and cried uncontrollably.

Earl Pharr, Gene discovered over the next week, was no longer a foreman at the foundry in Chattanooga. He and a partner now owned a foundry—Southeastern Tool and Die—and he was quite wealthy.

Gene's mother, Louise, and his aunt Elizabeth met Gene and Evelyn at the Chattanooga airport a week later and as they walked across the tarmac, Gene heard his aunt say, "They walk alike." Earl Pharr was waiting inside.

"I remember looking at him the first time," Gene said. "He was a shorter man than me, a stout man, and he wore a hearing aid and had a battery in his shirt pocket. He had had an operation for an inner ear problem and there was a scar. Black hair. Kind of ruggedly handsome. We reached for each other and hugged. My heart was racing. I was so happy. I had looked forward to that moment for so long."

From the airport they drove to the foundry and toured the tool and dye plant where presses were stamping out metal spoons and forks and pans and things. Gene's dad, workers told him, was one of the best tool and die men in the southeast. He had a patent on a burner for stoves. His foundry covered about two blocks.

Earl didn't offer Gene a job, exactly, but suggested that he should consider that possibility, consider moving to Chattanooga. "There are four people who would never be fired at the plant," his father said. "My three sons and a man who stuck with me all these years."

It was a tempting suggestion. "But I didn't even know what a press was," Gene said. "I knew nothing about that business. I couldn't do it."

He went home to Raleigh, bought into a Peddler's Steak House franchise in Hilton Head, South Carolina, managed it by night and played golf by day. The restaurant boomed, his golf handicap dropped to a two and his second marriage ended.

Earl Pharr eventually sold his half of the foundry to his partner and retired. Gene and his half brothers developed a lasting relationship that included North Carolina mountain retreats, brother-brother golf tournaments, reunions and storytelling visits. Only two things were now missing in Gene's life, a successful marriage and a reunion with his two children whom he hadn't seen nor heard from since they were babies. He got both.

Long after his second divorce when he was visiting a friend in Charlotte, North Carolina, the friend asked if he would like to have a date.

"No, thanks," Gene said.

"Ha! She said the same thing when I asked *her*," the friend said.

So naturally they made the date and that date eventually led to Gene's marriage to Kay Christmas, a pretty, kind and caring divorced mom with a school-age daughter.

"When I first met Kay I told her that I had two children in the world somewhere and I didn't know where they were," Gene said. "I had tried to see my children when I was discharged from the Army in 1959. I finally found out where they were living and talked to their mother on the phone about seeing them. But she said her husband wouldn't like it and she asked me to stay away." Her husband had adopted Paula and Gene. They had a different last name.

"I quit trying after that," Gene said. "I figured they didn't want to see me. But all those years I wondered about them. It was a hole in my life."

By now Gene had sold his thriving steak house in Hilton Head, had moved to Charlotte and was general sales manager at a Pepsi Cola bottling plant in Cherryville and Midland, North Carolina. One day in Charlotte he got a telephone call from a high school friend.

"Pat wants you to call her," he said. "She said your children want to see you and that she was sorry she had kept them away from you. She was sobbing and seemed desperate to find you."

Gene made contact immediately and made arrangements to see his children. First he called his daughter, Paula, and made plans to see her in three days. She was 39, a twice-married mother of three living in Cumming, Georgia. He hadn't seen her since she was a baby.

Then he called his 36-year-old son, Gene, in Munroe Falls, Ohio, and made plans to visit him. But first he told his boss at Pepsi, then called a staff meeting at the plant to tell his fellow workers that he would be gone for a few days, that he had found his children. Then he cried. Everybody at the meeting cried.

"I had driven through Cumming, Georgia many times," Gene said, "and had no idea my daughter lived there. I had played golf about six miles from her house. Kay and I drove down there to see Paula and the children answered the door when I knocked. That's how I saw my first grandchild, standing in the door looking up at me.

Paula was in her bedroom, a nervous wreck. "He came to my bedroom door with a vase full of long stem red roses and his wonderful smile," she said.

"Hey, Dad."

"Hi, sweetheart."

They hugged and cried.

The grandkids called him Grandpa and opened the gifts he had for them and they looked through a lifetime of photographs together and told their stories and took pictures of one another. Paula had a picture of her dad holding her when she was a baby, and one of him in a Phillies uniform. For several years after her parents' divorce Paula cried herself to sleep because she missed him so. When her mother or stepfather asked why she was crying, she told them her hip hurt.

"I started looking for him in 1967 when I was 14," Paula said. "I had wanted to find him for years but I didn't really know how to go about looking. I tried to find him in phone books and by calling information when I would go to Durham or Cary to visit relatives. I never knew to look in Hilton Head. The reason I was looking by myself is that I didn't want to rock the boat at home.

"My aunt LuRuth told me once that she heard he had remarried and moved, but she didn't know where. When I was little, my great grandmother told me the reason he had divorced was because he didn't want children. When I told him that, it was obvious it hurt him that she would say something so untrue. She was really an unhappy woman and tried to make everyone else miserable, too. But it has been so awesome getting to know him. He is one of the kindest men I have ever met and I admire him so much. I'm just sad because of all the years we missed."

Gene never knew that she had tried to find him.

They ate out together that day at Applebee's and went to the Community Bible Church the next morning where Gene was introduced to the congregation as her real father, whom she hadn't seen in almost 35 years.

Two weeks later Gene and Kay were in Munroe Falls, Ohio, a suburb of Akron, where his son lived with his wife, two children and a stepchild. They pulled into the driveway and saw the family looking for them through the front window. The front door burst open and the kids ran out to meet them before they could get out of the car. Gene hugged his grandchildren, then looked at his son for the first time since he was in diapers and they locked in a long, tearful embrace.

"A good looking boy, Gene thought, "a little bigger than his dad. Dark hair and brown eyes like his daddy's. And an athlete."

His son had been a high school football star, and such a good baseball player, a catcher, that he landed a baseball scholarship to the University of Akron.

"I didn't know what to expect," young Gene kidded his dad. "Being from Tennessee I thought you might be a hillbilly and drive up in some old dilapidated truck." He had been trying to picture what his dad would look like. "I didn't know if he was going to be wearing a polo shirt, or a coat and tie or a tobacco-spit-stained T-shirt," he joked. Actually, they had exchanged pictures before the meeting, so he knew his father was a handsome, well-dressed man.

But he knew almost nothing else about his father except that he had played minor league ball and that he was a good all-round athlete. His mother never talked about him when he was growing up, good things or bad; and young Gene never asked. He assumed his father had just run off.

"I always wondered what he was like," he said, "and my sister kept saying we need to find him and she couldn't understand why I didn't want to. But I had no problem with the way I was raised and I didn't think he wanted to see us. I was grown and married when my mom kinda sat me down one day and told me it wasn't that way. If I had known that, I would have tried to find him." He didn't know that his mother had contacted his dad, telling him that the children wanted to see him. His dad's telephone call came as a shock.

Their visit lasted three days in Munroe Falls and when they said goodbye in the driveway they wrapped their arms around each other and squeezed. When they let go young Gene stood back and said, "I've got to do this, Dad." He took his father's face in his hands and kissed him.

Gene and Kay drove home to Charlotte and began planning a reunion that would include all his children and his grandchildren and his mother and his half brothers and their children and his real dad. "After all these years, after all my prayers, it has all finally come together," Gene thought. "I'm no longer going to think about all the good times we missed. Now I want to see them and enjoy them for as long as I can. Now I want to see my grandchildren grow up and play soccer and swim and play golf and do all the things with them that I missed with my children. Today nothing is missing in my life, not one solitary thing."

Gene Pharr retired from Pepsi in 2005 at the age of 73 after 23 years there. He was inducted into the Oak Ridge Sports Hall of Fame in 2007.

Sophie's Secret

Although she was a year younger than most of us when she arrived in Oak Ridge in 1949, and although she had missed a full year of school hiding from the Nazis in wartime Hungary, Sophie Brody tested at the 10th grade level and was placed in our sophomore class. She had been separated from her family and arrived with a small suitcase, a pair of knitting needles and a secret.

Sophie Mary Brody was not in Oak Ridge during the war years. She was in the war. She was nine years old when German troops rolled into Budapest and into her life in 1944. For a year she ran from the Jew-hunting Nazis, sneaking from one hiding place to another, never knowing today where she would be tomorrow. While we were in elementary school watching Oak Ridge being built, she was in the streets watching Budapest being destroyed. During that time she witnessed the worst and the best of man—those who killed innocent people out of hate, and those who saved them out of love. She was still re-living that bleak experience in recurring nightmares when she arrived in Oak Ridge as a teen-ager in 1949.

Sophie, from a prominent Hungarian family, was separated from her parents and her 11-year-old brother during the last year of World War II, hidden by underground agents in the homes of strangers. Her mother and brother were hiding elsewhere separately. She didn't know where. The Nazis had taken her father away. She didn't know where. They were reunited after the war, but life for them would never be the same. The family was as broken as the war-torn country they lived in.

Four years after the war, after the new Communist government had taken away virtually every Brody belonging, the family split in three directions. Mother went to live with friends in Paris, brother went to a boarding school in Connecticut under the care of an uncle, and father sailed second-class with little

Sophie to New York City with no place to live, no job and little money. Sophie eventually landed in Oak Ridge alone, guest of a kind and caring family she did not know and had never seen. She was 14, knew no one and spoke little English. She was smart, humble, friendly and forever smiling. We didn't know that she was scared and insecure and that she had secrets. It would be more than 50 years before she would tell the story she is about to tell. She always thought she would write it herself but, she said, it just never happened.

"In truth," she began, "my going to Oak Ridge was an accident, and the truth about me has been a secret from all my classmates all these years. And, I think, from all my teachers, too. I never told anyone except my husband until now."

It was in July, 2004 when she began telling her story. She was by then Sophie Brody Ravin, a 69-year-old widow and retired teacher living alone in a tidy 42nd floor apartment overlooking Lincoln Park in Chicago. Two grown daughters and two grandchildren who lived in the Chicago area were among her infrequent visitors. She spent most days alone with her closest liberal friend, The New York Times.

She was frail and walked painfully and precariously on a crippled toe and with a dizziness that was with her always. She used a cane or a walker. Her lupus was in remission. A red squamous cell cancer on her nose soon was to be removed. Surgery for a cancerous kidney was ahead of her. As she spoke a quality of sadness invaded her dark eyes, a look of surrender, weariness that seemed deep and permanent. It is what life had done to her—the war, the Nazis, the broken home–and something else that she hadn't discussed with anyone except her family and her psychiatrist.

We classmates never thought about Sophie having worries and secrets. Everyone loved her from the time she joined the Class of 1952 as a 10th grader. She was so bright she immediately gained attention in class and began piling up scholastic awards.

She would graduate with honors, and the senior class would elect her the girl most likely to succeed. She earned a scholarship to the University of Rochester, where she graduated magna cum laude and was offered a Fulbright Scholarship her senior year.

- o –

Sophie was a timid, raven-haired little girl with flashing dark eyes when she arrived in America from Budapest in the winter of 1949 with her father, Janos, a once-wealthy grain dealer in Budapest. He was the son of Sandor Brody, a famous Hungarian novelist, playwright and short-story writer. A street is named for him in Budapest. Before the war the Brodys had a big, two-story home on a hilltop; No. 3 Sarolta Ucca, in the fashionable Rozsadomb suburb of Budapest. They had cooks and maids, an English-speaking governess and sometimes a valet and a dining room that accommodated 24 guests. From the top floor they could see much of Budapest. Janos and his wife, Lilly, hosted gala parties with string music and socialite guests. They drove fine automobiles and wore fine clothes.

Sophie's father grew up in a Budapest hotel with four brothers under the care of his famous father whose wife, also a writer, had left him. Both grandparents died before Sophie was born. Sandor's writings were naturalistic, mostly about poor people. He, too, was poor growing up and although he earned fame, he was never rich. He didn't take care of his money and in fact, except for his writing, he wasn't very responsible.

"My father didn't go to university," Sophie said. "He started out as a newspaper reporter. I don't know how he got into importing and exporting grain, but he was a very good businessman. He didn't have the writing gifts of his father, but he was a great storyteller. He was very good at helping you appreciate what you read. He loved reading to us and in that sense he was artistic. Mother was not college educated but attended art school and was quite a good painter. Her father, my grandfather

Elemer, was an eye, ear, nose and throat physician who also taught at the University of Budapest Medical School.

"My father was a handsome man," she said. "He met mother through mutual friends and mother waited 10 years for him. She fell in love with him when she first met him and wanted to marry him. I think father married her for her money. He had started his grain business but I think it was a humble operation. He used the money from mother's dowry to enlarge it and he became big and successful. Both became terrible spend-thrifts."

The problem, Sophie said, was that her father was unfaithful. They had terrible rows. Her mother would wake her in the wee hours of the night, crying because her father hadn't come home. "My father used her in a lot of ways," Sophie said. "He used her for giving parties and then he wouldn't pay much attention to her. She kept a very nice house and knew how to entertain.

"My brother Alexander and I played a game at their parties. We would watch my father flirt with other women and try to guess which one he had picked out for that particular night and we were always right. It was that obvious. He was not discreet about it and my mother had to live with that humiliation. That was the terrible part. Mother gained weight after the marriage after having two children. She was not a slender babe."

The parties and the spending ended once the war began. Budapest was bombed by the Americans and British long before the Nazis invaded, because Hungary had taken a position allied with the Nazis. Hungarian laws were changed to persecute Jews even before the Nazis arrived, and Sophie's grandfather Elemer lost his position at the medical school.

"My father had a bunker built in our yard for our safety," Sophie said, "but we weren't able to use it much because we eventually had to leave the house. I remember the first time we were bombed there were already the sounds of bombing when the sirens sounded. We immediately went to the underground bunker. We had some food out there and blankets and flashlights. We were underground not very long before the all-clear sounded and I remember coming out of the bunker and going up on the terrace to see the fires where the bombs had fallen. It was very scary. I had the feeling that if a bomb had exploded in our yard we wouldn't have survived in that bunker. It wouldn't have protected us. It wasn't deep enough underground. We lived pretty much on the alert for those bombardments. They tended to be at night."

As the German army approached Budapest, Janos and Lilly Brody sat down with Sophie and Alexander and explained some things about the Nazis. They would round up Jews, they said, and take them away, so everyone had to be very careful about what was said to anybody about their Jewishness or about anything they were planning. Without the children's knowledge, Janos made plans for an escape and for hiding. The Germans moved into Budapest on March 14, 1944.

"One day some German soldiers came to our door," Sophie said, "and arrested my father and took him away. Somehow, mother found out where and was able to send him food. The person who took the stuff to him was our governess, who was still living at our house. She didn't want to leave, but later she had to because Jews weren't allowed to have servants. Father was in a labor camp someplace close to Budapest. I don't know why he wasn't sent to a concentration camp, or put in a ghetto. That's how it started. They put Jews in a ghetto and hauled them off to a concentration camp. I suspect that my father paid somebody off to be in the labor camp. Later he was released and went into hiding. I never knew how he got out, maybe influence, maybe money, and I never knew where he went into hiding.

"After my father was taken, a German officer and his Austrian mistress occupied our house and we moved down to the basement to the servants' quarters. We became their servants. The officer and the young woman were very nice to us. She let me sunbathe with her on the balcony and she covered up the railings with towels so no one could see us up there.

"One day she told my mother that we should get out of the house right away because someone was coming to arrest us. My father had made arrangements for a place to go and we left immediately. We went with nothing. No possessions, just ourselves. We went to somebody's house, some important people in the underground. There were a lot of other people there, other Jewish people. I knew some of them. They were settled down in the floor of the living room. We slept there that night, about 15 of us.

"The next day some underground workers came to take us to our hiding places. They said we would have a better chance of surviving if everyone hid separately. So I had to say goodbye to my mother and brother because each of us was going to different places. That was the last I saw of mother until after the war. I saw my brother about a year later just before Germany surrendered. I was nine and very frightened."

For more than a year Sophie ran from house to house every few days under the noses of the Nazis, darting through the fiery streets in the confusing aftermath of nighttime bombing raids. Someone she didn't know would come for her, take her by the hand and hurry her through the burning streets to yet another hiding place in the home of someone else she didn't know.

"The bombardments were so frightening," Sophie said. "I knew it was the Americans and the British trying to get the Germans out, but I was so afraid of the bombs falling on me. When we changed hiding places I could see the destruction and the fires. We would take circuitous routes to get where we were going. It was always at dark when they came for me, after the bombers had gone. I never knew when they were coming or where we were going. It was better to move after the bombardments when the all-clear sounded, because people were all over the streets coming from their various shelters and trying to get home, so there was always confusion. The people who came for me were members of a Christian underground, sometimes a man and sometimes a woman. I wouldn't stay in any one place too long.

"Wherever I went people were kind to me. But always there was an injunction against talking. I had to be quiet, because no one should know that there was a child in the house. At one of the places there was a picture window and I had to crawl under the picture window so that I didn't show up in the window outside. Neighbors were always close by and nobody could know about me."

For most of 1944 and into the spring of 1945 Sophie remained in hiding, never knowing where she was or with whom, and never hearing about her family. She wore the same clothes every day for a year—a gray and white plaid skirt and jacket. She had some underwear and a pair of knitting needles. She outgrew her oxford lace-up shoes and they hurt her feet when she ran.

"People sometimes gave me stuff to knit with." she said. "If there were books, I could read. If there were no books, I would just sit quietly. There was a game I played, a grid game. You played it with two people really, so I pretended to be two people. What happens is that you make one line at a time and then the aim is to create a box. The opponent can interfere with your box, trying to send the line in a different direction."

Toward the end of the war Sophie and her brother Alexander were taken to an apartment building in Budapest's busy 15th District. The bombing had worsened and now the Russian army was inside the city, fighting the Germans house-to-house. Sophie and Alexander hid in a one-room apartment on the ground floor, occupied by a German-speaking single woman. She was the building custodian. It was Sophie's most dangerous hiding place.

"We were supposed to be very quiet always," she said. "We had a fight one day when I was knitting. He kicked at me and hit the needle and the needle stuck in my hand. I was in such pain. But I couldn't cry or make any noise. I had the scar for years."

The war taught Sophie not to cry, to maintain her composure. Even today she has difficulty crying. If she cries, it usually is on someone else's behalf.

"Early one morning two German soldiers came to the apartment and wanted to come inside to look around," Sophie said. "I heard the knock on the door. I couldn't see the soldiers but I could hear them talking to the woman. She spoke German with them and she was doing most of the talking. I don't know what she said, but she wasn't letting them in. I think she told them she was too busy and that they would be wasting their time and her time and to please go somewhere else and let her work. If they had come inside they would have found us because we were still in the bed she had made for us in the living room. We were very still and held our breaths. I was shaking so hard in my bed. I have never shaken like that before. We were both very quiet. We just hunkered down in bed, not knowing what would happen. The lady finally persuaded them that there was nothing to see and they went away. I think it was just a general inspection because they checked other apartments in the building. I don't think they had any idea that we were hiding there."

Outside the fighting soon moved onto their street as Russian soldiers began pushing the Germans back. Gunshots cracked like firecrackers, artillery shells screamed and shook the ground as they exploded. Now and then there were shrieks from fallen soldiers.

"I stood back from a corner of the window and watched." Sophie said. "It was cold and there was snow on the ground. I could see the soldiers' breaths. They were running back and forth from building to building, finding places to hide. I could hear the shots and I saw soldiers get hit and fall. It was horrifying—the leaking blood, the sudden quiet of the person. Utter quiet, a stillness of death. I had nightmares about it all the time, that and my hiding. I lived in constant fear of being caught, especially when we would run through the streets to a new hiding place. It was so difficult to keep moving around, but I knew it was necessary, it just had to be done.

"I could never go to the shelters during the bombing raids because it would be too risky. People would ask questions about who I was and what I was doing there. The worst place was the last one because of the danger almost every minute. There was the bombing almost every night and fires everywhere and the street fighting all day.

"Things got so bad one night there was no choice but to take us downstairs to the shelter. It was in the basement. I don't know how the woman who hid us explained our presence. But no one said anything to us. The streets were like a battlefield and we couldn't go out. We slept on planks and our only source of light was a candle made out of shoe laces and animal fat. They took a shoe polish box and put animal fat in it and then used the shoe lace as a wick and lit it.

"The power was off everywhere and the water pipes had been destroyed. That was the only time I was ever really hungry. All we had were some beans. Somebody would go outside with a pan and get some snow and that's how they got water to drink and to cook the beans. I don't remember what we did about the bathroom. There was nothing to do. Mostly we just sat all day staring into the darkness. I don't know how long we were down there, but it was weeks."

When they finally left the basement, the Russians had driven the Germans from the city and soon after, on May 8, 1945, Germany surrendered to the allies. Sophie and Alexander soon were reunited with their parents. The running and hiding were over, but not the horror. Undisciplined Russian soldiers were now everywhere and Hungary was under communist control.

"The Russian soldiers got drunk on vodka and plundered and raped and burst into homes and took what they wanted," Sophie said. "I knew about intercourse and I knew what rape was. I was scared all the time. One time they broke into our house and ransacked it and poked holes in a bag of flour so that it leaked out. For no reason, totally senseless waste, just to throw their weight around. But were they worse than the Germans? No, because the Germans hunted down Jews and killed them. The Russians had to fight very hard to liberate Budapest so they celebrated by drinking and stealing and doing whatever they pleased. They particularly liked watches. They would take them right off your arm."

Soon after the Nazi concentration camps were liberated, a bus carrying some surviving Budapest inmates arrived. Expecting to see her grandfather Elemer, the physician, Sophie went with her grandmother Margit to meet the bus. They watched as the gaunt survivors stepped slowly off the bus, but her grandfather wasn't among them. Instead, someone approached Sophie's grandmother and handed her some pieces of paper and trinkets. Grandfather Elemer was dead, he said. The papers were scraps of various sizes on which he had written Hebrew prayers and kept track of the temperatures and the health status of many inmates he had treated in prison; a doctor to the very end.

"He must have had to search for those little pieces of scrap paper," Sophie said. "His things also included three primitive pendants made by another inmate. They were inscribed with the names of Grandpa's three grandchildren—my brother, a cousin and me. We never knew how he died."

What Sophie saw during the war, what she heard and smelled and felt and thought, would haunt her throughout her life. It ended her childhood prematurely, destroyed her faith in mankind and in her God. And it filled her mind with doubts about her worth and her reason for being. For much of her life she would drive herself in search of respect and acceptance.

"The war left me with a constant worry," she said. "I worry about everyone and everything. Even now. I imagine the worst things. If somebody is late, I always worry that the person has met with an accident. And I worry about my grandchildren walking to school. I worry about everything. I don't trust people because I know how bad they can be."

Four years after the war the Brodys had virtually nothing left of value. The Russian-controlled communist government had systematically taken over private land and businesses. "After the war my father went to work buying horses for the Hungarian Trotting Association," Sophie said. "The Germans had either taken or slaughtered all the horses for food. He made several trips to the United States to buy horses; and he managed to get some money out of Hungary each time. On one of those trips he took Alexander with him and enrolled him in a boarding school in Connecticut–Edgewood School. From there my brother went to Princeton. I, on the other hand, never had enough money to buy clothes for myself."

In 1949 Janos Brody gave the Hungarian government his few remaining assets in exchange for passports, with the idea of taking his family to live in the United States. Since America's Hungarian immigration quotas were subscribed for years ahead, he devised a plan of deception. He would take Sophie to the U.S. with him using visitors' visas, then find a way to stay permanently and send for his wife.

"In order not to look like we were trying to immigrate," Sophie said, "my father decided to leave mother behind. It would look better to immigration officials. Mother was a painter and spoke fluent French, so she went to Paris to live and paint until we sent for her."

Sophie and her dad sailed in the winter of 1949 with their visitors' visas and secret plans. They had some clothes in their suitcases, a little money and little else. Janos spoke no English so he coached little Sophie, who spoke a little, on what to say and how to lie to immigration officials.

"I didn't want to say anything because I knew we were going to be in trouble," Sophie said, "but my father insisted. I couldn't deny my father so I spoke to them the way he told me. When we arrived, immigration officials came on board and they suspected us of not being genuine visitors right away. So my father decided to come clean and told me to appeal to the officials, to tell them that America is a place where everyone has a lot of compassion and to please have compassion and let us stay. They didn't listen. They refused us entry and sent us to Ellis Island. It was like an arrest. We were prisoners. We couldn't leave. They were going to send us back and we had no place to go. By now we realized that America wasn't going to be the dream we had envisioned."

Sophie was separated from her father at night at Ellis Island and slept in a large, stark women's dormitory-like room with strangers. There was nothing to do. People milled about and sat for hours on the many benches. Meanwhile a bill was working its way through Congress that would allow displaced persons to apply for citizenship. The Brodys qualified. After weeks of detainment, they were released and admitted to America.

"We lived in a hotel in Manhattan until the money ran out," Sophie said, "then my father asked some distant relatives of my mother if we could stay in their apartment while they were away at their summer home on Long Island. It was a big apartment on Fifth Avenue. All their furniture was covered up. They only left one little bedroom for us to live in, plus the bathroom and kitchen. My father slept in one corner and I slept in another."

Janos got a job boxing Channel perfume and Sophie became his maid. "We had no friends and there was no money to do anything," Sophie said. "He became very depressed and was very hard on me. I tried so hard to please him and take care of him. I did the grocery shopping, the cooking, washed and ironed his shirts and cleaned and scrubbed the floors. But he was verbally abusive to me and I don't know what else. I can't remember if he ever hit me or did anything else. In Budapest he used to spank us–hard. But we left Budapest on good terms and I dreamed of being a good housekeeper for him. I took such pride in what I did. I didn't know what to do when he lost his temper. During the day when he was gone I walked to the Catholic Church, Saint Patrick's Cathedral, sat in the back and cried. I don't know why I went to the Catholic Church. I can't explain it. Because it was quiet, maybe. I don't know what else."

One June afternoon in 1949 Sophie was found unconscious on the kitchen floor. She had swallowed all of her father's sleeping pills. She was rushed to an emergency room and eventually admitted to a psychiatric hospital on Long Island where she remained through the summer. That was the secret she kept in Oak Ridge, and for all the years since, until now. She also never mentioned that hospital officials wouldn't permit her to return to live with her father, or that she was a displaced person and had no real home, or that she was penniless and owned little more than two knitting needles, a dress and the shoes on her feet.

"I never revealed to anybody in Oak Ridge that I came directly from having attempted suicide and having been hospitalized in a mental hospital," she said. "I used to tell others that my father got TB and I had to leave him and that he was hospitalized and that's how I came to Oak Ridge.

"What really happened is that when I was ready to be discharged from the hospital I had no place to go. There was a doctor from Oak Ridge at the hospital visiting a medical school classmate who was one of the directors at the hospital. She overheard some conversation about my problem and asked, 'Why doesn't she come and live with me?' "

The doctor was Agnes Flack, an industrial physician and obstetrician at the Oak Ridge plants. It was Labor Day. Sophie was on a plane to Tennessee the next day and arrived just in time for the opening day of school at Oak Ridge High. She lived with Dr. Flack for a year, until the doctor left Oak Ridge to become medical director for a women's reformatory in New Jersey. Before she left, the doctor arranged for Sophie to remain in Oak Ridge; to move in with her brother, George Flack, his wife, Doris, and their three children.

Oak Ridge was no longer a secret when Sophie arrived, and there was no secret mission. The security gates had been open to the public for five months; and the normalization of the government war town was under way. Oak Ridge was getting major attention from a curious national media, which was calling it the world's most unusual city. The hustle and bustle and the mystery were gone, and for the first time Oak Ridge appeared on public maps.

Sophie knew virtually nothing about the town when she arrived. But whatever it was and had been, Oak Ridge was the best thing ever to happen to her. Compared to bombed-out Budapest, compared to Communist rule, compared to Ellis Island and the psychiatric hospital, it was beautiful.

"It was a very different setting and an exceptional experience for me," she said. She was talking not only about the town, but about the Flack family. "I had never known a family like that. I didn't have very good parents. I mean, even aside from the war, I didn't have a good childhood. It was never conducive to a good warm and fuzzy home life. It was a roller-coaster life. Live high, live in poverty. The Flacks became the family I could only imagine and to this day I call them Mom and Pop Flack. When I came home from school Mom Flack would stop what she was doing and sit down and talk to me. And she made my clothes because I didn't have any money. She even sewed an evening gown for my first prom. She found baby-sitting jobs for me so that I had some money for myself. They were not well off and with three children, you know, it was hard for them. Originally the arrangement was that my father would pay $50 a month toward my upkeep, but he got sick and was hospitalized and didn't have any money. I called Dr. Flack and mentioned it and I think she paid her brother for me."

After testing, school officials placed Sophie in the 10th grade at Oak Ridge High, even though she had missed a year of school during the war. By the time she was a senior she had accumulated an arm load of academic accolades and was the darling of her teachers because of her sharp intellect and hard-work attitude. She became a heroine of sorts with classmates.

"I had no idea about Oak Ridge, what to expect," she said. "Oak Ridge High School had a good curriculum, but I thought everything was very loose. I remember in one of my classes a student was sitting near the teacher's desk and she had no work and her stockings were down and she had shoes that she could easily remove. She took her shoes off and she played with the waste basket under the teachers' desk with her feet. I was so shocked I couldn't believe it. Because, you know, I had come from European style teaching, stiff and rigid.

"So I thought this is a different world. I remember the teachers asking me to go to different classes to tell about my experiences in the war. I enjoyed it, but I felt different because of my war experiences, and because of my being hospitalized. I felt different because, after all, I had attempted suicide. That was a big deal. I took pills, my father's sleeping pills. I lost confidence."

There was little about Sophie in high school to suggest that she was troubled, but she was never quite pleased with herself. Privately she felt too chubby, graceless and unfashionably dressed. Despite her world-class smile and friendly manner, she was hurting inside.

"Actually, my years in Oak Ridge are not really clear to me now," she said. "Someone mentioned at our 50th class reunion that I had been part of the Penguins, a girls' social club, and when she said 'Penguins' it woke me up. I was a Penguin but didn't remember.

"A lot of my problem was my trying to be somebody that I wasn't, trying to fit in. The biggest yearning I had always was for boys to recognize me and ask me out for dates, and that didn't happen very much at all. My teachers wanted to help me have a relationship with boys. Some of the proms were such that you didn't have to have a date and I would go to them and I would stand around and nobody would ask me to dance. And that made me feel terrible. But each time my teachers would prop me up again and get me to go. At the end of my junior year I started going with a classmate, Bill Greer. Bill was my first date with an American boy. I think he was the only person who asked me out. But I felt uncomfortable with Bill because I couldn't tell him the truth about me, about my suicide attempt, and that was very important."

"After the war I never made room in my life for religion. I didn't think that God, if there was a God, would allow the things that happened in the war. All the carnage. What I saw. I couldn't believe God would let that happen. I had always heard that God was merciful, good and just, and involved in the lives of people.

"The Flacks invited me to go to the First Presbyterian Church with them. I had never been to a Christian church before. I thought it was beautiful and I loved the music. But I couldn't understand the talk about God's Son and I didn't really believe the talk about the Trinity. I just thought it was people wanting to believe what they wanted to believe. I was only going through the motions. I didn't feel right about being in the Presbyterian Church. I did what was expected. I just went there because I wanted to please the Flacks and because I wanted to pretend to myself that I wasn't Jewish.

"After the war I really didn't want to be known as a Jew because I thought I would be subject to prejudice again. Whatever religion lessons I had were always about Jews being persecuted and I just always thought that was part of it. I knew that Jews didn't believe in Christ, so I thought that was the biggest reason, probably, that Jews didn't acknowledge Christ as the savior. And I knew that in Hungary before the war, Jews had a lot of money. There were poor Jews, too, but the Jews had much of the wealth and that was resented.

"My family wasn't very religious, so we weren't really brought up in religion. However, my mother was. Her family was kosher and she observed all the Jewish holidays. Father got a minimum of education in the Jewish religion and never did go to Hebrew school. His father wasn't religious at all. At some point we had some private lessons in the Jewish religion, but we never had bar mitzvah."

Sophie's romance with Bill slowly dissolved when she went away to college. She graduated high school at 16, won a full-tuition scholarship to the University of Rochester, graduated magna cum laude at age 20 and was offered a Fulbright Scholarship. All that despite working after school and weekends to pay for room, board, clothing and incidentals. During the summers, she worked as a telephone operator at the psychiatric hospital on Long Island where she had been a patient years before.

Early in her senior year at Rochester she was among a group of students asked to serve as a hostess for a faculty social, and there she met her future husband, biology professor, Arnold Ravin. He was 14 years her senior. They were engaged within months; and Sophie had to choose between marriage and her Fulbright Scholarship.

"If you accept the scholarship and go to Europe, the engagement is off," Arnold told her. So Sophie got married, started a family and a teaching career. She taught for more than 25 years, the last 19 at the Laboratory School of the University of Chicago, where her husband had become dean of the Arts and Sciences Department.

"The thing I'm most proud of in my life is the way my Lab School students remember me," she said. "They really appreciated my teaching. Many of them were faculty children and the children of doctors and professional people. They had to pass an arduous admissions test. It was a real bonus to be able to teach that kind of student. I learned from them. My emphasis was on a certain way of reading. It involved looking at fine details, images in particular, and trying to solve what I call the inner secret of the characters. I took a very psychological approach to teaching literature. I loved English. It is so much more expressive than Hungarian. It gave me so much freedom. I always thought that was a gift to me. Teaching those bright kids were the happiest times of my life."

Religion, the globalization of terror and the globalization of big business causes Sophie to worry about her adopted country.

"The Christian right," she said, "supposedly acting under the aegis of Christ, is very un-Christ like. They attack people who don't believe what they believe and they do it in the name of Christ." It is an attitude, she said, not unlike the radical Muslim terrorists.

"The United States has the power to incite violence everywhere," she said, "and what we have done is very scary. It encourages countries like North Korea to obtain nuclear arms. We are the greatest country in the world and so we think we have the God-given right to do what we want, to police the world. We haven't tried accommodation. It's not out of the question that we could have a religious war—Islam vs. Christian.

"If I could address the nation, I would plead that we return to the constitutional guidelines that have served us well in the past, among them the protection of individual rights and the separation of church and state—not just preaching, but prescribing. Take away the tax advantages of the ultra rich and return to a compassionate way of government. Make a good life available to the poor and middle classes. Reinstitute some of the safeguards against corporate power. I believe if some checks aren't made that in 10 to 15 years we will have gone too far and that it will be difficult to ever turn back.

"After having seen and lived through the war, I want to work for a better world. I believe that a better world is possible. But right now I'm at a low point as far as that is concerned. I'm so upset with what's going on in this country. I don't feel that it will turn around. Not anymore.

"I think the United States is about to lose its leadership in the world. We are close to it now because of the moral leadership we have lost. Morality should be an important part of our leadership. I think perhaps we are in the greatest crisis in the history of this country. I don't know why more people don't understand that."

They Sent Him Home to Die

Gladys McGinnis married classmate Herrell Akers a year out of ORHS and divorced 21 years later. They had three children, Jerry, Nancy and David. Gladys married Bill Edwards of North Carolina in 1984.

I came in from the evening shift and saw Jerry's forest-green Cutlass Supreme Oldsmobile in the driveway. So I thought he was at home, asleep. I got something to drink, showered and went to bed. At about 1:30 in the morning the telephone rang. Jerry was in the emergency room at a hospital in Harriman. A swimming accident. I was out of the door in a minute.

Jerry Herrell Akers was 23, the oldest of my three children. He was divorced with a 3-year-old daughter, Jasmine, whom he adored. He was an Air Force veteran, a jet mechanic, blond, blue-eyed, athletic and all muscle. The very first time he was on skis he dropped one ski and kept on going. He was only seven. "Look, Mom, I can fly," he shouted. He could do almost anything in the water.

I don't remember driving to the Harriman hospital, but it was in record time. When I got there they were getting ready to transfer him to the University of Tennessee Medical Center in Knoxville. A head injury, they said. When they rolled him out to the ambulance I saw his right arm slide off his chest and dangle beside the gurney. I felt my heart sink. I fell in behind the ambulance, and followed it. I could see the doctor and nurse taking turns trying to keep him breathing. I was praying, a mom trying to hold onto her son.

I parked and ran inside. He was on life supports. There were three small scratches on his forehead—no brain activity. This was a kid who had life saving and spent his summers on the water. What happened?

He had been out with four friends, and they talked to me while we were waiting. They were just goofing off. They were on someone's little backyard dock on Watts Bar Lake in Midtown near Harriman. It was around 10:30 on a Sunday night.

Jerry decided to take a quick swim, they said, and dived off the dock into the dark water. A minute passed and no Jerry. He didn't surface, or at least no one saw him surface. Two minutes passed. He's playing a game, his friends thought. He's hiding under the dock—three minutes.

Some work was being done at the dam and the water was lower than usual, somebody remembered. Had Jerry hit bottom on his dive? One of his friends jumped in to look for him. He landed on Jerry. Nobody really knew exactly how long he had been in the water—five or six minutes maybe? Each of the four seemed to remember things differently. An emergency squad that didn't seem to know what to do with him transported him to Harriman, and a doctor there said he must have hit his head in the dive. They drained his lungs before transporting him to Knoxville and found very little water. A day passed and there was no change—then two days. I still didn't know the details of what happened. Nobody seemed to know.

While I waited, I began thinking of Jerry's entry into this world and his narrow escape from death. He was born three weeks early and came by C-section. He had a very faint heartbeat and his blood count was so low all I was told was minus five. In less than four hours his weight dropped from 6.7 pounds to 5.11. Next morning it was 5.2 pounds.

His doctor gave him blood transfusions in his feet and ankles with a hypodermic syringe and ordered one every four hours. But Jerry continued to lose weight and there was nothing anyone could do. After two weeks, we were told to take him home. I was so afraid. My thoughts were, "OK, little fellow, nothing will happen to you on my watch." I didn't know it, but they were sending him home to die.

He couldn't tolerate milk or regular formula. I found a place selling goat milk, put a bigger hole in the nipple of his bottle, mixed some strained liver baby food in with the goat milk and fed him one sip at a time.

We lived in an E-1 apartment then, one of the wartime fourplexes in Oak Ridge, and we had a small range. I turned the oven on warm, wrapped Jerry in a blanket, and placed him on the oven door. I smacked the bottom of his feet and gave him a sip of the concoction. I did this all day and all night for eight days. Every few minutes a smack and a sip. He was so white from lack of blood, but after eight days I saw a little pink in his cheeks. I was still so afraid, but that night I slept all night.

His doctor had given me an appointment in two weeks, and I kept that appointment. She said she could hardly believe the baby was still alive. "What have you done to this baby?" she asked. "He's all pink and I can see that's he's gained weight." Jerry had gained a pound.

Then she told me that three doctors had wanted me to take him home to have a little time with the baby, to hold him and to love him before he died. She started crying.

I told her what I had done and all she could say was, "We never expected to see this little fellow alive for his two-week appointment." She said she wouldn't have thought of what I did. I don't know how I thought of it. I guess that's what moms are for. I can still see those little feet. These days, I would probably be in jail for abuse.

Now here he was 23 years later, back in a hospital; and he was dying again. But I couldn't do anything to stop it. Except pray. Two days passed. A letter came for him in Monday's mail from Roane State College. He had been accepted for the fall term. Another letter confirmed that he had been accepted for a job at U.S. Nuclear where I worked.

Jerry never knew. He died on the third day after the accident, August 20, 1978. The cause of death: "Swimming accident." There was no autopsy. No investigation.

A part of my mind shut down that day, and I've kept it that way for 32 years until now. I never thought I would be able to talk about it, or write about it. A place in me will always be shut down. That's the place where I carry Jerry. This is the first time I've tried, and it has helped.

God let me keep him for 23 years and four months, up to the day we buried him. I guess I forgot that he was on loan from God. I am so thankful for all those years.

Years later I lost my daughter, Nancy Carol Akers Freels. It's a little easier talking about Nancy because we know how she died. But it was still earth shattering. She was 49, divorced with four children. She had an enlarged heart with complications.

I still have David, 53, and five grandchildren, so my children live on.

Gladys McGinnis Edwards

Oak Ridge, Tennessee

Some Rules to Live By,
Some Rules for Dying

Donald Wentworth Lane had one of the highest IQs in the ORHS Class of 52, a friend found out from a front office contact. If he knew it, he never let on and one would never have guessed it. After graduation, he proceeded to flunk out of the University Tennessee after two freshman quarters, having failed 31 consecutive academic hours. For the longest time, he seemed always to be looking for happy hour. Until one day. He told this story in 2004 while he was dying from brain cancer.

On a hot summer day in 1944, Tom and Jean Lane boarded a train in Boston en route to somewhere in Tennessee with nine-year-old me, two teen-agers, a toddler and a baby in diapers. Only Dad knew we were going to Oak Ridge, Tennessee, a new town where he had been working secretly for almost a year. Now he had come for us. We would live in a brand new house, he said, with a view of distant mountains. We could hardly wait.

Our train stopped in Washington D.C. and, unbeknownst to its civilian passengers, hooked on several rail cars filled with young soldiers. Essentially, from that point on, we were on a troop train. We had to walk through the troop cars to get to the dining car, and it was a trip my 16-year-old sister, Mary, didn't want to make a second time. She was horrified when she stepped into the first troop car and was greeted with whistles and "hubba hubbas" and catcalls.

"Well," she explained years later, "the soldiers were half naked because it was so hot and there was no air conditioning, so they had their shirts off, and whatever; and they were laying in their berths, hanging over the sides, bare legs hanging out over the aisles. I was so embarrassed. I grabbed little sister Charlotte by the hand hoping they would think I was her mother."

A few years later Mary would marry a soldier, a member of the Army's elite Special Engineering Detachment (SED).

When we finally got to Oak Ridge somebody drove us up this winding dirt road to the crest of a big ridge; and I thought we were going to see our house. But what we saw was a huge mound of dirt.

"There," a construction supervisor told us. "That's where your house will be in about a month."

We were all disappointed; but I remember mom standing on that huge mound of dirt and looking out over the Cumberland Mountains. It was a beautiful sight and she was really excited about it.

While we were there, Dad talked the construction supervisor into knocking out a wall or something and to add a fourth bedroom. They were supposed to go strictly by the specs, but the guy told dad he would do it.

While our house was being built, Dad rented two side-by-side cabins on the banks of Norris Lake at Norris Dam State Park, some 35 miles from Oak Ridge. I thought I'd died and gone to heaven. We had a floating dock, and we lived in that lake every day. The water was so clear and pristine you could see your feet on the bottom. But the chiggers! My God, you've never seen such chiggers. All of us looked like we had the measles. Dad blew up like a balloon and had to be hospitalized.

About six weeks later our house was ready, but the bulldozers had cut deeply into the ridge top, new houses now lined both sides of the dirt road; and the once grand mountain view was obscured. That dirt road would become a major artery running for nearly seven miles along the ridge top on the northern border of residential Oak Ridge. My job every afternoon was to hose down the road in front of the house just before shift changing time to keep down the dust. The government provided Dad with a car, but often he couldn't drive it home because of the mud or the deep ruts in the road. After a rain, mud collected on the running boards, smeared across the windshields, oozed from beneath the doors, stuck to door handles and stained seat covers. Tires sank down to the axels and spun hopelessly. On rainy days, Dad left the car in a dormitory parking lot at the bottom of the ridge and took an Army bus up the hill.

That muddy road was named Outer Drive, and it would be home for some of the world's brainiest scientists, including Hungarian Nobelist Eugene Wigner. Our house, 19 Outer Drive, was on the eastern end of town, a choice type D cemesto; which was about as close to a status symbol as there would be in wartime Oak Ridge. We didn't know it then, but the D cemestos were mostly assigned to people important to the operation. In early Oak Ridge, not even medical doctors could get one.

They were one-story, ranch style with light grey prefabricated fiberboard siding bonded with a cement-asbestos mixture called cemesto. They were shipped in by sections on trains and trucks, and some were put together in two days by large construction crews rotating in assembly-line fashion. They circulated house to house in waves. By the time a bulldozer leveled a lot, masons were putting down cinderblock. Then came the framing carpenters, then the electricians and the plumbers and the painters in swarms. Houses could be wired in a matter of hours. Same with plumbing. Then on to the next house, and the next and the next—20 or more houses finished in a single day during some peak periods. Yet there was a housing shortage right up to the day the war ended. The cemestos, the most permanent of the Oak Ridge houses, had a life expectancy of 25 years. More than 60 years later virtually all are still occupied.

Construction crews stretched out for miles up and down the ridges, working dawn to dusk, seven days a week. The constant hammering and sawing and the roar of trucks and heavy equipment scared away wildlife. For the longest time there were no birds in Oak Ridge.

By the summer of 1945, the government had spent $110 million just building the town. It had installed a 35-mile railroad line with five locomotives; and a crew of 105 men kept 3,000 cars of construction material rolling to the plants every month. It operated a farm on the area with a herd of 800 beef cattle and thousands of chickens to help supply meat to Oak Ridge residents. The town had 12 schools, a 300-bed hospital, 20 fire halls, nearly 10,000 residential houses, 34,000 dormitory spaces, more than 5,000 trailers, 13 supermarkets, 9 drugstores, 4 theaters, 9 cafeterias, 5 restaurants, 23 tennis courts, 6 recreation halls, 36 bowling lanes, a 9,400-book public library, 18 ball parks, 12 playgrounds, a symphony orchestra and one of the largest municipal swimming pools in the nation.

I loved Oak Ridge from the beginning; and no matter where else I lived; I always knew I would return and die there. Not that anyone would care. I left no legacy at Oak Ridge High, graduating somewhere in the academic middle in 1952. I was not an athlete, not a thespian, not an artist, not a scholar. I didn't like to read; and I didn't join clubs. I got through my classes with passing C's and B's and an occasional A without studying. I had a part-time job after school, my only hint of discipline, and hardly ever missed a party. I was butt mooning from car windows before mooning had a name.

My gait was slow and easy, my shoulders slightly slumped, and I ignored a shock of auburn hair that seemed always to hang in my freckled face.

I pretended to be gruff sometimes, but I was probably just looking for attention. Anyhow, the girls seemed to like me; mainly because I could dance. I could also play a little boogie-woogie on the piano, and I could get the family car for dates. Not every family had a car. Beneath my roguish bluster I tried to be kind and fair. I always thought I had a special quality for something, but it took a long for me time to find it.

I spent four years in the Navy, married my pretty high school sweetheart, Joan Collins, then graduated from the University of Tennessee with a business degree in personnel management. We had four children and settled down, eventually, in Oak Ridge; after a stint in Paducah, Kentucky. Like my dad, I was in industrial relations. I was the personnel department superintendent at Y-12—labor relations, wages and hiring. All salary actions, whether promotion or new hires, had to go through me. I was also an alcoholic, but I didn't think anyone knew it. I hardly noticed myself.

It's funny how it takes an alcoholic so damn long to wake up. If you get in the car and start it up, and smoke starts coming from under the hood; you know you've got a problem. You call Triple-A and get it fixed. But you won't get yourself fixed. It took me three years to come to the decision that I had a problem, and to admit that I couldn't handle it. I couldn't believe me anymore. I was mixing Hydrocodone and bourbon, and it finally hit me that I was going down the sewer. I had about three doctors I was lying to. Addicts learn to lie.

Every alcoholic in every Alcoholic Anonymous meeting in the world couldn't take care of things or they would have. It takes an alcoholic forever to come to that decision. If you want to keep drinking, fine, keep drinking. But if you want to quit drinking, Alcoholics Anonymous has found a way out. The proposition is so simple it's astounding. I almost lost everything dear to me—my family, my wife, my God.

After a failed first trip to a rehabilitation clinic in 1983, I went back for seconds in 1986, and became a model AA success story and one of its hardest working leaders.

One of the things I'm proudest of is that after more than 30 years, this old drunk went back to school and, like my wife, got a Masters degree in rehabilitation counseling. And, mister, I put it to use.

I retired from Y-12 at age 59 in 1993 after 25 years, and went to work full time as a United Way volunteer; helping hundreds of disabled men, women and children at Emory Valley Center, an Oak Ridge training school for the handicapped. I worked side by side with them in hotels and fast food kitchens—flipping burgers, scrubbing floors, busing tables—training them on the job until they could work on their own. I did it for more than three years, 8:30 a.m. to 5 p.m., five days a week or more.

You can read about seizures and Down's Syndrome; but you don't really know about it until you work with their victims in human terms; like sitting down with a 35-year-old Downs patient and showing him how to put a nut on a bolt.

Once I was job coaching an adult woman with a very low IQ who couldn't remember numbers. We were training her in a hotel kitchen, and her job was to take breakfast orders to rooms. No matter how many times I went up the elevator with her to the rooms, she could not figure it out herself. If that tray went to room 433, she could not figure out how to get there. She couldn't get on an elevator and punch 4. Numbers meant nothing to her. I worked her shift with her for months. If she got behind busing tables, I'd go help her. Officials from the Y-12 plant often had lunch there and I'm sure they couldn't figure out why I was busing tables in my retirement.

I had a young man in training at a hamburger joint. His job was to toast the buns and cook the meat. It was my job to train him, and I followed him along to make sure everything was right. He could do the job, but he couldn't keep up; so I started helping him during lunch hour. I determined after a few days that there was no way for one person to do the job they were asking of him. I couldn't do it. So I approached the manager and explained that it wasn't a one-person job. The manager was a young girl, and she admitted that she was on a cost-cutting scheme and wanted to see if one person could do that job. I pulled him out of there that day. We had been there a month. How thoughtless. How uncaring. How unfair to him.

That incident gave me an idea. Why not have a training kitchen at the Emory Valley Center? We could teach our own how to become cooks. Emory Valley Center already had an old cafeteria, so I wrote a grant seeking funds to renovate and equip it. The grant was approved by the state, and trainees soon were generating daily meals for 30 to 40 little ones, ages eight and under. Then the cafeteria was opened to the public for one-dollar lunches, and soon trainees were landing jobs in restaurants.

I also became a non-rowing member of, and one of the busiest work volunteers for, the Oak Ridge Rowing Association; where my wife rows competitively in the Masters program. I helped set the ORRA's Melton Lake course and helped make it one of the best competitive facilities in the nation. I worked in committees, cleaned the clubhouse, officiated at races, cut grass. Everything I did, I did for someone else.

Like AA says, life runs on improvement, not perfection. If you're on the improvement curve, you're fine. You get rid of the old garbage, and make your amends and get into living life in an appropriate way. Every high school senior should be required to take a two-week AA course. It would save a lot of them a lot of grief.

Almost nobody has any rules in his life. You live like you damn well want to. It's a self-centered life. I am so fortunate to have finally learned that.

One late summer day in 2003, I was cutting grass along the lake banks at the rowing club, lost my balance, fell into the water and the power mower rolled in on top of me. Some path walkers rescued me. I had been losing my balance a lot lately, and having headache and vision problems. Not long after that I was celebrating my 69th birthday with friends at a restaurant in nearby Clinton. I excused myself to go to the men's room and couldn't find my way back to our table. A waiter found it for me. Driving home that night I veered into an oncoming lane twice and narrowly missed head-on collisions. Then I turned onto the wrong street to my house. That was the last time I drove a car.

Two days later, on Sunday, Sept. 1, my wife Joan convinced me to see a doctor. Joan was a social worker at the Methodist Medical Center in Oak Ridge, and she could drop me off at the emergency room as she went to work. We walked into the emergency room together, and Joan went upstairs to work. I was immediately taken to X-ray and soon the radiologist had the film on his screen.

"Mr. Lane, he said, "I'm going to tell you that this is not good news. Looking at this picture you can plainly see the big area here and these two lighter spots."

The doctor was pointing toward the top of my skull. "We have found three and maybe four brain tumors."

I didn't know what to say.

"What does this mean?" I asked the radiologist.

"First let's get your wife down here," he replied.

When Joan got there, that radiologist laid it out cold. I don't remember his exact words but it was something like: "If you don't have a will, you need to be drawing one up now."

Maybe not so harsh as that, but he didn't mince words. And that's not all bad. Why dance around it? He told us both very plainly. There was this instant shock. The doctor is standing there with a couple of X-rays in his hand, and he's handing me my rear end on a platter. The interesting thing is—and I credit the AA's 12-step recovery program for this—I thought about it for about two minutes and then there was immediate acceptance.

These are the facts. Can't change facts. Now what can we change? What's next?

Joan and I sat there and looked at each other for a while and finally I said, "Well, that's what the deal is. What are we going to do? Let's don't sit and wail and cry, let's get a plan."

There were three tumors. Melanoma. The largest, 3 centimeters, was removed in surgery. The other two were inaccessible. To compound matters, I developed pneumonia while I was recovering from surgery and later learned that the cancer had metastasized to the lungs. I went home and, between radiation treatments, sat on my front porch for long talks with old friends, poking fun at myself and my surgical scars, my lost hair and my worsening bag-of-bones appearance.

Cards and letters began pouring in from friends all over the country as word of my illness spread, so many the postman sometimes had to hand deliver them to my door because there wasn't room in the mailbox. My former classmates at Oak Ridge High formed a work party, mowed my lawn and raked leaves, cleaned my windows and washed my truck. There were picnics in my honor and backyard cookouts. Scores of friends visited; some daily. One flew in from Chicago just to spend a few minutes with me. A small chorus of carolers sang to me from my front yard one evening as Christmas of 2003 approached. I peeked out the living room window in disbelief, then walked onto the front porch and listened until the December chill sent me back inside to the window. "Unbelievable," I told Joan.

I've been thinking of the serenity prayer a lot lately: God give me the serenity to accept the things I cannot change, the courage to change the things I can and the wisdom to know the difference.

I'm fortunate. I found the wisdom to know the difference and the wisdom mainly lies in not having the capability to make decisions. So you just turn decisions over to God. Let go, let God handle it. There is a lot of comfort in that. I don't have to run the whole world any more. One of the neat things about recovery in the 12-step program is that they outline a ballpark guide on how to live life well. Most people have no rules in their lives. They live the way they damn well want to. Well, I found some rules to live by, and now I'm going to find some rules for dying.

You know, people accept unpleasant things and live with more of them than they realize—crabgrass, beer bellies, hemorrhoids. But they can change all that. I cannot change what's happened to me so I fall back on the 11th step of AA which is that we continue to make conscious contact with God. I can and I do.

In the days that followed, I talked about the things that had been most important in my life; and it started with Joan and my four sons. Our second son, David, was badly injured in a freak accident while he was on liberty in the Navy at Virginia Beach, Virginia. David was half sitting, half leaning on a friend's car fender when the driver suddenly put the car in motion. David lost his balance and pitched backward. His head slammed hard against a cement curb, leaving him unconscious. For two years he was in a coma; first in a hospital in Norfolk, Virginia, then in Nashville and, eventually in Oak Ridge. Joan or I—or both— were at his side virtually every day, including the day he died in 1980 at 4 o'clock in the morning. He was 22.

That took my mind off of drinking and off of myself. I didn't drink through that whole ordeal. It brought Joan and me closer and closer.

But soon after David died, I had dental implants and the dentist gave me Percodan for pain, and I found out real quick that one of those pills and a couple of drinks not only got rid of a lot of physical pain, but psychological pain as well. I was angry. I would shake my fist at the sky, and ask if there's anybody up there who would strike down a boy like that, doing what he's supposed to be doing with his fellow shipmates. I was mad at God. Then somebody told me that it's hard to get mad at something you don't care about. It's hard to get mad at a dog peeing on a fireplug because you don't care about it. So I must have cared. It was a pretty strong message, but it took me a while to get it.

For the longest time I was a disgusting person. Miserable. I couldn't even believe my own lies. If anybody else had treated me like I treated myself, I'd want to kill them. I was awful. I didn't know what I was doing half the time. At one point I was filing for a divorce against Joan. I found out about it a year into recovery. An attorney called me and said the judge wants to know if you want to go ahead with this or not. I didn't even know about it, didn't remember any of it. That's an indication of how far out I was. I finally realized that you can't change the facts, but you can change your mind.

When I hit bottom, I hit it hard. I don't remember going to the hospital. They rolled me in on a gurney and kept me three days. They weren't sure whether I was going to live or die. Finally they transferred me to the detox unit. But, just like an alcoholic, a few days later I was sitting up in bed wondering where I could get a drink. I knew when shift-changing time was for the nurses; and I knew at that time they huddled around and talked for about 30 or 45 minutes. So at shift-changing time I got up, got dressed, slipped down to the back door at the hospital and walked over to Charlie Robinson's liquor store. I bought a fifth of 100-proof vodka, slipped back in the hospital, got in bed and started drinking. I drank the whole bottle. I got away with it. But when I was done I had a problem. What to do with the bottle?

The next morning I got up around 5 or 6, went down the stairs to the employees' lounge, slipped into the toilet and got a bunch of paper towels. I wrapped the bottle in the paper and stuck it down in the bottom of a garbage can and covered it up. The janitor would take care of my problem. I went back to bed and fell asleep. When I woke up, I was startled to see that empty vodka bottle staring me in the face. They had found the bottle and somebody had sneaked into my room and placed it on one of those little rolling hospital trays and eased it right up under my nose.

Visiting hours were 1 to 4 p.m. and next day at 2 o'clock, no Joan. Three o'clock, no Joan. Finally at about 3:30 she walked in. There were twin beds in the room. I was sitting on one and Joan sat on the other. She looked sternly at me, eyeball to eyeball.

"I want you to clearly understand what I'm going to tell you," she said. "You are no longer the most important person in my life. Do you understand that?"

I said I did. It came down hard and clear.

"We just weren't on the same page," Joan remembered about those sad times. "He was into his insanity, his deceptiveness. It was a total meltdown. Typical alcoholism. He was at the end of his rope and I was *way past* the end of my rope."

I was sitting there in that empty room thinking of all I was about to lose. I thought back to three years earlier when I first went to treatment. I expected to see a lot of sick people rolling around on the floor. But instead, everyone there seemed happy. I knew right then that I wanted what they had. But here I was, right back where I started.

That bottle of vodka in the hospital was my very last drink, a bottle all to myself. The problem is when you're an alcoholic or an addict, you reach a point when you've drunk the fun out of the bottle. There's no more fun, no more euphoria in that bottle. At that point when you drink you just go from being sober to being drunk. And that's it. It's like opening and shutting a door. The euphoria is gone. And that's what gets a lot of addicts in trouble. They're chasing that God almighty euphoric high and it's not there anymore. Ever. But they still go looking for it. Before, when I tried to quit, I thought of all the things I couldn't do. I couldn't go to a football game because there's drinking. I couldn't go to certain restaurants because there's a bar. I couldn't go to parties where there's drinking, I couldn't hang around with people who drank. All negative stuff. This time I turned it around. I said I can do anything I want to do, go anywhere I want to go. There's only two things I cannot do. And that's drink and drug.

That was the beginning of what became a rock solid marriage. From that point there were 18 years of care, attention and love. Now my wedding anniversary is very important to me, because I spent our 30th wedding anniversary in a treatment center. It was just another day in treatment for me. It was a heartbreaking day for my wife.

I'll tell you how strong this marriage is now. Statistically, couples who lose a child for one reason or another go at each other. They have to blame somebody. Somebody has to be at fault. It's in the 90 percentile that they get a divorce. But we drew closer and stronger. I was helped a lot by something I read in a book. It puts things in proper perspective. The book is *The Present*, a best seller by Spencer Johnson.

My past was the present and my future will be the present. The present moment is the only reality I ever experience. As long as I continue to stay in the present I am happy forever, because forever is always the present. The present is simply who I am, just the way I am. Right now. And it is precious.

So no matter what, I plan to stay in the present. This is who I am.

In the months following surgery, I was not sleeping well. The headaches continued. My sight worsened. There was apprehension over what was coming next; not apprehension of the radiation treatments, but the after effects of them.

I go into dark holes. It's almost like a seizure. I feel it coming on about five minutes before it gets here, and then I'm in trouble with anxiety and it builds and builds. Each one is always worse than the last one. I have some medications that kind of string me out of that and eventually I'll just fall asleep.

Sometimes I see things in my mind, bad things. But they're not always bad. One time I saw the notes for a piano recital I did when I was a kid. I was playing it, and I heard the music and all. And once I saw a replay of a Boom's Day fireworks display, the big sparkles coming off a bridge like a waterfall to the tune of the Blue Danube. It's like a permanent recording there in your brain. My doctors call them brain poots. Those things come and go and you live with them.

One morning I got out of bed and couldn't tie my shoes. I had forgotten how. Another day I couldn't tell time. I would look at the big hand and then at the little hand and their placement no longer made sense to me. Every day it was something different.

When the spring sun was warm and there was no wind, I sat in my back yard with whomever happened by. Sometimes I would talk, and sometimes I would sit silently and look curiously about as if I were seeing my house and my yard for the first time. Or the last.

It is a private yard, with woods on either side and not a neighbor's house in sight. Behind me, hidden by trees and underbrush, is an old rusty single-track railroad bed that led to the Y-12 nuclear plant some four or five miles away. During the war, when my yard was part of a small forest, millions of pounds of raw uranium ore were hauled in from Canada over those tracks for processing and enrichment. The rail cars always were empty when they returned. Nothing ever came out of the plants that anyone could see. What came out were precious grams of weapons-grade uranium—green salt—carefully packaged in small, gold-plated nickel cylinders, placed in cadmium- lined wooden boxes and carried out in briefcases handcuffed to the wrists of armed government agents by automobile and train to Site Y—Los Alamos.

240

There's only seven-tenths of a pound of bomb-grade uranium in a hundred pounds of raw uranium ore, and they processed thousands upon thousands of tons of uranium at Y-12. So what happened to the tons left over from the processing? It never came out. It's buried somewhere inside those plant fences. Some we know about, but nobody knows for sure where all the waste was buried in the war years or how much, because accurate records weren't kept. The Secret City still has some secrets.

Down the street from me rests the tombstone of old John Hendrix (1865-1915), for whom this subdivision, Hendrix Creek, was named. Hendrix, a John the Baptist kind of eccentric in overalls, considered himself a prophet and often wandered through the wooded hills of Bear Creek Valley alone for days, sleeping on the ground, at a time long before it became Site X. He emerged from the hills one day and told of a vision in which Black Oak Ridge becomes a bustling city overrun by thousands of people. "Bear Creek Valley someday will be filled with great buildings and factories," he said. "And they will help to win the greatest war that will ever be." Hardly anyone paid attention to Hendrix until some 40 years after his death when the construction of Oak Ridge began.

Some people don't believe that. You can believe the vision or not, but what he said would happen, happened. I have to laugh when I hear about visions. I had a few visions in my day.

My resolve is fading almost daily now, and every radiation treatment seems to deepen my depression. I only have so much stability left, and every treatment takes another cup or two out of the bucket. There are no guarantees that the doctors can extend my life one day. You think to yourself that after the treatments are completed, maybe all the things you're giving up will come back. I really don't know what radiation does or is supposed to do. It's one of those things where you just throw your body to the medical community and tell'em to have at it. It's like betting the keys to the chastity belt.

I don't know if I'm going to live, or if I'm going to die. The jury's still out. I've done everything that modern medicine has to offer. Neurosurgery, laser knife surgery, brain testing. I've decided not to take any more radiation treatments. I told them I've had all the fun I can stand with those things, so this is kind of a turning point. Now I've got to be prepared to live or be prepared to die. Well, I'm preparing to live. I don't count days. I count today. I have all this equipment in the house for body construction. I'm just a bag of bones right now. Starting tomorrow, I'm going to build my body back up. I can't plan to die. It's a bridge too far. But just in case, I showed Joan where all the policies and papers are. Death may come, but it holds no power over me. None. I don't think God is up there waiting for this old hillbilly, but if He is, He is. Now, will He let me in heaven, or will He hang my ass on the gates of hell? I just remember what He says: Don't be afraid. Just follow me. I don't know if there's life in the world to come or not. My church says there is. Somehow I don't believe in the human soul, when you peel off the skin, the ego, and get down to the id. For some reason I just can't believe that part is true. Some call it a soul, some call it a spirit. But I think there's something else out there. If not, it's just a long, long, long quiet rest. I prefer to think there's something beyond that. And that's why death has no power over me. Physical power sure. But that's all.

Returning from a funeral of a friend one day, I told Joan how I want my funeral. I want a little bit of dancing, a little bit of singing, a little yah-yah and go home.

I know I shouldn't get down like this, but I can't help it. I can't sleep. I lay down and my mind goes into dark corners; places I don't want to go. With all the medication I'm taking, my mood swings get wider and wilder. Sometimes I don't know where I am or where I'm supposed to be. I just keep getting beaten down with something every day—sore throat, fever, headaches. It's always something. Sometimes Joanie and I will

242

just go to bed and hold each other for a long time. It's about the best thing that happens to me now.

I had been a recovering alcoholic for 18 years when the brain tumors were discovered. I became a respected member in the AA, and a successful sponsor for many seemingly hopeless alcoholics. I got so much from AA, and so I give a lot back. I am two years short of receiving one of the organization's most coveted awards; the 20-year sobriety medal. I'm looking forward to that day. I didn't accept the one-year medal, or the one you get after five years or 10 years. I told them to just hold them. But I am really looking forward to accepting the 20-year medal.

I sank deeper into depression. Hospice came.

My last AA meeting was at my house with several of my fellow recovering alcoholics. "We've decided to give you a couple of years," one of them said, and presented me with my 20-year medal.

By April, Don's fingers could no longer hit the proper keys on his computer keyboard, so he decided to shut it down. But first he sent a final e-mail to his 1952 ORHS classmates.

"As you all know by now, my finl curtain call is soon. but I couldn't let the time go by without—m no wrdsd can wxpress it, all th cards, letters, love, and compassion

As yo have given Joaan and and me,—hureds ang hungreds of hthem. You will all be remmemberd until yhe end of time God willlig

Love to all and thanks so mich for so much ovwe rhe years—it wa sone hell of ride....Smoooch!'

Don Lane

1934- 2004

Don died on May 26, 2004. Twenty days later, on June 16, his 48th wedding anniversary, a large bouquet of flowers arrived at Joan's front door with an attached card "Love, Don," it read.

It happened again the following June and the June after that and every June since. Joan doesn't know where they come from or for how long, but she knows they are from Don, and that it was his idea.

How to Say Goodbye

Don knew from his first visit to the doctor that he could not survive the malignant tumors in his brain. He was having headaches and confusion with numbers and distance-type judgments. From then until his death in May, we were struggling with acceptance of the inevitable, and, of course, his deteriorating health and abilities. We went through many peaks and valleys.

Classmates had a part in those peaks, never letting us face it alone. There are simply no words to describe what that tender love and care meant to us. So many wonderful things happened. Classmates raked leaves, washed cars and windows and staked out "I love you" messages during the holidays. There was a Christmas carol event and spring picnics, dinners, visits from distant classmates, front-porch chats and an awesome card-writing campaign that all arrived on one day. Just remembering this all again makes me realize how truly blessed we were.

Don and I used to talk about this journey that we didn't wish on ourselves, but nevertheless, had to take. I sometimes joked with him saying that he had the better part facing his last days because he was still young and pretty and had lots of good friends and family, and he had me to be with him and help him out; while I'll probably last into my 90s, a dried up forgotten old hag with everybody else gone and have to go it alone. I feel very close and connected to my dear old best friend and believe in the inscription on the garden sundial that he gave me years ago: "Grow old with me, the best is yet to be."

Joan Collins Lane

Nov. 14, 2004

Oak Ridge, Tennessee

Living a Hot Life—with Uranium

Depending on the isotope of uranium, and at a certain recovery stage, you can handle uranium with your bare hands and it won't hurt you—unless you get a lot of it together. Your skin will stop alpha and most beta rays from entering your body. Gamma is the hard stuff that penetrates. Neutron radiation goes right through you. You have to know what you're doing; you have to know the good stuff from the bad.

To do a small analysis, you put organic solvents on top of liquid samples and shake it really well. Do that with a certain acidity and the uranium goes from liquid to organic. It is a common every day practice, common everyday stuff—collecting enriched uranium, plutonium and other valuable elements. It comes right out of the reactor.

Herrell Akers, a quick-footed football player at Oak Ridge High and Maryville College in the Fifties and a longtime road-runner, worked for 23 years in such a hot spot at the Oak Ridge National Laboratory. He was a chemical analyst. He knew how dangerous it was. He wore pocket meters, an alert gadget called a chirper and a radiation-recording badge to gauge his exposure to radiation. He checked his hands each time he went into a lab, which had hand and foot counters at every door. He wore protective clothing, had urine and fecal analysis periodically and a full body count check once a year.

He was in the hot-cell group at building 3019 until it was shut down after a major alpha radiation incident. He moved to building 2026, then became a shift foreman at the transuranium building, 7920. At 7920, the element CF was recovered from radiation facilities. They used remote master manipulators in cells behind four-foot glass shielding. Herrell and co-workers had to go into the cells periodically and clean them out. There was a time limit for safety. They could work only so long; and then they would have to leave or risk getting too much radiation.

Nobody knew for sure what the safe limit was, but company officials had it set at five roentgens (5R) when Herrell was working there, so that workers were allowed to get a 5R reading before being pulled off the job. Over the years it was discovered that the so-called safe level was way too high. Now it's probably less than 500 miliroentgens (500 MR). A miliroentgen is 100th of a roentgen.

It wasn't that anyone was doing something wrong. The bad thing was that you had a lot of guys who, being the way men are, and the bosses wanting to get things done, would take off their meters and work until the job was done. The work had to go through.

Herrell's blood count was perfect when he went to work at the Lab in 1957. He was checked regularly by Dr. Tom Lincoln at ORNL and Dr. Gino Zanolli at Y-12.

Gradually, his blood count began to drop—lower, then lower and lower—until, after 23 years, he became anemic. He had virtually no bone marrow. He was lethargic and weak. He would have to take a nap when got home from work, and had to have at least eight hours of sleep nightly.

In 1980, he was transferred out of the Lab, and sent to Y-12 to another nuclear building; away from the hot stuff, but not away from toxic chemicals. Among other things, he ran an electron microscope checking material from St. Helen's volcanic eruption; and he checked moon rocks. He was also among the first to do radiation checks on deer and other animals that ran around the nuclear plants. He liquefied their body parts and analyzed the sample with a gamma spectrometer.

In 1990, at age 56, he retired from work but tried to continue running. For 10 years he had run about 40 races a year, some of them marathons. But now a race would lay him up for a day or two. He dropped down to 10-mile races. No improvement. His wife Barbara finished ahead of him five times in six races. He was hurting and he had to quit.

Then Barbara noticed a shuffle in Herrell's gait. He wasn't walking straight. He lost strength in his legs. A doctor listened to his symptoms. "Write something on a pad for me," his doctor said. Herrell scribbled some lines. His letters were tiny and tapered at the end, hardly legible. Parkinson's disease at age 72. And anemic.

By the time Parkinson's is discovered, the victim has lost more than 80 percent of the dopamine producers in the brain. There is a miracle drug now that furnishes the dopamine. But there is no cure.

Soon Herrell could hardly walk. If he came to a pothole in his path, he would freeze, not knowing what to do. It was the same when he made exits through doorways.

He's using a rolling walker to get around now. He can't walk without it. He can't walk and carry anything. He can't lift anything above his shoulders. But he does 20 pushups every day and 20 butterflies. He uses a scooter if he has far to travel and rides in electric carts at the grocery store.

Once a week a male nurse goes to his house on Outer Drive, part of Herrell's job compensation, and helps him do things. He grooms him, trims his toenails, helps him with the flowers he grows and the yard that he keeps. Herrell gets physical therapy twice a week and massage therapy twice a week at home; all part of the Department of Energy's compensation for his anemic condition and skin cancer.

Now, at age 75, there are still Parkinson's issues to be settled. Parkinson's never gets better. It just gets worse. "But I don't let it get me down," he says. "I keep plugging away. I keep going and doing."

A Day in Hiroshima

Clyde "C.W." Ramsay moved to Oak Ridge from Knoxville with his mom, dad and three brothers in 1945. In June, 1951, the summer before his senior year at ORHS, he was called to active duty by the Naval Reserve and returned to graduate in 1954.

In 1982 I accepted a position as a senior quality engineer with Nissan Motor Manufacturing Co., a Japanese company that was planning a new plant in Smyrna, TN. We moved to Murfreesboro, TN and assisted in the design and start-up of the new plant. Things went well for me there. It was a very good company to work for, and the work was interesting and rewarding. I was promoted to product engineering department manager in 1990. In 1995, I was selected as project manager to lead a team of engineers and technicians to Japan to conduct the first engineering trials on a brand new Nissan truck that was to go into production at the Smyrna plant in 1998. The major parts of an engineering trial are usually handmade prototypes and sometimes difficult to assemble. The team knew the truck as the QW Project. In 1998, the truck came off the Smyrna line as the Nissan Frontier.

While with Nissan, I made about 16 trips to Japan; and my first was to Kyushu Island to visit our truck plant for three weeks. The city we were staying in was the original target for the atomic bomb. But the city was fogged in on that historic day and the alternate target was Hiroshima. I was traveling with another engineer, and we decided to go to Hiroshima for the weekend and see the sights and visit the Atomic Bomb Memorial Museum. We took the bullet train; and it was packed with school kids of all ages. They entertained us the whole trip. They said "hello" and "how are you?" practicing their English. A teacher told us that most schools were out for a holiday. When we got to Hiroshima Station, just about everybody on the train got off. We settled in our hotel and went sightseeing.

This all took place in August, 1983 and at that time Hiroshima was the most ultra-modern city I had ever seen. It did not have any resemblance to a Japanese city and was more modern than most American cities. Of course, they started with a blank page because almost 90 percent of its buildings were destroyed or damaged by the atomic bomb. Streets were four to six lanes wide, and the buildings were beautiful. And the place was bustling with people.

The next morning we went to the Atomic Bomb Memorial Museum and discovered that about 400,000 Japanese were there; including the schoolchildren from the train and the people we saw on the streets the night before. Then it dawned on us. It was August 6, 1983, the 38th Bomb Day of Remembrance for Japan; a national holiday.

Here I was, a hillbilly from Tennessee who had no clue what 8/6/1945 represented to the people of Japan, the 38th anniversary of the atomic bomb drop. I had a very uneasy feeling about my safety at first, but the people were very gracious and friendly. I experienced many guilty feelings as I viewed the photos and artifacts of the hardships, death and destruction that occurred on that day. If you visit Japan you must see the Atomic Bomb Museum at Hiroshima. You'll see things you will not believe.

Clyde Ramsay

Cookeville, Tennessee

Everybody Thought I was Dumb, Including Me

Betty Stinson was a pretty, jumping jack cheerleader at Oak Ridge High in 1952, a popular but puzzling student who had trouble making conversation and answering questions in class. It surprised many when she founded one of Oak Ridge's most successful businesses after she was well into her fifties. Hardly anyone knows the problems she had to overcome. For 21 years she hardly understood a word anyone said.

It was the winter of 1978 and Betty Stinson Hurt had just been granted a divorce after 25 years of marriage. She had a daughter in college and a son in high school. She had no job and no income. She got the house in the divorce settlement, but she wasn't sure she could sell it. She was 45 and she didn't know what she was going to do. She had worked since she was 15, starting at McCrory's dime store in Jackson Square, then at Hamilton Bank and at the hospital and at Rust Engineering, and at Union Carbide; all in Oak Ridge, all office jobs.

While she was married; she worked off and on for about 12 years in the family heating and air-conditioning business, which she helped establish. "I took two weeks off to have babies and I'm not even sure I got two weeks," she said, laughing. There were no vacations.

After 25 years she ended the marriage, not knowing what she would do. When she returned to the office a final time to collect her things, she broke down at her desk and cried.

A friend and businessman, Bill Robinson, who happened to be in the office that morning, asked what was wrong. "I don't have a job," she said, sobbing, "and I have no income. I don't know what to do."

And he said, "Well, we'll just take care of that, won't we?"

And he did. In a manner of days, Betty had an office job with Union Carbide and in less than a year she was in business for herself. It was the start of a new life that would eventually turn her into one of the more successful businesspersons in Oak Ridge, as owner of Apex Office Supply and Design. She started the company on a shoestring, despite warnings from friends and her boss.

"I was in Purchasing at Carbide," Betty said, "and this guy from Knoxville was making all these deliveries, filling big orders and I thought, 'My, he's got it made.' So I decided if he can do it I can do it. I could start my own office supply business. I had worked at Carbide before and needed only two more months there to qualify for pension benefits, but I wanted to get out on my own and I didn't want to wait. When I told my boss I was quitting he said I must be mentally retarded. I guess I was stupid, because I really didn't know what I was getting into."

Once Betty got an idea in her head, she held onto it, even in the face of reason itself. She was confident that she could do it but, as she said, "I always had to work twice as hard as anyone else to achieve the same thing."

There was a reason for that. She spent much of her childhood being laughed at because she was not responsive in conversations and could rarely answer questions in the classroom. She couldn't hear the questions. She didn't know it, but she was virtually deaf. Incredibly, no one knew it, not even her parents.

"Everybody just thought I was dumb," she said, "including me."

She was a pretty, brown-haired girl with apple cheeks and sparkling brown eyes, but terribly insecure, intimidated, withdrawn and too shy to be comfortable around people. She was 21, working at the Hamilton Bank, before she discovered the problem. The bank manager, Hoyt Mason, pulled her aside one day.

252

"I believe we need to see a doctor," he told her. "People are talking behind your back and you don't know what they're saying." They were making fun of her.

Betty saw a doctor immediately and discovered that she was born with a dead nerve that caused her hearing problem. There's nothing that can be done, she was told. All she could hear, tests showed, was noise. Not words, not music.

"All those years I never knew that people could hear better than me," Betty said. "I thought my hearing was normal. I just thought I was dumb, because I didn't learn much of anything."

Hearing aids in the 50s were mostly big and uncomfortable and, in Betty's case, just exaggerated the noise. So she became an expert lip reader and used amplified telephones to get by until her divorce in 1978. "Then I finally decided that I'd like to be comfortable in conversations," she said. "I still have a hard time understanding women because their voice is more shrill, but I can understand most men. I have to have subtitles when I watch movies."

It turned out that Betty wasn't dumb at all, that she was, in fact, very bright. Leaving Carbide, she bought a little rundown house on Sutherland Avenue in Knoxville but saw right away that it wasn't going to work. Her mother told her she should go back to Oak Ridge where she knew people. So she loaded up, sold the house, returned to Oak Ridge and set up shop in a one-room rental in Jackson Square, making deliveries in an ugly, beat up, 10-year-old, brownish yellow Dodge Dart with the back seats removed.

"That was the toughest time of my life," she said. "At times I didn't have any money and interest rates were 20 percent. My daddy would lend me money, and I always paid him back. Barry, my son, was out of high school, then and he came in and helped me. Then my daughter Sheila went to work in sales for me. If it hadn't been for them, I probably wouldn't have made it. Sometimes Barry and I would work all night long packing and getting ready for the next day deliveries.

But soon she was delivering supplies under contract to Y-12 and X-10, and she was selling office furniture as well. She learned quickly that she could never relax, could never take a customer for granted because, she said, "As soon as you do, they're gone." She was courteous, eager to please, dependable, and she delivered complimentary doughnuts along with orders to the guys at X-10. "I never went out there without doughnuts," she said.

Her clients quickly became her fans and wanted to see her succeed. When the old Dodge quit running, she got a loan and bought a used van. When she made her first van delivery, the guys at X-10 clapped and cheered as she unloaded their ordered supplies.

She has now been in business 31 years, has her own office building on Administration Road with 14 employees, none of whom lost his job because of the recession. Single for 27 years, she re-married in 2005, becoming Mrs. Tom Smith. He was a fellow motorcycle enthusiast. Betty rode a trike, a three-wheel Harley Davidson and a *Boss Hoss* with a powerful Corvette engine. Life couldn't have been much better.

On an April Saturday morning in 2007, she and Tom were cycling to Busch Gardens and stopped for gas on Highway 321 near Interstate 75 in Lenoir City. The throttle stuck as she pulled away and the cycle shot forward like a rocket. Betty could hardly hold on. She veered right to avoid hitting Tom, who was in front of her, and was headed toward the Interstate when she slammed into a double-post sign . "I felt like I was going a thousand miles an hour," she said. "I couldn't stop it."

The sign stopped the runaway cycle but Betty's right leg got pinched between the cycle and the sign. She was conscious but couldn't move. She was rushed to the University of Tennessee Hospital in Knoxville. In the following days, doctors told her she would have to lose her right foot. She cried for three days, then faced her fate. "It could have been a lot worse," she reasons now, "I could have been brain damaged."

She was hospitalized three months and was home another three months before returning to work. She had to learn to walk again and to drive again. At 76, she still runs Apex Office Supply and Design. Every day.

Betty Stinson Smith
Oak Ridge, Tennessee

"I'll Be Seeing You . . ."

Classmate Tom McCulloh -- actor, playwright, producer, songwriter, and theater critic, died in a Hollywood, California hospital on March 28, 2004 from heart disease. He never married and had no family, so on his deathbed he phoned his best friend, former Oak Ridger Ted Lehman:

"I'm going to have all life supports removed," he told Ted. "I just wanted to say goodbye."

"I'm sorry, Tom," Ted Replied. "I'll be seeing you in all the old familiar places."

"Yeah," Tom said.

A Dark, Disturbing Dream

Of the 140,000 or so who worked or lived in wartime Oak Ridge at one time or another, relatively few were scientists. Most Oak Ridgers would never see the inside of a nuclear building. There were some 44,000 construction workers and nearly that many administrative and blue collar plant employees and a few thousand soldiers and merchants, plus thousands of moms and kids. About 10,000 were needed to run the city. Susan Bowman's father, Arthur B. "Ott" Bowman, was one of those. Susan was an honor student at Oak Ridge High, class of 1952, bursting to succeed—National Honor Society, yearbook editor, Student Council, art, music, dance. She was voted "Friendliest Girl" by the Class, then blossomed fully at the University of Tennessee where she was named to Who's Who in American Colleges and Universities and Torchbearer, the highest honor given to a UT student. She left with degrees in liberal arts and education.

Daddy was a bookkeeper primarily—part accountant, part manager. His wartime job was to help keep Oak Ridge buses running, inside and outside the security gates—work buses, commuter buses, school buses, city buses, olive drab Army buses, obsolete buses, shuttle buses, trailer buses and even the free buses that transported Oak Ridge children to Vacation Bible School. He worked for Roane-Anderson Company, which managed the town, supplied electricians, carpenters, painters and plumbers, collected garbage and rent, maintained 300 miles of roads, operated 11 cafeterias and a laundry service that handled 100,000 pounds of flatware a week. It was also responsible for overseeing commercial businesses, housing and transportation.

Daddy joined the transportation department at a time when Oak Ridge was growing so fast that bus drivers sometimes got lost on their routes. It was not unusual for a driver to stop and ask for directions, driving down a street today that wasn't there yesterday. Some parents marked their look-alike houses and streets with colored ribbons or signs so that their children would know where to get off.

We moved to Oak Ridge in 1944, when the town was about half completed—Mom, Dad, sister Nancy, age 3, and me, age 10. We were assigned to a just-finished, two-bedroom cemesto house on Pennsylvania Avenue that was ear-marked for essential personnel. Other than the scientists and certain military brass, Ott Bowman was about as essential as anyone, because Oak Ridge had to have buses and people to run them. There were fleets of them, more than 800 vehicles in all, operated by several bus companies under government contract. They carried an average of 120,000 passengers a day, from as far as 50 miles away, and covered 2.4 million miles a month. At its wartime peak, it was the ninth largest bus system in the United States.

Our house was not a pretty one. There were no pretty houses. They were made of unpainted, light gray panels coated with cemesto, a mixture of cement and asbestos, and attached to wooden beams. The back porches, kitchen and bathrooms purposely faced the street to save plumbing pipe footage to street hookups. A huge red clay ditch stretched across the front of our house, and there wasn't a blade of grass in the trampled front yard. Lumber and brick and sewer pipe rested in stacks along the unfinished gravel road and in the yards of unfinished houses. Sewer ditches looked like open wounds on the landscape. Coal was delivered house to house every few days by workmen who carried large canvas coal bags over their shoulders from the street and dumped them into furnace room bins. Coal dust stirred through the house with every dumped load. Mother stuffed towels beneath doors and placed cheesecloth over vents to contain it. Black smoke from thousands of coal furnaces darkened the Oak Ridge sky in winter. Coal deliveries were included in the rent, along with electricity, water, trash pickup, house repairs and painting.

I think we were more appreciative of Oak Ridge than most. We moved from Jacksboro, a timber, farming and coal mining community in northeast Tennessee's Campbell County, about 40 miles from Oak Ridge. Campbell County was the poorest of Tennessee's 95 counties; and its schools were grossly underfunded. The student restrooms at Jacksboro elementary, where I entered as a second grader, were permanently stained from years of use and wreaked of old urine. I avoided them, holding everything all day until I got home after school. And every day after school Mother put me in the bathtub and scrubbed me for lice with Lifebuoy soap. Lice were common, but I never got them. Little Genie Dossett walked by our house every morning on the way to school and on some days mother would see her scratching beneath her sweater. "There goes Genie," she would say. "She's got the itch today."

My father was from Jacksboro and had first worked for the railroad in neighboring Jellico. He left there to work as circulation manager for a newspaper in Birmingham, where I was born, and later in Nashville and Knoxville. Just before we moved to Oak Ridge, he was back in Jacksboro managing a large commissary in Turley, one of several coal mining hamlets in the Jacksboro area. He sold everything from shoes to sugar, slept in the store weeknights and spent weekends at home. Home was a large two-story white house that had been converted to a duplex. It had a big eat-in kitchen and one large bedroom where everybody slept. The bedroom was also the living room. There was no heat in the bathroom. Lights had to be off by 8 p.m. and Jacksboro's civil defense warden, a teen-age boy, walked the streets and alleys enforcing the wartime blackout rule. "Turn out the lights!" he bellowed. "Pull down the shades!"

My mother, Lottie, was from Lot, Kentucky, about three miles across the Tennessee state line from Jellico, where she went to high school. Her maiden name was Faulkner, as in William

Faulkner, whose roots were in Kentucky. She was a distant relative of the famous author.

Mother became a school teacher like her father, and as a young woman taught first grade in Habersham, a little coal mining community between Lafollette and Jellico. On a good day, she would have about 30 kids in class. But on Monday, wash day, she would have 45 or more, because mothers would send little siblings to school with their big brothers and sisters so laundry could be done in the wash kettle more easily at home.

One day some of the children got up during class, walked out and headed for home. "Gotta go, Miss Lottie," they said, but nobody would say why. Through the classroom window Miss Lottie noticed two men dressed in suits walking up the railroad tracks and then she understood. They were government men, revenuers. The children were going home to warn their moonshining parents. Those were depression times, and moonshine was a major source of income for some.

I sometimes think how different our lives would have been if we hadn't moved to Oak Ridge. In Oak Ridge I started fifth grade in a brand new school, Cedar Hill Elementary, and it had everything. We had music classes and art lessons in an art room with long tables with metal sheeting across the tops. Oak Ridge was ugly but it didn't matter and I hardly noticed. You rose above the ugliness. To me it was beautiful, exciting. The freedom there was fantastic. We could go anywhere and be safe. We played "queen of the jungle" in the woods and marched through the erosion ditches making Tarzan-like sounds. I was always the queen of the jungle. We had Girl Scouts and went to day camp. It was like living in fairyland day after day. It just never ended.

My parents absolutely loved Oak Ridge, They were very community involved. All of us in Oak Ridge were in the same boat and helped one another. There were so many knowledgeable people around who were so helpful. You can't really tell people how it was at that time because they don't get it. Even

259

the people I went to college with didn't get it. You never lived in a real house or in a real city, but you didn't care. I missed it for years after I moved away. I never had that kind of connection when I went back. I think, "Oh, my gosh!" I see those buildings and I feel like the person living on the outside looking in. I'm like the clerk in the stores in Knoxville looking down disgustingly at the Oak Ridger with mud on his shoes. Those years were just treasures.

Kids 12 and up had to wear a badge—I still have mine—and had to show it to the guards to get in and out of the security gates. Dad was a gardener and on weekends he drove the family to see our grandparents in Kentucky and brought back a trunk load of manure. We didn't have any trouble getting through the security gates with that. The guards would open the trunk, get one whiff and wave us on. We always got a laugh and we always had a fabulous garden.

I don't remember a lot about the war but I do remember VE Day. Mother said we're going to sit right here by the radio and listen while we paint this little Mexican chair. We listened all day. There were constant prayers on the radio that day. And I remember the day Japan surrendered, looking out the window and thinking. "What a day this is!"

After college I worked at the Oak Ridge National Laboratory, where I met and began dating Richard Keely, a chemical engineer who had just accepted a job in Minnesota, his home state. He was scheduled to leave in two weeks. A little single-engine airplane saved our romance. Rich was a pilot and flew his little Piper PA back to Tennessee often to see me. After several months, he flew down one weekend with a special message. "If you don't say you want to marry me, I'm not coming back." he said.

"You haven't even asked!" I said.

"But I've been trying."

I guess I was dumb and just didn't get it. Anyhow, I said "Yes!"

We were married a year after we met, and I began a roller-coaster ride though life that lifted me to great happiness and, later, shocking sorrow. We lived first in Minneapolis, then in Sioux Falls, South Dakota, population 75,000, the biggest town in the state. It never got above 15 degrees below zero the entire month of January that year, night or day. Twenty-five inches of snow fell one weekend and buried traffic signs so that motorists had to stop at every intersection. We would also live in Washington State, New York and South Carolina before settling in Orinda, California, San Francisco's East Bay area, with three school-age sons.

Before leaving South Carolina, I had an unusual and troubling dream about my husband that popped up in my mind now and then, like a reminder. It followed me to California.

It's muddled now, but it was a dream that things weren't the same with us, that we weren't together. It wasn't a divorce kind of thing. Nothing like that. It was like a feeling of disconnection. I don't know if there were other people in the dream, but I know it always woke me up and I was always frightened by it. The message was that Rich wasn't there, that we weren't going to be together. I never told him about that. I didn't think about it a lot, but I never forgot it.

Years later in California I was out walking with a lady friend who mentioned how happy she was with her marriage, her life and how she wanted to keep everything just as it was.

"So do I," I thought, but I didn't think that was going to happen to me. A strange, uncomfortable feeling swept over me. I was happy with my life and my family, but there was something dark and disturbing that kept me from looking into the future. It was that feeling of disconnection again, a nebulous kind of thing, the South Carolina dream. I was tempted to discuss it with Rich, but I didn't. That's a worrisome kind of thing to say to someone, and how did I know what that dream was connected to? I didn't want to upset him.

In California, Rich worked for Bechtel Corporation, headquartered in nearby San Francisco. Shortly after the highly publicized accident at the Three Mile Island Nuclear Generating Station near Harrisburg, Pennsylvania in March, 1979, he was sent there to write and administer a cleanup procedure. For six weeks he worked at Three Mile Island and flew home on weekends. On the eve of the Memorial Day weekend, Friday, May 25, he left Pennsylvania for home thinking he probably wouldn't have to return to Harrisburg.

While he was flying home that Friday, I was attending a meeting at the Orinda school district office helping to select two principals for the next school term. When the meeting ended at about 4:30, I got in my Chevrolet station wagon and started home. Something told me to turn on the radio. There was a breaking news story. A plane was down in Chicago. American Airlines Flight 191, a McDonald DC-10 aircraft bound for Los Angeles. It crashed on takeoff at O'Hare International Airport, killing all 271 aboard and two people on the ground. It was the deadliest single-airplane accident ever on U.S. soil. The newscast included a Red Cross telephone number for passenger information.

Rich's scheduled flight was not routed through Chicago; it was through Denver or someplace. He told me the night before on the phone "I'm due in at 8 o'clock," he said, "and I don't think I'll have to come back. The cleanup is going well."

He needed to get home because he had so many things to do. We had just moved from one neighborhood to another in Orinda when the Three Mile Island accident occurred and there was still some moving to do. Also, as president of the local swimming pool association, he needed to be home for the big Memorial Day party that opened the summer season.

All those thoughts raced through my mind as I drove home. But while I was waiting at a stop light, the radio announced a phone number. I grabbed a pen and wrote down the Red Cross emergency number on a scrap of paper.

"Rich is dead," I thought. I was sure. Instead of driving home, I turned toward the Meadow Swim and Tennis Club. "Rich will not be here for the opening tomorrow," I told the coaches there. "I'm sure he was on that plane." I can't imagine now how I could have done such a thing; how I could have said that with such certainty. But I just knew.

Rich always said he had extrasensory perception with people close to him. He told me once that he and a high school friend had successfully transmitted information using mental telepathy in experiments with cards and numbers. When he was growing up in Minnesota he had a dream that his older brother, Al, was dead. He saw him lying on the floor, he said, saw the blood, saw the gunshot wound in his head. Soon after there was a call from Fargo, North Dakota, where Al, a bright, 24-year-old college graduate, lived and worked. Someone needed to go to Fargo to identify the body, the caller said. He had been found at home on the floor, shot in the head; an apparent suicide. Rich accompanied his father to Fargo and saw the room, much as it was in his dream. I always thought it was coincidence. "Hogwash," I called it. But now something or somebody was telling me that my husband was on a plane he wasn't supposed to be on, that he was dead. Was it Rich telling me?

I drove home from the pool and called the Red Cross emergency number. It wasn't working. I called a friend whose husband was an American Airlines pilot and got some telephone numbers, but no one knew anything more.

I went out and worked in the yard, digging in the dirt and thinking. I mowed the lawn just to keep busy. When our oldest son, Mike, got home from school I told him what I thought, but I didn't tell the two younger boys. Mike, 16, was a junior in high school, Rick, 13, was in junior high and Colin, 9, was in fourth grade. Some kids came over and wanted Mike to go to the movies. I thought no, but said, "Go ahead." He would have to find out when he got home.

There was still no word from the airline or from Rich by dinner time. Colin and Rick watched the Chicago crash on the evening news. Someone at O'Hare caught the accident on video and it was being shown repeatedly on television—the liftoff, the nosedive, the raging black-and-orange smoke fire. I turned off the TV. "Oh, come on. Let's have dinner," I said.

I looked at the clock every few minutes. Eight o'clock came and went. No Rich and no phone call from him. He always called if he was running late. Nine o'clock, 10 o'clock. I got on the phone and called every place I could imagine, searching for a passenger list. Then at 2:55 in the morning a spokesman from American Airlines at the Los Angeles airport returned my call.

"Mrs. Keely," he said. "I'm calling to tell you that your husband was not on that plane."

"Thank you, for calling," I said. "I certainly hope you're right and I hope you don't call back in five minutes and say he was on the plane." I didn't believe him.

In exactly five minutes the man called back. Rich *was* on the plane. His first and last names had been misspelled on the passenger list, but it was Rich. He had changed planes at the last minute and taken a flight through Chicago that would have him home five hours early.

The phone rang all night and the kids slept through it, but that last call woke Mike. He walked into my bedroom crying. "I knew it," he said. He slept beside me the rest of the night while I stared into the darkness. I couldn't sleep. I asked for strength.

The next morning I told the younger boys. I can't remember what. You don't remember things that hurt that much. Rick, the 13-year-old, blamed himself for the crash. "It's the only night I didn't pray that Dad would come home safely," he confessed. Colin, the little one, was stoic and remained stoic. He had a baseball game that day and Mike was scheduled to take the SATs that day at school.

"I'm going to take those tests, Mom," Mike said.

"I'm going to play that game," Colin said.

I didn't want them to but I said OK. After Colin left for the game, I followed him to the ball field and called the coach aside to alert him. He already knew.

The airline did nothing for days. Never called me, never offered to take me back there, didn't tell me if there were any remains. I didn't hear anything for the longest time.

It was two weeks before the airline told me that Rich's body had been identified. So now I could have a memorial service. Someone from a local mortuary called and said the body was there and did I want to see it?

"How was the body identified?" I asked.

"Fingerprints," she was told.

"You mean there were fingerprints left?"

"Yes, would you like to see the remains?"

"Yes," I said.

"Are you sure?"

I thought about it, about how mangled Rich's body would be, whatever was left of it. I didn't want to remember him that way.

"No," I said.

Later that summer I was attending a brunch at my church and someone, a man I didn't know and had never seen, walked into the church and asked to see me. He had a message for me. I excused myself from the table and went to meet him.

"I wanted to tell you that I was at O'Hare Airport when flight 191 went down," he said. "I was looking through a window and saw it all. I want you to know your husband didn't suffer. It was too quick. The plane went straight up and straight down."

I was in such shock that somebody knew where I was and knew that Rich had been on that flight and that this stranger found me in this church. It's like an angel had come to see me. I couldn't believe it was happening to me. It was so comforting. I haven't seen him since or heard from him and don't know his name. It was like he was there, and then he was gone.

By then I had read details of the crash in Chicago newspapers sent to me by friends in Chicago. Shortly before liftoff, I learned the number one engine under the left wing of the DC-10 separated and flew up and over the wing and smashed onto the runway. The plane continued its climb to around 600 feet as fuel and hydraulic fluid spewed a trail of white vapor.

"Damn" a crew member was heard to say just before the cockpit recorder went dead. The plane, with a full load of fuel, stalled, pitched left, rolled over uncontrollably and skidded into a field. It struck an abandoned hangar and burst into a huge fireball. Some of the wreckage was thrown into a nearby mobile home park and killed two residents.

Almost two years after the accident I was sound asleep when, at 5 o'clock in the morning, my eyes suddenly popped open. Once more, something or somebody told me to turn on the radio. I never get up at 5 o'clock and if I did, I wouldn't think of turning on a radio. But I did, and once more I was startled by what I heard. It was a news story about an American Airlines mechanic committing suicide. He had been a supervisor when the ill-fated DC-10 received its last major overhaul. (Incidentally, the news report stated that the suicide victim had tightened the bolt and thought he was at fault.)

I tried to get that news report again later in the day and there was none. It wasn't on the nightly news or in the newspapers, either. It was like it was broadcast just that one time. To this day I've never heard another word about it. It was as if it had been orchestrated.

Earl Russell Marshall, 47, the suicide victim, had worked at American's fleet maintenance facility in Tulsa, Oklahoma. He took his life the night before he was to have been deposed by lawyers for McDonnell Douglas, the plane's manufacturer, in a civil case brought by relatives of Flight 191 victims. The Federal Aviation Administration had blamed the crash on a defective bolt in the engine pylon. An investigation into the suicide led to new information about the cause of the crash.

It was discovered that, after the crash, American Airlines had conducted a private internal investigation of the maintenance history of the Flight 191 aircraft. The probe showed that the company had developed a cost-cutting shortcut in servicing engines on DC-10s. The shortcut involved lifting the engine with a fork lift for servicing rather than removing it from the pylon as recommended by the manufacturer. The shortcut saved up to 200 man hours per aircraft. The Flight 191 plane was last serviced in Tulsa eight weeks before the fatal crash. By chance, the hydraulics on one fork lift were faulty and the engine slipped when the lift truck was used to hold up the engine overnight. The drop led to hairline cracks in the pylon attachment that holds the engine to the wing. The plane made several successful flights before the stress of takeoff at O'Hare finally caused the engine to break loose.

When American Airlines lawyers saw the private company report, they ordered it destroyed, fearing American would be held solely responsible for the crash. But the damaging information was leaked to the media after the mechanic's suicide. Continental and United airlines also were found to have been using the maintenance shortcut and similar hairline cracks were found among their fleets. All 138 DC-10s in the United States were grounded by the Federal Aviation Administration for two months and foreign based DC-10s weren't admitted in the U.S.

There were many strange stories related to Flight 191. Actress Lindsay Wagner, TV's "*Bionic Woman*," was on the flight list but as departure time drew near she felt uneasy and walked away as passengers were boarding. A musical group called *Shoes* also switched to another flight in the last minutes.

Earlier that month, before the crash, a man named David Booth, an automobile mechanic from Cincinnati, had a series of recurring premonitory dreams that tormented him for 10 consecutive nights. He saw an American Airlines plane take off from an airport, bank steeply and crash. On May 22, three days before the crash, he called American Airlines about it and was told to see a psychiatrist. Federal Aviation Administration officials at the Cincinnati airport took him seriously and guessed from his description that the plane was a DC-10, but could do nothing about it. Where? When? When Flight 191 went down, it happened almost exactly as David Booth had seen in his dreams.

Long after the crash I was given the name of a contact person for American Airlines, who was attempting to reach financial settlements with surviving families.

They wanted to know how much I expected. I gave them a figure, a relatively low figure, and they said no. I didn't want to sue, didn't want to put the children through it, but I had to. Three weeks before the suit deadline I filed. The children had to go on the stand. I was awarded the same sum I had asked for. But the airline appealed and an appeal could drag on for five years and I thought, "What am I going to live on?" I ended up settling out of court for less and had to pay legal fees. They knew that. They're all in cahoots, but that's another story. Rich would have been appalled.

Rich was a vibrant 51 when Flight 191 went down, as adventurous as he was when he took me flying in his little two-seater plane some 18 years earlier. I eventually became Rich's navigator, using church steeples, rivers, highways and such as guides. I wasn't licensed to fly, but Rich taught me how to get the Piper down, just in case.

We had two narrow escapes. Once in Minnesota the engine began making strange loud noises immediately after we were airborne and Rich quickly returned to the airstrip. He had tied down the Piper the day before and someone apparently tampered with it during the night. Another time we flew to Florida and back with little Mike in my lap. The Piper had been inspected and painted just days before takeoff. When we returned Rich had the plane checked out again and discovered that the fabric was rotten. "You're lucky to be alive," we were told.

Rich and a mechanic friend took off the wings, removed the engine, put it on a flatbed truck and drove it down South Spring Street and into our two-car garage. There, warmed by a rented heat blower in the 25-below zero temperatures of South Dakota, he and I sewed on the new Seconite fabric, painted the Piper PA-12 and sold it.

Rich was so curious, and enthusiastic and chatty with everybody; he wanted to try everything, whether he could do it well or not, and he was so full of surprises. Once I told him I was going to take a pottery course and he said, "I'll do it with you." I took Mike home to visit my mother one summer and when I came back I noticed we weren't on the right road going home. Rich and his sister had moved us into another house and that was my surprise. He decided that we needed a bigger place.

During World War II when he was too young to enlist, he knitted socks for the Red Cross. Once he tried oil painting while he was recovering from pneumonia. He hunted wild game and fished with his boys.

Near the end of summer after Rich's death, 13-year-old Rick went to Canada as a guest of a neighborhood friend and his family. When he returned the absence of his father struck him like a crippling disease. He had a fabulous time in Canada but when he came home he couldn't face the fact that his dad was gone. It almost killed him. He vomited for days, had ongoing diarrhea, became dangerously dehydrated and lost 15 pounds.

Doctors treated him but couldn't explain his illness. We almost lost him...

Now, 31 years later, I still wonder occasionally about those early premonitions, about my uncharacteristic impulses—where they came from, or from whom—and whether I could have done anything about them. I know I couldn't have. But maybe Rich was right about his ESP thing.

At the time of the accident I had not worked outside the home since we lived in South Dakota, when I did some substitute teaching. Now I was 45 and had three boys to put through college. I had no fear, I don't know why. What I felt was responsibility. I knew it was mine now. I had to take care of things, so I went about making plans to do that.

I went to work, part-time at first, then full-time. For 18 years I taught children with learning disabilities, and for five years operated a catering business out of my home on weekends. I invested Rich's insurance money and set a scholarship course for the boys, each of whom was a varsity water polo player. Two of them got athletic scholarships and Colin, the youngest, narrowly missed making the U.S. Olympic team. Mike and Rick graduated from the University of California at Berkeley and Colin from Stanford.

Today Mike is regional director of leasing for C.B. Richard Ellis Investment Group in Oakland. Rick is a vice president at Colliers International, a real estate company in Oakland. Colin is a director at Knight Trading Company, a brokerage firm in San Francisco. I still live in the same house on Heather Lane in Orinda, grandmother of six girls, a chorus singer, a church lady, a bridge player, a traveler, a tutor and a widow for 31 years. My motto is, "Live life to the fullest with a song in my heart."

Susan Bowman Keely

Orinda, California

270

Grief, a Scar and a Butterfly

Jim Hodges, the starting center on the '52 ORHS basketball team, was a technical illustrator at the Marshall Space Center and later opened a creative graphic and design shop.

Sherry and I had become soul mates through 38 years of marriage; living and working and having our two sons in Huntsville, Alabama. She could start a sentence and I could finish it. She was cute and bubbly, a striking dresser and for years a sharp computer programmer for National Cash Register.

I had never given much thought to death. I always believed she would outlive me by many years, so I was whistling along in a world that was in great order. Life was good.

Sherry didn't accompany me when I drove to Tennessee for the 50th Reunion of the Oak Ridge High Class of 1952. She said she wasn't feeling well. That was October in 2002. In November she went to the beach for a month, and when she returned home for Thanksgiving she still wasn't feeling well. Then in December she began losing weight—like 30 pounds that month. And she tired easily. By January, she was suffering severe pain and walked around the house late at night until the pain subsided. We both knew there was a serious problem.

Searching the Internet I discovered that her symptoms matched those of pancreatic cancer. Victims of pancreatic cancer, the article stated, usually live about three months from the time of discovery. I printed the article, but didn't want to show her what I had found. But she insisted. When she read it, she seemed to accept her fate immediately. She looked up at me and said, "Everybody has to go some time." Then she added matter-of-factly, "I want no chemotherapy or life-support machines."

Soon after that we were out to dinner one evening and I said to her, "At least I have a chance to tell you just how much I love you," and tears began rolling down my face. I had to go to the men's room to dry my red eyes, and when I returned she smiled and said, "You're not going to last three months."

She was tough, and she never let her situation beat her down. I believed that we would beat it, that we could make her well again. I bought herbs from Canada that were formulated to boost the immune system and fight off cancer. I bought other remedies until she finally said stop.

The pain became so great that her doctor prescribed morphine patches, and she slept a lot after that. I brought her soup at lunchtime, but she couldn't eat and she just kept getting weaker. When I came in from work, my drafting chair would be in the kitchen where she had been sitting, looking out the window.

I finally talked her into taking some mild chemo to see if it might slow the cancer, but after the third treatment the doctor basically told me to take her home to die. I had been remodeling our home and everything was a mess, so I leased a two-bedroom apartment in South Huntsville near my work so people could visit. When I drove her there from the doctor's office she asked to sit in the car for a while. She napped alone in the sunshine for about hour, and then I helped her into her wheelchair and rolled her into the apartment. I lifted her into bed and opened the windows. It was now March and a warm breeze blew through the open window. "Oh," she said. "I can hear the birds singing." I thought how sad that she never again would enjoy such simple pleasures of life.

By now I had gotten a grip on numbing my emotions and was handling it. I took a leave from work; and tended to her needs all day and night. I rigged a wireless doorbell for her in the living room so she could ring it when she needed me. Soon Hospice was called in and was very helpful. Two weeks after we moved into the apartment, Sherry died. It was April 1, 2003. The hard part for me was about to begin.

Sherry Raley Hodges made her last trip to Gadsden, her hometown, in a hearse down Highway 431 from Huntsville to Crestwood Cemetery. Later, after the funeral services, I returned to the cemetery alone, and as I approached her grave all the strength suddenly drained from my body. I dropped to my knees, overwhelmed with grief. I must have been there close to an hour, wiping tears, trying to dry my eyes so I could see to drive home.

Hospice called, offering support and group therapy. I thanked them, but explained that I had a large supportive group of family and friends, and that I thought I could manage my emotions alone.

Back at work it was difficult to focus. My thoughts drifted to Sherry several times throughout the day causing me to tear up. My evenings back at the apartment were no better. When I drove somewhere and glanced at the passenger seat, where Sherry should have been, it brought more tears. I avoided restaurants that we had frequented together, and the friends that we often saw there. Things would happen that I wanted to share with Sherry, but she wasn't there. Emptiness would then swallow me, reminding me that I was alone, and sometimes I felt that my life was over also.

Going back to our old house on Acklen Drive caused such strong feelings of emptiness and sadness that sometimes I would have to leave. During the first year after Sherry's death I frequently dreamed of her, only to awake to more disappointment.

Strange, unexplainable things began to happen at the apartment. One evening I heard a doorbell ring. The apartment didn't have a doorbell, only knockers. I had taken the batteries out of the wireless doorbell and kept it in a kitchen drawer. It happened on several occasions. Then a friend from Knoxville, visiting for a few days, was sitting at my computer when he heard a doorbell ring. I explained that I didn't have a doorbell.

"It's coming from your phone," he said. And it was. To our amazement, it rang several times.

One morning, walking into the Sparkman Center where I worked as a creative designer, a beautiful pale yellow butterfly lit on the collar of my shirt behind my ear. As I passed through the security checkpoint I asked the guard if the butterfly was still on my collar. It was. I took an elevator down one floor, walked a long corridor to my office and the butterfly was still there. One of the girls at the office told me that it was Sherry, telling me that everything was okay. I walked back outside, shook my shirt and watched the butterfly fly away.

I stayed in the apartment for the next two years and the doorbell never rang again. I went back to our old house only to empty it before retiring and moving to Georgia.

I can't tell anyone how to cope with grief. You just do. One day at a time. I've always heard that time heals all wounds. You eventually begin to get back into the flow of living and, for the most part, the pain goes away. But you still have some teary moments, and you always wear a scar.

Sherry's niece, Cathy Kessler, reminded me that I still had a lot to live for—two sons, two grandsons and a large loving family. "Get on with it," she said.

And so I do.

Jim "Cowboy" Hodges

Greensboro, Georgia

"I'll Take You Home Again, Kathleen"

Lewis Thomas Hardin was a starting forward on the basketball team, a member of the National Honor Society, Student Council vice president, Senior Banquet speaker and one of the true gentlemen of the class. He and Kathleen Myers were married 51 years.

I have lost a dad, a mom, my sister Carol (ORHS class of '54), many pets and many friends. And on April 18, 2009, I lost my wife, Kathleen. It was the worst and the hardest loss of all. I guess that's to be expected because of our 51 years of marriage, plus the three years of togetherness before we became man and wife. I had seen her at church for a couple of years, but we never spoke until she was 18, the summer after she graduated from ORHS and after my sophomore year at UT.

A friend used to say when he saw an attractive woman: "I wouldn't be ashamed to walk down Gay Street with her." And so it was with Kathleen Garrison Myers, from Crossville, Tennessee. I was impressed, to say the least, the first time I saw her walk into the First Presbyterian Church in Oak Ridge. She had been in five high schools during her sophomore year as her dad, a civil engineer, followed a pipeline that was being built across Texas and Louisiana. Her mother felt she needed a more stable high school experience, so she sent her to Oak Ridge to live with an uncle and aunt to begin her junior year and to finish at ORHS in 1954.

We had a very ecumenical youth fellowship group at First Presbyterian in the summer of '54, and the males of the group, especially those of us who graduated in '52, swept those pretty young girls from the '54 class off their feet. Or so we imagined. Anyhow, a lot of marriages resulted between the '52 boys and the '54 girls.

I knew I would never be ashamed to walk down any street with Kathleen. We were married on the longest night of the year, December 21, 1957.

On Memorial Day, 2006, my mom died. On the same day, Kathleen was diagnosed with small cell lung cancer. It had spread to the lymph nodes in her chest. The Internet mentioned "mean time between discovery and death is four months". She almost made it three years, the time at which we were told she could have an 85 to 95 percent chance. We made many trips to the emergency room after that because of her illness, most of the times on holidays. Excluding weekends, she began daily doses of radiation for six weeks, plus three concurrent weeks of chemo treatments at three times a week. Treatments stabilized the cancer, at least temporarily. After a few months, the tumor began to grow again, requiring another round of 20 radiation treatments. It stabilized again, but appeared again, this time at the base of her skull. More radiation; but the tumor continued to grow and brain surgery was soon necessary, followed by a gamma knife procedure of highly concentrated radiation on Dec. 12, 2008.

Kathleen's final ER visit was on March 20, 2009. On the following day we learned the brain tumor was still there and growing. It was the birthday of my sister, Carol, who died in 1996.

My hardest times began shortly before Kathleen died, but I'll never forget our trips for treatment during the nearly three years. She had to lie in the back seat of our 2006 Ford, and she required a wheelchair at the hospital. She resisted all efforts to get her to eat and drink, so she became dehydrated and required several hydration treatments. Her sole source of nourishment was four or five daily bottles of Boost, a nutrition drink.

She never liked to talk about it. She didn't want phone calls or the many get-well cards she received. I was always hopeful, but now and then she would mention that she wouldn't be around much longer.

After being told there might be more radiation and not hearing anything for a couple days, I called the surgeon and asked about further treatment. He said, "There will be no further radiation. You need to call Hospice." That hit me like a ton of bricks! I often have wondered what went through her mind when our younger son Scott broke that news to her. She became weaker by the day before she died 15 days later.

She was born on April 5, 1936 and died at home in Florissant, MO, a suburb of St. Louis, at 4:05 p.m. on Saturday, April 18, 2009. Scott and I lay weeping on either side of her, stroking her arms, until the mortician, a friend of ours, arrived. Joel, our doctor son who has seen death up close many times, watched over us. Family and friends, with tears rolling down our cheeks, lifted our glasses in her honor as the black hearse drove her down Castle Drive for the last time, then turned left on Old Jamestown Road en route to Washington University Medical School in St. Louis, where she had donated her body.

I shared Kathleen's thoughts about funerals. We thought they are too hard on the family. "They" say we need a visitation to obtain closure–whatever that is. I never have wanted to sit or stand beside a body for hours while friends drop by to say they're sorry, or "how good she looks." Nobody looks good dead! So nine days later we had a memorial service in which our sons, sister Mary Kay and friends told stories about her cleverness, her good humor, her goodness, her spirit. The service began with a recording of Bette Midler singing, *Wind Beneath My Wings* and ended with a local songstress singing, *I'll Take You Home Again, Kathleen.* Many attendees complimented us on the service; and said they would have a similar service as a result.

Kathleen always loved to throw a party, whether it was at home, or when she was in the catering business; or at our club, where she planned functions for all the women's events. The day after the memorial service there was a bottle of wine on every table for Kathleen's lady's golf group luncheon after their weekly round. They, too, lifted their glasses in her honor. I appreciated that very much, and I become misty-eyed each time I think of it.

I call them "moments" when the misty eyes occur. There are many such moments. A few of them included riding my little orange Kubota tractor around the yard mowing and remembering her coming out on the front porch to point to a strip I missed; wondering what her thoughts were during the sickness; discussing her and thinking of the frequent trips we made to the Siteman Cancer Center in the Center for Advanced Medicine (CAM) at Barnes Jewish Hospital in St. Louis. There are moments even now when I visit the CAM for my own ailments.

I have made one trip to Oak Ridge since. On the return I had a big-time moment as I passed through Crab Orchard, where she spent a lot of time with her paternal grandmother. Grandma Myers was a huge influence on Kathleen, including matters of clothes, which might explain the 72 pairs of slacks in one closet and many other clothes and shoes in three other closets, plus four large storage bags in the basement.

At this writing, it has been a year and 11 days since she died. Saturday April 17th was the end of the 52nd week, and Sunday the 18th was a year. I had a hard time each day as 4:05 p.m. approached. I decided to clear her bed and lie on it while the dogs rested on the floor beside me as 4:05 came and passed. It worked both days.

My sisters and friends have been terrific support. One couple has been especially helpful. If you give your family and friends the opportunity they can help. Scott comes to town to check on me and to drive me to Florida—I think he feels I can't drive that far alone—and Joel calls frequently. A grief session at church also helps. Classmates have supplied a lot of support with phone calls and emails, even to this day.

A friend told me after his wife had been gone for six years that he still talked to her. I've never felt that way, but I did feel Kathleen was present in the house one time. A large portrait hangs on the family room wall, and I say "Hi" as I pass. While that's the only time I talk to her, I'm never alone at home. I talk all the time to my two Faithful Canine Companions, Louie and Molly, the prettiest white lab in the world and a very sweet black lab mix, respectively. I strongly recommend Faithful Canine Companions.

We all know that handling grief varies with each individual and that time probably eases grief—at least for some. My former next-door neighbor lost a daughter several years ago. He said one never really gets over it, which was echoed by a friend who was widowed last December. Some follow the one-day-at-a-time philosophy. Others live by the "keep on keepin' on" slogan. A lady who was widowed four years ago told me that we don't ever get over it, but we learn to accept it.

Of two things I'm sure: People are different and the world doesn't stop. We can get off or continue the ride. I choose the latter. It's tough, but not as tough as what KH went through. Having said all that, she said she would go through it again, and I am of the same opinion. We would take another chance, given the same situation, for a cure, over just giving up.

Tom Hardin

Florissant, Missouri

Majorette Dottie Hawkins Shelton at 75

Reunion Surprise!
Dancin' Dottie

The last reunion started with some fiddling and guitar playing. There was a concert in the park. Trombones serenaded us at a cocktail party. Then there came the surprise. In the middle of a dinner program that featured speakers and song and video, there came a shocker.

The air filled suddenly with band music, Glenn Miller's St. Louis Blues, and out of nowhere appeared a 75-year-old majorette, high stepping and twirling a baton the way she did 60 years ago. It was Dottie Hawkins, the same Dottie Hawkins who was a majorette nine straight years from junior high through college, the same Dottie who led a six-mile parade down the Oak Ridge Turnpike the day the city opened its gates to the public in 1949.

She was a star then and she was a star at the last reunion in the summer of 2010, prancing back and forth in black tights, sequined black sweater, white boots and white hat. She was wearing the same smile she's worn all her life. No classmate ever had more spirit. She had red hair and freckles and green eyes that had smiles in them and she just loved everybody.

When she was five she was singing on the radio. When she was 9 she was selling lemonade and Hershey bars on the Turnpike to construction workers, and when she was 10 she opened up a booth and sold kisses for 10-cents per smooch in the Middletown trailer park. For an extra dime, she gave kissing lessons. At 13, she had her own dance studio teaching baton and tap dancing.

On D-Day, the 6th of June, 1945, she organized a parade. She didn't know what D-Day was, but she broke off the handle of her mother's new mop and made a baton out of it, then led a dozen or so children who were beating on dishpans and buckets with spoons through the trailer park. She starred in Saturday morning kiddies shows and got to know movie stars such as Lash LaRue, Fuzzy St. John and Bob Steele, who produced live shows at the Middletown Theater. And when she was a student at Memphis State, she met Elvis Presley and helped him distribute some of his first recordings to radio stations across East Tennessee.

"It wasn't all fun," she said. "It took me four years to get a divorce after a 20-year marriage. I had two daughters and there were times when I didn't have enough money to buy a loaf of bread. But you can't let it get you down. "

She worked 20 years with the Havana, Florida Police Department, retired briefly then returned to work for the state commissioner's office in Tallahassee. She's still there, and still dancing and prancing. They know her by her married name, Shelton—Shellie Shelton. She's still Dancin' Dottie to us.

Senior Class 1951 – 1952

Adams, James Martin
Adkins, Barbara Estelle
Akers, Wofford Herrell
Alexander, Billie Joy
Alexander, Gilbert Blake, Jr.
Alexander, Martha Sue
Ammons, Donald Rogers
Amos, Bobbie Jean
Attkison, Betty Jean
Aurin, Bebe
Baer, Juanita Alleen
Bagwell, Bobby Lee
Baker, Frank Alphues
Baker, Loventris
Barger, Thomas Howard
Barto, Bruce Irwin
Batch, John Marvin
Bell, Charlene Bosworth
Black, Nancy Jett
Blakely, Carolyn Temple
Bonifacius, Barbara Joyce
Bowman, Mary Susan
Boyd, Joshua Rieff, Jr.
Brewer, Dawn Marie
Brewer, Lois Andree
Brody, Sophie Maria
Brown, Dorothy Ann
Bryan, Nancy Ferrell
Buchanan, Carl Dean
Buchanan, Virginia Emma
Buck, Frances Wilson
Buckley, Jan
Carr, Eleanor Mae
Carver, John Robert
Clayton, Johnnie Faye
Clinton, Sammie Dale
Clowers, Reta Janet
Conner, Bobby Jean
Conner, Bobby Gene
Conner, Harry Gene
Cooley, Betty Sue
Cooler, Montie Rose
Corbett, Walter Dugan, Jr.

Cornell, Sally Clair
Cotham, William Earl
Counts, Charles Richard
Cowan, Peggy Jo
Craig, Una Fay
Craven, Clyde Wesley
Cromer, William Rice
Cunningham, Elbert Claxton, Jr.
Davis, Gary Wayne
Day, Billy Wade
Dean, Vivian Rose
Dickenson, Jean Evelyn
Dixon, Harold Eugene
Donald, Melba Nell
Dripps, Joseph Wensel
Eads, Pearlie Elizabeth
Easier, Carol Patton
Edwards, Jimmy Carroll
Edwards, William Jackson
Elder, Mary Virginia
Ellis, Opal Hope
Ethridge, Fredrick Alien
Eve, Joseph Edward
Febuary, Jacqueline Peggy
Finch, Stanley Johnson
Fisher, Philip Neal
Fisher, Thomas Justin
Fitzgerald, Paul Terrence
Foster, Sara Dean
Fox, Thurman Lee
Freels, Geraldine
Freels, Juanita
Fulkerson, Rea Marie
Galloway, James Michael
Gardner, Ronald Eugene
Garland, Thomas Jack
George, Melvin Douglas
Gick, Martell Louise
Gilliland, Robert L.
Goad, Billy Haze
Gragg, Geraldine Louise
Gragg, Mary Joan

Senior Class (con't)

Grant, Maynard Fuller, Jr.
Gray, James Don
Griffin, Jesse Keeton
Griffith, Adam David
Gulley, Gerald Lee
Gustison, Myrna Lee
Haese, Lois Anne
Hale, Mary Ann
Hale, Merelyn Yvonne
Hall, Esther Voleen
Hall, Wesley Catron
Hardin, Lewis Thomas, III
Harris, Norma Ruth
Hart, Mary Ellen Lucille
Hawkins, Dorothy Shellie
Helton, Billy Wayne
Hemphill, Bennie Elizabeth
Henderson, Kenneth Donald
Hendrick Richard Lloyd
Hendrick, Robert Mack
Henley, Martha Rose
Hensley, Maxine Marie
Hickey, James Charles
High, Jimmie Gray
Hitchock, Sylvia Anne
Hobson, David O'Brien
Hodges, James Wesley
Hollingsworth, Leland Stanford
Home, Faye Iona
Home, Robert Eugene, Jr.
Horton, James Jackson
Howard, Frances Joan
Hughey, Betty Ann
Jackson, Norma Jeanne
Jackson, Frances Sabelia
Jago, Robert Anthony
Jarvis, Walter Monroe, Jr.
Johnson, Bobby Lynn
Johnson, Joyce Evelyn
Johnson, Lois Ann
Jones, Bettie Mary
Jones, Clyde (Jack)
Keith, Troy Lemuel

Kendrick, Billy Ray
Kilgore, Sammy Henry
King, Henry Hayden
Kitchin, James Edward
Kite, Jewel Evelyn
Lane, Donald Wentworth
Lay, Delmas Lee
Layne, Ronald Pierce
Long, Betty Walton
Loudermilk, Roy Lee, Jr.
Luckett, Margaret Anne
Lynch, Don Wilson
Mahood, Cecelia Kate
Mance, Fredric Russell
Mason, Dorothy Cole
Mason, Kay Eugenya
Matlock, Donald Anthony
Matteson, Claire L.
Matties, Robert Laroy
Maxwell, Bernaida Sue
Miller, Emmett Donald
Miracle, Patsy Marie
Moore, Yvone Dagmar
Morris, Joel Anne
Morris, Violette Maxine
Morton, Thurston Wilbur, II
Mullins, Bobbie Jean
Murrin, Bobby Faye
Myers, Dorothy Anne
Macdowall, John Douglas
McCulloh, Thomas Hugh
McDougal, Doris Helen
McFall, Paul Russell
McGaha, Dorothy Irene
McGinnis, Gladys Marie
McMaster, William Murry
McPeters, Roland Eudean
McPeters, Wayne Kyle
Neal, Barbara June
Neubert, Barbara Jean
Nicholson, James Lazenby
Norton, Mary Carol
Okes, Delores Butcher

Senior Class (con't)

Oliver, Billy Eugene
O'Neal Palestine
Parker, Willa Dean
Parsons, Bobby Dean
Payne, Rama June
Peach, Patricia Alene
Peacock, Annie
Pearce, Malissa Ernestine
Perrin, Margaret Ann
Peters, James Clair
Pharr, Ernest Eugene
Phillips, Dolores Jean
Pierce, Willlis Idol
Pleasant, Norman Oliver
Plummer, Mary Ellen
Potts, Loretta Estelle
Powell, Marolyn Wynelle
Pressnell, William Wayne
Pullen, Wylodean
Raines, Katherine Eugenie
Rathbone, Emma Sue
Ravage, Dorothy Elaine
Rawlings, Edgar Lee, III
Redden, Betsy Lou
Reece, Mary Sue
Reece, Richard Lee
Reynolds, Karen Ann
Roach, Douglas Hardy
Roberts, Betty Lou
Robinson, Donald West
Roseberry, Ronald Thomas
Rosenbaum, Frankie Lynn
Rowan, Sheila Clare
Ruble, Norma Jean
Rust, Mary Van Zandt
Savage, Priscilla Mae
Schubert, Gertrude Lillian
Searcy, Jarrell Dutton
Shackelford, Edgar Patton
Sheldon, Anne King
Shook, Colleen Kay
Smith, Martha Jo
Smith, Sylvia

Smith, Wade Cothran
Spalding, James B., Jr.
Stinson, Betty Jo
Stubblefield, Robert Edward
Tate, Frederick Gene
Teague, Lyie Thompson
Terry, Daniel Lloyd
Thomas, John William
Trotter, Frank Samuel
Upchurch, Joan Merle
Valliant, Beverly Ann
VandenBuIck, Charles Franz
Vandergriff, Bobby Lynn
Van Fleet, Robert Simon
Vaughn, Joyce Marie
Verner, Thomas Edward
Waldroup, Mary Dell
Walker, Douglas Truman
Wardley, James Alan
Wayland, Richard Donald
Webb, Hazel Eugenia
Wheeler, Johnny Clay
Wheeler, Margaret Sue
Williams, Peggy Ann
Wilson, Mary Jane
Woullard, Jimmie Lee
Wright, Ada Jans

About the Author

Jarrell "Jay" Searcy, a newspaperman for 44 years, is a national award-winning sports writer and feature writer who lived in Oak Ridge as a child during World War II. Both of his parents worked at the nuclear plants. Jay has been collecting Oak Ridge stories most of his adult life. His newspaper career, which started at The Oak Ridger when he was in high school, took him to The Kingsport Times-News, The Chattanooga Times, The New York Times and The Philadelphia Inquirer, where he was executive sports editor. He twice was named Tennessee Sportswriter of the Year and is a member of the Chattanooga, Oak Ridge and Tennessee Sports Writers Halls of Fame. He lives in retirement in Loudon's Tellico Village with his wife of 55 years, Jackie Hildebrand, an Oak Ridge schoolmate.